"A Handful of Mischief"

Evelyn Waugh in his library at Piers Court in 1950. This photograph by Douglas Glass appeared in "Portrait Gallery" in the *Sunday Times,* January 7, 1951. Waugh had recently published *Helena* (1950), and he was about to start writing *Men at Arms* (1952), the first volume of the trilogy that became *Sword of Honour* (1965). © J. C. C. Glass

"A Handful of Mischief"

New Essays on Evelyn Waugh

Edited by
Donat Gallagher,
Ann Pasternak Slater,
and John Howard Wilson

Madison • Teaneck
Fairleigh Dickinson University Press

Published by Fairleigh Dickinson University Press
Co-published with The Rowman & Littlefield Publishing Group, Inc.
4501 Forbes Boulevard, Suite 200, Lanham, Maryland 20706
www.rlpgbooks.com

Estover Road, Plymouth PL6 7PY, United Kingdom

British Library Cataloguing in Publication Information Available

Library of Congress Cataloging-in-Publication Data
Library of Congress Cataloguing-in-Publication Data on file under LC#2010016424
ISBN: 978-1-61147-048-2 (cl. : alk. paper)
eISBN: 978-1-61147-049-9

♾️™ The paper used in this publication meets the minimum requirements of American
National Standard for Information Sciences—Permanence of Paper for Printed Library
Materials, ANSI/NISO Z39.48-1992.

Printed in the United States of America

To Alexander Waugh,
who keeps the show on the road

Contents

Acknowledgments

THESE ESSAYS WERE ORIGINALLY PRESENTED AT THE EVELYN WAUGH CENtenary Conference, held at Hertford College, Oxford, September 24–27, 2003. Many people contributed to the success of the conference, and we would like to thank them.

Craig Dean Willis, then President of Lock Haven University, and Roy Stewart, then Provost of LHU, both provided grants that helped to pay for planning, printing, and facilities. A grant from the LHU Faculty Professional Development Committee enabled one of the editors to travel to Oxford.

The conference began with a visit to Castle Howard in Yorkshire, one of the locations used in the 1981 television series and the 2008 film based on *Brideshead Revisited* (1945). Heather Eisenhut organized a private tour of the house and grounds, and Michael Johnston secured accommodations at the Old Lodge Hotel in Malton.

At Hertford College, Julie Dearden, the Director of International Programmes and Conferences, arranged rooms and meals for fifty people. Sebastian Perry, K. J. Gilchrist, Peter Christensen, Eulália Carceller Guillamet, Mark Dittman, and Marcel DeCoste chaired sessions devoted to film, travel, religion, modernism, *Brideshead Revisited*, and the Second World War. Patrick Denman Flanery and Sebastian Perry gave tours of the city and the university. Through Patrick's membership in the Oxford Union, confreres were able to enter the library, where Evelyn Waugh wrote part of *Rossetti* (1928), and the debating hall, where he spent many evenings as an undergraduate. Fr. Gerard Hughes, SJ, and Fr. Nicholas King, SJ, guided groups through Campion Hall, still supported by royalties from Waugh's *Edmund Campion* (1935).

Waugh wrote part of *Black Mischief* (1932) at Madresfield Court in Worcestershire, and Lady Morrison opened her home to the conference. We also visited Waugh's home, Piers Court in Gloucestershire, and the owner, Mrs. D'Arcy, refreshed us with a cream tea. That evening, at a gala dinner in the Hall of Hertford College, Alexander Waugh gave a rousing speech; renewed his grandfather's attack on his tutor, C. R. M. F. Cruttwell; and answered numerous questions. One of Evelyn Waugh's granddaughters, Claudia FitzHerbert, also attended.

On the last evening of the conference, we dined at the Spread Eagle Hotel at Thame. The proprietor, David Barrington, served Alexandra cocktails and Mavrodaphne trifle (among other things), as in *Brideshead Revisited.*

For permission to use copyrighted material, we thank the Estate of Evelyn Waugh, the Estate of Laura Waugh, the Wylie Agency, the Orion Publishing Group, the BBC Written Archives Centre, Penguin Books Ltd, Oxford University Press, J. C. C. Glass, Jeremy Front, and Little, Brown and Company.

Abbreviations

ALL	*A Little Learning*, 1964
ALO	*A Little Order*, 1977
BM	*Black Mischief*, 1932
BR	*Brideshead Revisited*, 1945
Campion	*Edmund Campion*, 1935
CSEW	*The Complete Stories of Evelyn Waugh*, 1999
CSS	*The Complete Short Stories and Selected Drawings*, 1998
D&F	*Decline and Fall*, 1928
DEW	*The Diaries of Evelyn Waugh*, 1976
EAR	*The Essays, Articles and Reviews of Evelyn Waugh*, 1983
EB	*The End of the Battle*, 1961
Helena	*Helena*, 1950
Knox	*Ronald Knox*, 1959
Labels	*Labels*, 1930
LEW	*The Letters of Evelyn Waugh*, 1980
MW&MS	*Mr Wu & Mrs Stitch: The Letters of Evelyn Waugh & Diana Cooper*, 1992
RuL	*Robbery under Law*, 1939
Scoop	*Scoop*, 1938
SoH	*Sword of Honour*, 1965
TL	*Two Lives*, 2001
Tourist	*A Tourist in Africa*, 1960
WiA	*Waugh in Abyssinia*, 1936
WTGWG	*When the Going Was Good*, 1946

Introduction

Robert Murray Davis

DURING THE 1980S, AS VARIOUS SCHOLARS WERE TRYING TO COME TO informed if not definitive conclusions about values, structures, and meanings in Evelyn Waugh's work and about its possible place in the canon of twentieth-century fiction and, more broadly, of comic and satiric fiction, more and more material was becoming available. Since then, scholars in various countries have published hundreds of books, articles, and notes on Waugh, more than a hundred listed in the *MLA International Bibliography* since 2003 (with an unaccountable gap between that date and 1998), and one veteran Waugh scholar maintains that nothing more remains to be said about him. Fortunately, participants at the Evelyn Waugh Centenary Conference at Hertford College, Oxford, came to a different conclusion in 2003. Since Waugh's memory could not be fully honored without at least a touch of irony, the conference was organized by an American scholar, and most of the speakers were from the European, North American, and Australian continents, none held in high esteem by the subject under discussion. Meals and some sessions were conducted under the glowering portrait of C. R. M. F. Cruttwell, Waugh's disapproving tutor, whose name became a byword for incompetence or worse not only in Waugh's prose but also in the speech by Waugh's grandson, Alexander.

This selection of papers from the conference, aptly entitled "*A Handful of Mischief,*" shows that there is much more to be said about Evelyn Waugh. Four papers study the contexts in which Waugh's work was written and by which it can be better understood. Another five use recent theory to illuminate and, in some cases surprisingly, to defend Waugh against tired charges of snobbery, racism, religious intolerance, and other politically incorrect attitudes laid against him by Edmund Wilson, Conor Cruise O'Brien, and a host of less talented stylists going back more than sixty years.

For at least half of that time, Donat Gallagher searched libraries all over the world to discover long-buried work like an article for *Catholic Mother* and an interview in the *Uganda Herald*, and he dug even more deeply in the archives of the Vatican and the War Office. As a result, he knows more about Waugh's life and work than all of his biographers put together. Much of Gallagher's labor has consisted of attempts to correct gross and at times seemingly willful misstatements of fact. He has been particularly diligent in trying to correct the numerous errors in Martin Stannard's two-volume biography, notably about Waugh's testimony before the ecclesiastical court that finally granted the annulment of his marriage to Evelyn Gardner and about Waugh's much-maligned war record. Waugh served with the Commandos in Crete and wrote about his experience in the *Sword of Honour* trilogy. In "Guy Crouchback's Disillusion: Crete, Beevor, and the Soviet Alliance in *Sword of Honour*," Gallagher considers whether Waugh and his commanding officer, Robert Laycock, acted legally and honorably in leaving the island, thus avoiding capture. Gallagher admits, "It may seem ponderous . . . to counter this lively story with documented argument. But to answer one assertion with another is not productive." His argument is based on four issues: what Laycock did during the evacuation and whether Waugh recorded those actions truthfully in the War Diary, whether the historian Antony Beevor's charges have any merit, why Waugh reacted so strongly after the Cretan campaign in referring to dishonor, and whether or not Beevor increases our understanding of the trilogy.

John Howard Wilson's "A Walking Tour of Evelyn Waugh's Oxford" is no less detailed, but it is geographically rather than intellectually complex, literally pedestrian, since it stemmed from an actual tour during the conference. For those not familiar with Oxford, two points become apparent. First, to those accustomed to the sprawling campuses of American universities, the colleges that compose the university are surprisingly compact. To reach the Union from Hertford, Waugh would have had to walk about two blocks. The Bodleian Library is across the street, Blackwell's Book Shop just around the corner, C. M. Bowra at Wadham College half a block up Parks Road. Wilson very usefully traces the movements of characters in *Brideshead Revisited*, points out important landmarks in Waugh's university career—not all of them on the map, but easily located—and identifies people and places that Waugh used frequently—some, such as Cruttwell, almost promiscuously—throughout his career of four decades.

Richard W. Oram provides a different kind of walking tour, of Waugh's library, now at the Harry Ransom Center (known to old hands as the Humanities Research Center) at the University of Texas at Austin. Waugh's taste for Victoriana seemed odd until it became fashionable just before the middle of the last century, and Oram notes the number of books that "relate in some way to ornamentation, because this is precisely what Waugh valued so much in Victorian books, furniture, and art." Oram concludes that Waugh's love of books and other possessions was, as were his relationships with people, tempered by his fear "of being swallowed up . . . and thereby losing his identity."

As do Gallagher and Oram, Patrick Denman Flanery dives into archives—in this case of the BBC to examine Lance Sieveking's radio script for the 1956 broadcast of *Brideshead Revisited*. Both the script and preliminary publicity, Flanery demonstrates, present "the story as a chiefly secular microcosm of upper-class life, with reference neither to Roman Catholicism nor to Charles's adulterous relationship with Julia, and only a deftly inconclusive description of Charles and Sebastian's friendship and their Oxford milieu." Anthony Blanche, Celia, and less colorful secondary characters are diminished or deleted entirely; added dialogue introduces "arch class caricature." Flanery notes, perceptively, that the broadcast version plays an important part in the study of the novel's reputation. The Home Service, a middlebrow outlet between the more prestigious Third Programme and the Light Programme, gave *Brideshead* a "downward positioning in the popular consciousness," and "its further popularization at the hands of Granada Television's ITV-broadcast adaptation has aided its construction, at least in Britain, as rather mediocre melodramatic entertainment: a window on the eccentricities of the English upper-classes, and specifically on that even smaller minority of the Catholic upper-classes."

General readers and more advanced students of Waugh may be attracted to essays that offer new or more complex interpretations of his work by using new or neglected critical approaches. Peter G. Christensen's "Homosexuality in *Brideshead Revisited*: 'Something quite remote from anything the [builder] intended'" offers a provocative new interpretation of the relationship between Charles Ryder and Sebastian Flyte, and readers who become fully engaged in his argument will find themselves surprised and enlightened. Christensen argues that whereas Sebastian is gay, Charles is not; that Charles's narration is guided by unconscious "homosexual panic"; and that Sebastian's apparent withdrawal from Charles is due less to his alcoholism than to depression resulting from his awareness that "Charles [has] escaped from Sebastian's 'solitude,' his feeling of isolation as a young gay man." Furthermore, Charles's journey to faith occurs not through his successive loves for Sebastian and Julia but through Lord Marchmain's deathbed conversion, facilitated by the celibate Father Mackay. It is clear that the end of the novel, in which there will be no dynastic heir to Brideshead Castle, supports Christensen's case that "conversion, not procreation, ensures the survival of the Christian church."

The concept of conversion includes not just formal submission but also spiritual awakening; it can also be a thematic and structural device, as in John W. Mahon's "'A Later Development': Evelyn Waugh and Conversion." *Brideshead* is only a small factor in Mahon's argument that conversion is central not only to this novel, *Helena*, and *Sword of Honour,* but also to Waugh's biographies of Edmund Campion and Ronald Knox, to Waugh's own conversion to Catholicism, and indeed to his view of the church as providing not a refuge from the outer world but a whole new universe in which the world and the individual can be transformed. Mahon shows that Waugh presents the actual process of conversion only for secondary characters, normally preferring to show the effect in characters' lives.

Both Irina Kabanova and Marcel DeCoste maintain that *Helena* offers clues to reading Waugh's work as a whole. Using Michel Foucault as a starting point for analyzing institutions of power, Kabanova examines Helena's statement about "Power without Grace"—who better qualified than a Russian to do so?—in light not only of that novel but also of *Edmund Campion.* Her analysis of the marionette/dummy metaphor can be applied not only to Queen Elizabeth and Constantine, foils to Waugh's eponymous saints, but also to characters such as Professor Otto Silenus in *Decline and Fall* and in much of Waugh's later work. DeCoste argues that *Helena* "seriously challenges the simple equation of Waugh's faith with elitist nostalgia" and that its "flagrant and obtrusive anachronisms foreground an historical sensibility at odds with this equation," showing not decline and fall but recurrence relieved only by incursions of the divine into the temporal.

DeCoste concludes that *Helena* "offers us a Waugh interestingly at variance with portraits, not excluding his own, depicting *him* as an anachronism, a Jacobite lost in the twentieth century and mourning the irreparable passing of a worthier culture, a truer civilization." This project of redeeming Waugh, even from himself, is continued in Lewis MacLeod's "'That Glittering, Intangible Western Culture': 'Civilizing' Missions and the Crisis of Tradition in Evelyn Waugh's *Black Mischief*" and Dan S. Kostopulos's "Eyes Reopened: *A Tourist in Africa*." Unlike many critics, who view Waugh's travel books as revealing racial and class snobbery—an attitude analyzed and, as far as possible, refuted in Baron Alder's "Violence, Duplicity, and Frequent Malversation: *Robbery under Law* and Evelyn Waugh's Political Critique"—Kostopulos concentrates on what he got right in his trips to Africa. Oddly—Waugh would no doubt have thought so—he anticipates some observations of Frantz Fanon and Edward Said about the effects of colonialism on the colonized and, in the words of recent postcolonial theorists offering a definition of their approach, "foregrounds a politics of opposition and struggle, and problematizes the key relationship between centre and periphery." One can imagine Waugh's Pinfoldish reaction to "problematizes." Kostopulos concludes that *A Tourist in Africa* should "be thought of as a significant work of postcolonial discourse because it demonstrates a shift in consciousness, a new awareness that the relationship between the colonized subject and the colonizer is in the midst of a profound transformation."

Lewis MacLeod draws even more widely on postcolonial theory to illuminate Waugh's view not only of Africa but also of the traditions of England's landed gentry: "Both must deal with the fallout that results from an under-considered effort to 'modernize' the cultural and physical spaces they once considered their own." Seth's desire to modernize Azania stems from "self-loathing" and the belief that the closer it moves to "the universalist dimensions of modern thought, the more civilized the country becomes." But as MacLeod demonstrates, *Black Mischief* refuses to equate modern with civilized and primitive with barbaric, and "Tradition, even African tradition, earns Waugh's respect; modernity arouses his suspicion."

The longest critical essay in the collection, Ann Pasternak Slater's "Waffle Scramble: Waugh's Art in *Scoop*," interweaves factual material drawn from Waugh's nonfiction, letters, and diaries with analysis of literary sources and recurrent situations that become structural devices holding the novel together. As in *Labels*, where the author observes a honeymoon couple clearly based on Waugh and Evelyn Gardner, Waugh divides himself into the fashionable novelist John Courtney Boot and the naïve countryman William Boot, and, as Pasternak Slater indicates, the confusion of one with the other initiates the plot devices of mistaken identity and reversal used throughout the novel and embodied rhetorically in anagram and metathesis.

Students and even more casual readers of Waugh will find in *"A Handful of Mischief"* much to stimulate rereading and reconsideration not only of Waugh's work but also of long-held, even ossified, attitudes toward it.

The hope I expressed twenty years ago for new approaches to Waugh has been answered beyond my expectations and certainly beyond my fears. But like many wishes, it cannot be finally fulfilled, and we can look forward to new and provocative readings of a writer whose work has survived him and his century.

"A Handful of Mischief"

Evelyn Waugh, Bookman

Richard W. Oram

In a piece written for *Life* in 1946, Evelyn Waugh confessed that he collected old books in an "inexpensive, desultory way."[1] The statement is deceptively modest, for Waugh was in fact a discerning bibliophile and book collector for most of his life. The principal evidence resides in his 3,500-volume library, now a part of the Harry Ransom Humanities Research Center at the University of Texas at Austin.[2] Not surprisingly, the contents of the Waugh Library reflect the collector's own fondness for Victoriana and the grotesque, as well as its highly opinionated owner's personal tastes and prejudices in modern literature. It also reflects his lifelong love affair with the book arts, and ornamented bindings, calligraphy, and illustration in particular. Waugh's interest in finely produced books led him to pay careful attention to the appearance of his own works, most notably the limited editions prepared for friends and fellow authors. Books as physical objects (and not just beautifully illustrated or handsomely bound ones) always fascinated Waugh, and they were prominent features in his homes and those of his parents and grandparents. In the novels, the books owned and read by various characters often provide us with subtle insight into their intellectual and interior life. Although it will not be attempted here, a study of all of the references to books and reading in the novels—this is especially true of *Brideshead Revisited* (1945)—would be revelatory.

Waugh's enthusiasm for books was formed very early in life and began with excursions into the library, chockablock with medical specimens, stuffed birds, and other exotic curiosities, at Midsomer Norton, the home of his paternal grandparents. He was fortunate to have access to the extensive library of his father, Arthur Waugh. Evelyn retained around 250 volumes typical of an Edwardian man of letters, sets of Thackeray and Dickens (one of which, the *Nonesuch Dickens*, Arthur had coedited), as well as many signed copies of books by Chapman & Hall authors. It was a source of youthful delight but in later years would symbolize the novelist's sense of difference from his father. This distancing is obvious in an article entitled "General Conversation: Myself" (1937), which refers to an episode "on one of my rare, recent visits to my home" in which Evelyn "inadvertently set the house on fire, destroying the carefully garnered fruits of a lifetime of literary friendships" (*EAR* 190). According to Arthur's diaries at Boston University, the fire took place at Highgate on January 29, 1935. The fruits to which Evelyn refers are the "hundreds of inscribed copies" by some of the "numerous, patronizing literary elders" (*EAR* 190) who frequented the Waugh house. A few days later, Evelyn flippantly remarked to Mary Lygon, "I set my booms [i.e., father's] house on fire last Monday."[3] There is no indication that Evelyn felt much remorse about setting his father's books on fire (most likely with his cigar while he was tipsy); on the contrary, one finds a strong undercurrent of hostility toward his father. "General Conversation: Myself" is about the shared family occupation "man of letters," which bonds him to his father, but it is also about the son's rejection of the stuffier world of the previous literary generation and the books they produced.[4]

Evelyn Waugh began to assemble his own library as a very young man, while still at Lancing College. His adolescent bibliophilia peaked in the autumn of 1919, to judge from entries in the *Diaries*. On September 27: "I have found another of Andrew Lang's book-collecting books. My opinion of the value of my much valued Elzevir has been rudely shocked."[5] A few weeks later, on another book by Lang: "It is printed very well on the most beautiful handmade paper and the feel of its crisp edges made me feel that I could buy no book on anything else again" (*DEW* 24). And another: "I have spent a lot of today pondering on the very important question of bindings. . . . I have just thought what an excellent binding could be made of half black morocco, and half cloth of gold, but I have only enough of it to do a very small book and it would only be suitable for certain sorts, such as Oscar Wilde. . . . If only I could do it myself" (*DEW* 23). Here is evidence of Waugh's early fascination with the pure sensuality of books, especially finely bound ones, not to mention his crush on the greenery-yallery books of the 1890s, typified by the book designs of Charles Ricketts.

Calligraphy was another passion. One of his early heroes was Edward Johnston, the great English calligrapher best known as the teacher of Eric Gill and as the designer of the crimson initial letter *I* that travels down the first page of Genesis in the Doves Press Bible. When Waugh was only fourteen, he was taken to the socialist community at Ditchling to meet Johnston. The calligrapher inscribed a copy of the eighth edition of *Writing & Illuminating, & Lettering*, now in Austin, to the young man. In later years, Waugh could still "treasure the memory of the experience of seeing those swift, precise, vermilion strokes coming to life" (*EAR* 536). Through Johnston, Waugh was to discover Eric Gill, whose typography and craftsmanship he consistently admired. In late 1919, not long after presenting a paper on illumination and decoration at the Lancing Art Club and winning a school prize for his own illuminated letter, Evelyn met the calligrapher, illuminator, and aesthete Francis Crease, who exerted a strong influence on the young bibliophile. Thereafter, his Thursday sessions with Crease became sacred events, until the relationship soured after Evelyn broke a prized penknife he had used without permission. Crease taught him the basics of calligraphy and illumination, further encouraging his already considerable love of the decorative arts in all forms. Waugh bestowed his highest possible praise on Crease's work in his 1927 preface to the artist's *Thirty-four Decorative Designs* when he wrote that Crease's "fineness of perception" was comparable to Ruskin's.[6]

The Lancing housemaster E. B. Gordon, who introduced Waugh to Crease, was also responsible for teaching him how to print on a small handpress. This formative experience was later fictionalized in the autobiographical fragment "Charles Ryder's School Days." The housemaster, Mr. Graves, takes an 1824 stationer's press, complete with a bag of jumbled type and ornaments, to school. Charles priggishly claims to be more interested in calligraphy than typography, yet he is actually enchanted by the process of printing, daydreaming obsessively about "the tall folios, the wide margins, the deckle-edged mould-made paper, the engraved initials, the rubrics and colophons of his private press."[7] For Charles (and Evelyn), the world of books and bookmaking represented an escape from the banalities of school life.

At Oxford, Waugh's bibliophilia was partially diluted by his participation in the usual undergraduate pursuits and by his perennial lack of money. Nevertheless, visiting friends could find him in his Hertford College quarters luxuriating in the midst of finely bound volumes. Bindings were still an obsession. Regarding the Ricardi Press Rupert Brooke, Evelyn writes in a 1922 letter to Tom Driberg: "I cannot possibly afford it but sufficient for the day is the beauty thereof. I am having [it] bound—after much hesitation between levant moroccos, calfs, pigskins and Morris papers—in full vellum, bevelled boards, absolutely untooled anywhere."[8] In his last years at Oxford, Waugh polished his own artistic skills and earned some money to buy books by creating dust-jacket art for his father's firm (something he had been doing since his Lancing days) and bookplates for his friends. Unfortunately, Waugh's book buying had a sudden end during his last year at Oxford, when his rapidly mounting debts forced him to auction off the choicest parts of the library. This episode, fictionalized, forms the climax of the story "The Balance" (1926), in which the library of Adam Doure, a thinly disguised version of the author, is described in these terms: "Adam's book-shelves; it is rather a remarkable library for a man of his age and means. Most of the books have a certain rarity and many are elaborately bound; there are also old books of considerable value given him from time to time by his father" (*CSEW* 19). As did Waugh's, Adam's profligacy ends in a cataclysm; his prized volumes are sold off at a fraction of their value to the predatory Mr. Macassor.

After university, Evelyn's affinities for the book arts were still strong, and his father put up a premium so that Evelyn could become an apprentice at John Guthrie's Pear-Tree Press. The young artist's dreams of life at a fine press were deflated after one night's stay with Guthrie: "I was not exhilarated by what I found," he reported in *A Little Learning* (1964): "I had expected something like the austere and secluded St Dominic's Press at Ditchling [founded by Eric Gill and Hilary Pepler], but the cottage which gave the press its romantic name was a modern villa very near Bognor. The young son of the house, with whom I walked for a morning through damp lanes in search of lodgings, confided in me his ambition to become a fashion-designer."[9] Equally unappealing to Waugh was Guthrie's use of modern photo-etched process plates, rather than more traditional wood engravings like Gill's, for his illustrations.

Poverty and the pursuit of a career continued to be impediments to Waugh's bibliophilia, and it is only in the late 1930s, after his early literary successes and his marriage to Laura Herbert, that references to book buying begin once more to crop up with regularity in the diaries and letters. The move to Piers Court at Stinchcombe ("Stinkers") at last provided Waugh with a proper home for his books. The library was promptly outfitted with two "very fine carved pedestals which I am having converted at enormous expense into bookcase ends" (*DEW* 420) as well as a portrait of George III that stared down at Waugh from the opposite wall of the library; "I think of putting 'scribble, scribble' on a ribbon across the top," he writes (*DEW* 438). A couple of allegorical Victorian "problem paintings" by Rebecca Solomon titled *The Virtuous Undergraduate* and *The Dissolute Undergraduate* were added later, as was a trompe l'oeil painting on tin by Martin Battersby, presented to the author by Chapman & Hall and featuring elements from Waugh's books. Tom Driberg described this highly eclectic room, painted in bluish green, black, and white, as it looked during the 1950s in an article written for, of all places, *Housewife* magazine. After making his way past the brass plaque with the famous engraved notice "NO ADMITTANCE ON BUSINESS," Driberg penetrated to the sanctum sanctorum:

> The library is the finest room at Piers Court—indeed the only room of more than modest size. To make more space for his books, Mr. Waugh had a window blocked up at the end of the room behind his desk, and built bookcases out into the room at right angles to the outer wall, adorning these cases with Ionic capitals. His inkpot is a bust of Queen Victoria, and on his desk, too, is a bowl full of stone eggs. . . . Similar stone eggs are scattered throughout the house, even in the bathrooms, as ornaments or paper-weights. Mr. Waugh has collected them for years. "I like playing with one when I'm thinking," he says.[10]

At the beginning of the war in 1939, Waugh rented out Piers Court and sent his family to Pixton Park. The books remained for a time at "Stinkers," then leased to a convent. Writing to Laura in November 1940, Waugh made sure that she would ask the nuns to air his books: "That is to say take them all out shelf by shelf, dust them, open the leaves & bang them together. Otherwise they will get worm & damp in them" (*LEW* 146). Between his various military assignments, he often stayed at the Hyde Park Hotel. The bulk of Waugh's library was transferred there from Stinkers at some point and remained in London until November 1943, when, because of the threat of German rocket bombardment from France, the books were evacuated back to Piers Court, where they went into storage. The transfer of the books to the countryside occasioned a remarkably frank, even chilling entry in the *Diaries*. Waugh writes of the timing of the library move: "At the same time I have advocated my son coming to London. It would seem from this that I prefer my books to my son. I can argue that firemen rescue children and destroy books, but the truth is that a child is easily replaced while a book destroyed is utterly lost; also a child is eternal; but most that I have a sense of absolute possession over my library and not over my nursery" (*DEW* 555). We must take this admission at face value while acknowledging that Waugh's tendency to play agent provocateur lies behind it. Relationships with people were always messy for him and all too often ended in disastrous dustups; as he wrote to Graham Greene in late 1952, "It has been a year of lost friends for me. Not by death but wear & tear" (*LEW* 386). Children never behaved precisely as they ought. Relationships with collectibles, on the other hand, were predictable and orderly, hence reassuring (although even these ultimately failed him). Books established a sense of protective order and reassurance at war's end when Waugh returned to

Piers Court. Almost the first thing he did was to unpack all of the books he had placed in storage, positioning them perfectly on the much-missed library shelves. The function of the library as sanctuary was apparent in later years when Waugh frequently retreated there to eat in solitary peace, worlds removed from the tumult of family dinners (there might be, after all, six children at table!).

What books was Waugh collecting in the late 1930s and during the war years, when he was able to spend time in London bookshops? They were "shabby little new books and sumptuous old ones" (*DEW* 540), and the ones dearest to his heart were not modern but old ones, especially the Victoriana he prized so much. Chief among these books were the high Victorian chromolithographic masterpieces of Owen Jones, such as the lavishly illustrated *Grammar of Ornament*, and of Henry Noel Humphreys. At the time Waugh began collecting them, these books were still scorned by most serious collectors and could be procured for almost nothing—for example, he purchased a copy of the Owen Jones *Victoria Psalter* for £1 (*DEW* 551). Only in the late 1940s and early 1950s did this situation change; John Carter began pointing out that there were bargains to be had in Victorian fiction, and Ruari McLean produced the first of his groundbreaking reevaluations of the merit of Owen Jones and his contemporaries. Today, no man of Waugh's relatively modest means could possibly assemble such a brilliant collection of these works without expending tens of thousands of pounds. For Waugh, the chromolithograph represented the apex of illustrative technique. In one of his reviews he contrasts the modern color-illustrated book with its nineteenth-century predecessor: "The paint, though more opaque than one could wish, has not the solidity of most medieval manuscripts. This solidity, so brilliantly and arduously counterfeited early in the last century by the hand-colouring of Henry Shaw and the lithography of Owen Jones, was quite lost in the photographic, three-colour process at the beginning of this century" (*EAR* 463). In a Proustian moment recorded in the wartime diaries, Waugh compares the sunrise shining through the vines in Yugoslavia "to the border round a text, to my grandmother's illumination, to the tones of chromolithograph" (*DEW* 581). Here nature is seen through the eyes of a bookman.

Beside the color-plate books, there are a good many examples of Victorian caoutchouc (natural rubber) and papier-mâché bindings in the high neogothic style of the 1850s and 1860s. There are also many books on Victorian architecture; one of Waugh's particular favorites was Chambers's *Civil Architecture*, which he bought in 1939. Many titles in the Waugh library relate in some way to ornamentation, because this is precisely what

Waugh valued so much in Victorian books, furniture, and art. In the 1938 article "The Philistine Age of English Decoration" in *Harper's Bazaar*, Waugh notes that in the modern world, "ornament is vulgar" (*EAR* 220), but for Victorians decoration provided entertainment and relief from the ordinary. However, he predicts (rightly, given the late-twentieth-century revival of interest in Victorian furniture) that "the inevitable cycle of taste will restore all and more than all that was lost. Now is the time to form the collections of genuine pieces" (*EAR* 221). While he is speaking of furniture, he could as easily be expressing his view of books. Waugh's best exposition of the value of ornament is contained in a 1954 piece that compares the nineteenth-century home to modern domestic architecture: "the huge euphoria of the Victorian home may be attributed directly to the abundance of ornament. How much of the neurotic boredom of today comes from the hygienic blankness of offices, aerodrome waiting-rooms, hospitals? The human mind requires constant minor occupations to put it at rest. The eye must be caught and held before the brain will work" (*EAR* 466).

After the success of *Brideshead* and *The Loved One* (1948), Waugh could afford to make large investments in books and antiques. In the early 1940s, Waugh had established a close relationship with the firm of G. Heywood Hill, a well-respected bookshop still to be found on Curzon Street in London. Heywood Hill was called up in 1942, and the firm would probably have gone under were it not for the efforts of Nancy Mitford and some of her friends, who not only sold books but also packed them for shipment. In the postwar years, Waugh's principal contact at Heywood Hill was Handasyde Buchanan, a specialist in Victorian art books, who became Mitford's boss. Waugh corresponded frequently with Buchanan and bought both Victoriana and contemporary literature from him. "Handy" Buchanan was an opinionated Scottish socialist, so it is tempting to imagine sparks flying when bookseller and customer met, but the truth is that these two crusty men got along extremely well. At least, that is the impression created by Buchanan's amusing reminiscence in *Evelyn Waugh and His World*.[11] Waugh occasionally managed to include in his letters some aspersions on Buchanan's political views. For example, after Buchanan had thanked him for one of the special copies of *Ronald Knox* (1959), Waugh responded, "Greatly encouraged that Agnostic socialist can find interest in KNOX, thanks awfully for telling me" (*LEW* 225). On another occasion, Waugh returned a book to the shop, addressing the parcel to "the Secretary, West London Pornophilic Society, c/o H. Buchanan Esq" (*LEW* 225–26). Waugh once sent the following message on a postcard to another bookseller: "Could you please tell me, does 'spine repaired' mean rebacked by a competent binder or plastered with scotch tape by a governess? If the former please send."[12]

Though the Waugh Library demonstrates the collector's preference for books of the Victorian age, as opposed to those of "the darker and duller succeeding century" (*EAR* 635), Waugh did buy some modern books. He also received more than a few inscribed copies of works by his friends. The most notable series of books inscribed to Waugh are the twenty-odd from Graham Greene, in editions from the late 1940s to the mid-1960s. Greene's mistress, Catherine Walston, presented the Classic Comics version of *Crime and Punishment* bearing the inscription "To join the E.W. collection of Russian novels." By far the most interesting of the Greene inscriptions appears in *A Burnt-Out Case*, in which Greene has written "For Evelyn with deep affection & admiration from Graham." Below, Waugh has added in red ink: "Mud in your mild & magnificent eye. E.W. Epiphany 1961. Ever glad, confident morning again?" The allusion to Robert Browning's poem "The Lost Leader" says much about the declining state of the relationship between the two novelists at this time. "The Lost Leader" is addressed to the aging leader of a movement by one of his erstwhile followers, who once "lived in his mild and magnificent eye." In his later years, the "lost leader" has abandoned his youthful ideals and has sold out his troops. The poem's speaker condemns his former role model, usually identified as William Wordsworth, once revolutionary but by the early 1840s politically conservative. The speaker, betrayed by his idol, renounces him:

> Life's night begins: let him never come back to us!
> There would be doubt, hesitation and pain,
> Forced praise on our part—the glimmer of twilight,
> Never glad confident morning again!

Waugh's letter to Greene of January 5, 1961, the day before the inscription, alludes to the same poem in its attack on *A Burnt-Out Case*. Waugh had refused to review the novel for the *Daily Mail* and regarded it as a "plain repudiation" (*LEW* 559) of Greene's Catholicism: "You will find not so much 'hostility' among your former fellowship as the regrets of Browning for his 'Lost Leader'—except, of course, that no one will impute mercenary motives" (*LEW* 559). The inscription, however, is even more acerbic than the letter, since Waugh's version turns into an ironic toast: "Mud in your mild & magnificent eye."

Other major contemporary novelists are represented as well: Anthony Powell, Ivy Compton-Burnett, Henry Green, Muriel Spark, and Elizabeth Bowen.[13] The virtual absence of P. G. Wodehouse is a surprise; it appears that these books were held back by the family. Among the modern poets are John Betjeman, Waugh's contemporary at Oxford, and Edith Sitwell, who inscribed two books to Waugh: he had served as her sponsor when she was received into the Catholic Church. We may regret that Waugh was generally not an annotator of books, as Robert Murray Davis has demonstrated in his useful checklist of the marginalia in the library.[14] On the few occasions when Waugh did annotate and found the book contemptible, his comments could be merciless. The most celebrated example is the limited edition of *The Unquiet Grave*, written by Cyril Connolly, under the pen name *Palinurus*. Waugh heavily annotated his copy in red ink during the last year of the war (these annotations have been transcribed by Alan Bell).[15] Waugh's caustic remarks, some of them almost long enough to be miniature essays, emphasize Connolly's sentimentality, sloppy theology, and even sloppier writing. In 1971, Connolly visited the Humanities Research Center and discovered the rubricated copy in his old friend's library; the experience devastated him, and upon his return home, he sold all of his inscribed Waugh first editions.

After Catherine Waugh's death in 1954, Arthur's library was split between Evelyn and his brother, Alec. It included many presentation copies from Arthur's friends and contemporaries and long runs of his favorite authors, notably Dickens, Tennyson, and Kipling ("Terrible man my father," Evelyn once said. "He likes Kipling").[16] Evelyn's letters to Alec, now at the Ransom Center, indicate how the division of these books put further stress on an already strained fraternal relationship. Waugh moved from Piers Court to Combe Florey in early 1957. One of the attractions of the red sandstone house was that it had a spacious library. Here, copies of his manuscripts—the early ones bound by Maltby of Oxford, the later ones more sumptuously, with the family arms on the front, by Sangorski & Sutcliffe or Zaehnsdorf—joined equally sumptuous copies of the limited editions of his works on large paper. Chapman & Hall began preparing these, beginning with *Black Mischief* in 1932, for Waugh to present to friends; they were charged to his account. At times, Waugh was heavily involved in the design and typography of the large-paper editions—for example, in *Love among the Ruins* (1953), he consulted the printer for hours and then required that the entire special edition be pulped after it failed to live up to his expectations. When the cover design for the American reprint of *Brideshead Revisited* reached him, Waugh took care to write to Little, Brown: "It is a most incompetent and lamentable design. Pray suppress it."[17] Waugh took a close interest—unusual among major novelists—in the bibliographical niceties of his own works: he fretted that the limited edition of *Basil Seal Rides Again* (1963) appeared in two states (one with and one without a half-title) and that "the numbers of each were not recorded" (*DEW* 787).

After Evelyn Waugh's death in 1966, Laura Waugh found herself in financial distress; it later turned out that her situation was not as dire as it seemed. Her American son-in-law, John D'Arms, the husband of Waugh's daughter Teresa and a professor at the University of Michigan, contacted Harry Ransom, then the chancellor of the University of Texas, about selling the contents of Waugh's library to the Humanities Research Center. After further negotiations involving the American bookseller Lew David Feldman, alias "El Dieff," who played a role in many of Ransom's major acquisitions, the manuscripts of all but two of the novels were added to the deal. A few months before his death, Evelyn had taken Alec Waugh to task for donating manuscripts to Boston University instead of selling them: "Your gift of archives to America will cause a painful precedent. Most of your fellow-writers hope to support their declining years by sales to Texas."[18] Ironically, Evelyn's prediction of a sale to Texas came true a couple of years later, although hardly in the manner he had expected. Ransom agreed to purchase the manuscripts of most of the novels as well as the library, desk, bookshelves, pedestals, paintings, and some miscellaneous furniture and decorative objects. The probable intention was to reconstruct the Combe Florey library in a special room in the center's new building, but this in fact never came to pass.

No discussion of the Waugh library would be complete without consideration of an item that has consistently drawn more attention than anything else. A large oblong scrapbook, shown to scores of visitors to the Ransom Center over the years, has been nicknamed "The Blood Book." It contains collages consisting of carefully cut out and assembled engravings from eighteenth- and nineteenth-century books. The emphasis is on religious imagery and the Crucifixion interwoven with images of birds and snakes. Most of the images drip blood in the form of red ink. The "Blood Book" is an object of fascination, horror, and mystery. We know that it was created or at least commissioned by a Victorian businessman and politician named John Bingley Garland, and it was given to his daughter, Amy, in 1854. Nothing is known about its path to Waugh's library.

Apart from the mysteries of its creation, purpose, and provenance, there is the central mystery of the album's appeal to Waugh. What did he see in it? What does it tell us about him? Besides its appeal as an item of Victoriana, the wedding album is an astonishingly grotesque book, which clearly appealed to Waugh's well-known and lifelong obsession with collecting the bizarre, in the form of books or bric-a-brac. A piercingly honest observation that pops up in the *Diaries* indicates the function of grotesquerie: "By choosing preposterous objects as possessions," Waugh writes, "I keep them at arm's length" (*DEW* 610). Equally à propos is a note found after Waugh's death and identified by Selina Hastings as referring to Piers Court: "Everybody who comes in says 'What a lovely house you've got.' But I haven't got it: it has got me. How am I to impress my personality (if I have one) on a house whose atmosphere is not mine? And how long will it be before the place begins to impress its personality on me?"[19] In a wartime letter to Laura, Waugh refers to his "ineradicable love of collecting bric-a-brac" and his "collecting mania," one of two principal motivations in life, along with writing (*LEW* 190). Always fearful of being swallowed up in personal relationships, getting too close to other people and thereby losing his identity, Waugh was, it seems, equally wary of being consumed by his own possessions—houses, books, art, antiques. All of those objects must finally be kept "at arm's length." The first-rate library he built over several decades gave Waugh a sense of pride and afforded him a measure of protection from the world, but ultimately even it could not make him secure.

NOTES

1. Evelyn Waugh, *The Essays, Articles and Reviews of Evelyn Waugh,* ed. Donat Gallagher (Boston: Little, Brown, 1983), 301. Hereafter cited as *EAR.*

2. See Anthony Newnham, "Evelyn Waugh's Library," *Library Chronicle of the University of Texas at Austin* ns 1 (1970): 25–29, a useful overview of the library and its contents, particularly the literary works.

3. Evelyn Waugh, *The Letters of Evelyn Waugh*, ed. Mark Amory (New York: Ticknor & Fields, 1980), 93. Hereafter cited as *LEW.*

4. My interpretation of this episode is similar to those of Alexander Waugh, who regards it as yet another "father-son atrocity" of this period, and Martin Stannard, who misdates it. See Alexander Waugh, *Fathers and Sons: The Autobiography of a Family* (London: Headline, 2004), 230, and Stannard, *Evelyn Waugh: The Early Years 1903–1939* (London: Dent, 1986), 447. Both of them detect the hostility but miss Evelyn's ambivalence in his acknowledgment of the family bond.

5. Evelyn Waugh, *The Diaries of Evelyn Waugh*, ed. Michael Davie (Boston: Little, Brown, 1976), 21. Hereafter cited as *DEW.*

6. Evelyn Waugh, Preface to Francis Crease, *Thirty-four Decorative Designs* (London: A. R. Mowbray, 1927), vii.

7. Evelyn Waugh, *The Complete Stories of Evelyn Waugh* (Boston: Little, Brown, 1999), 308. Hereafter cited as *CSEW.*

8. Martin Stannard, *Evelyn Waugh: The Early Years 1903–1939* (London: Dent, 1986), 69.

9. Evelyn Waugh, *A Little Learning* (Boston: Little, Brown, 1964), 214.

10. Tom Driberg, "'Housewife' Visits Evelyn Waugh," *Housewife*, September 1955, 64.

11. Handasyde Buchanan, "His Bookseller's View," in *Evelyn Waugh and His World*, ed. David Pryce-Jones (London: Weidenfeld & Nicolson, 1973), 219–27. The letters are now at the Georgetown University Library. Nicholas Scheetz has informed me that almost all of them are routine orders or business inquiries.

12. Evelyn Waugh, postcard to Anthony Newnham, August 9, 1960, Evelyn Waugh Papers, Harry Ransom Center, University of Texas at Austin.

13. A more complete listing may be found in Newnham, "Evelyn Waugh's Library," 25–26.

14. Robert Murray Davis, *A Catalogue of the Evelyn Waugh Collection at the Humanities Research Center, the University of Texas at Austin* (Troy, NY: Whitston, 1981), 327–35.

15. Alan Bell, "Waugh Drops the Pilot," *Spectator*, March 7, 1987, 27–31.

16. Alec Waugh, *My Brother Evelyn, and Other Portraits* (London: Cassell, 1967), 169.

17. Evelyn Waugh, letter to Stanley Salmen, February 6, 1955, Evelyn Waugh Papers, Harry Ransom Center, University of Texas at Austin.

18. Evelyn Waugh, postcard to Alec Waugh, August 31, 1965 [postmark], Evelyn Waugh Papers, Harry Ransom Center, University of Texas at Austin.

19. Selina Hastings, *Evelyn Waugh: A Biography* (London: Sinclair-Stevenson, 1994), 361.

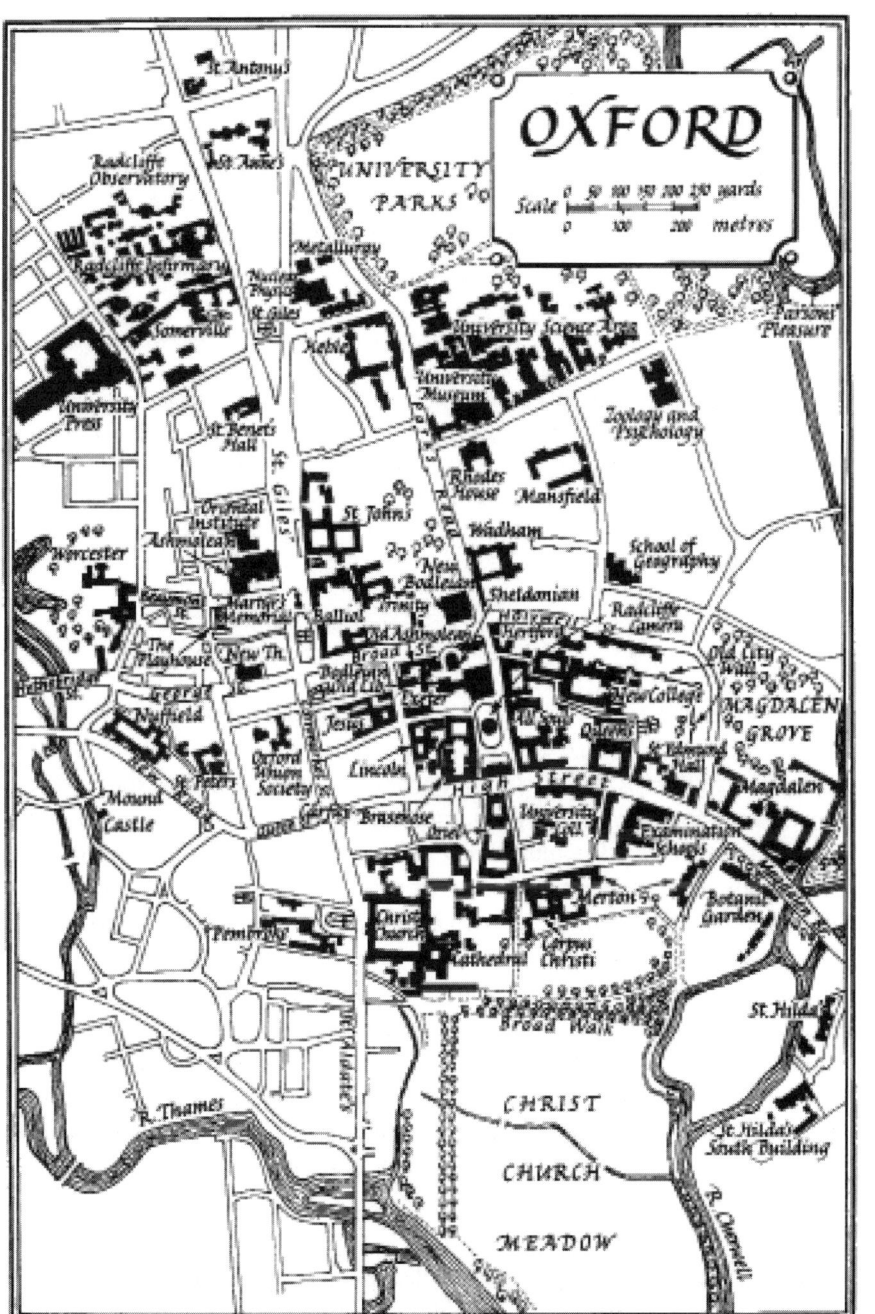

A Walking Tour of Evelyn Waugh's Oxford

John Howard Wilson

EVELYN WAUGH'S OXFORD COLLEGE, HERTFORD, DATES BACK TO THE FOUNDATION of Hart Hall by Elias de Hertford in the early 1280s.[1] Hart Hall was incorporated as Hertford College in 1740,[2] but it lacked endowment and ceased to exist in 1805.[3] Magdalen Hall occupied the site in 1822.[4] Thomas Charles Baring, "a partner in the merchant bank and a Member of Parliament,"[5] offered to endow several fellowships at Brasenose College, but BNC declined. Baring was a "staunch Conservative and strong Churchman," and the fellowships were "restricted to members of the Church of England."[6] Baring made a similar offer to Magdalen Hall in 1874.[7] The hall accepted, dissolved itself, and transferred its site and property to Hertford College.[8] (For the location of Hertford and other sites, refer to the map of Oxford.) Over the next several years, Baring spent £229,000 to endow twelve fellowships, thirty scholarships, seven lecturers, the bursar, and the dean.[9] These scholarships attracted Waugh when he visited Oxford in the early 1920s.

Waugh went to Oxford in December 1921 to compete for a scholarship. His father, Arthur Waugh, hoped that Evelyn would go to New College, where Arthur had been, but Evelyn knew that he was "not up to a New College scholarship," and he indicated that Hertford was his "first preference."[10] Hertford offered eighteen open scholarships, whereas New College offered only four; Hertford's were worth £100 per year, while New College's were worth £80. Waugh was desperate to escape from Lancing College, his public school, but Lancing probably directed him to Hertford. The founder of Lancing, Nathaniel Woodard, earned his degree at Magdalen Hall in 1840, and Lancing's captain of the school, Frank Edward Ford, went up to Hertford in 1921.[11] Conscious of these connections, Waugh selected Hertford, and he succeeded in winning a scholarship on his first try.

Waugh went up to Hertford in January 1922, and he lived a "solitary and quiet life" for two terms.[12] The college seemed "respectable but rather dreary" (*ALL* 164); a contemporary describes it as "earnest and lower-middle-class."[13] Waugh's rooms were in the "oldest building" and "looked out on New College Lane." These rooms were over the Junior Common Room buttery, and Waugh's "chief memory of the staircase is of the rattle of dish-covers on foggy afternoons and the smell of anchovy-toast and honey buns" (*ALL* 166). "Public-spirited senior men in Hertford" tried to recruit freshmen for the League of Nations Union, but Waugh "did not find much in common with these" (*ALL* 165). In *Decline and Fall* (1928), Paul Pennyfeather bicycles "happily back from a meeting of the League of Nations Union,"[14] only to run into the Bollinger Club. In *Brideshead Revisited* (1945), Sebastian Flyte supposes that he might mend his ways by joining the League of Nations Union.[15]

In his third term, beginning in September 1922, Waugh moved to "large rooms on the ground floor of the front quad" (*ALL* 171). He had become friends with Terence Greenidge, known for "eccentricities," such as "declaiming Greek choruses loudly, late at night, in the quad" (*ALL* 176). Waugh started keeping "open house for men from other colleges," and Greenidge "dubbed these assemblies 'offal.'" They "drank large quantities of beer and made a good deal of noise" (*ALL* 178–79). Beer was served at luncheon and dinner, though Waugh alone ordered "a tankard of beer for breakfast."[16] Drinking opened the breach with Waugh's tutor and the dean of Hertford, C. R. M. F. Cruttwell. Waugh had been "conspicuously drunk" at a "freshers' blind," and Cruttwell said he "had not chosen the best way of ingratiating [himself] with the college"; Waugh "became fatuously haughty" and declared himself "quite indifferent to college opinion" (*ALL* 175). Waugh and Greenidge accused Cruttwell of having a "sexual connection with dogs," and Greenidge bought "a stuffed one in a junk-shop in Walton Street," which they placed "in the quad as an allurement for him on his return from dining in All Souls," where Cruttwell had been a fellow before the First World War. Waugh and Greenidge also "used rather often to bark under Cruttwell's windows at night" (*ALL* 177). In *The Ordeal of Gilbert Pinfold* (1957), the voices claim that Mr. Pinfold was "sent down" because he had "accused the Dean of the most disgusting practices."[17]

Waugh began to make friends outside Hertford. Greenidge believed that Hertford men had been "lucky enough to hold him" as long as they had.[18] Hertford's gates closed at 9:05 p.m., though men could enter until 11:00 p.m. After that, one had to pay nine pence to the porter,[19] and the "list of late comers" was "submitted to the Dean. After midnight the only means of entering was by climbing. Both the possible routes . . . were tricky for drunks," and Waugh did not use "either more than a dozen times" (*ALL* 176). Hertford undergraduates disliked these habits, because "some participation by almost everyone was essential if a small college was to field teams of rugger, soccer, hockey, tennis, and cricket," plus rowing.[20] A "tipsy white colonial" asked Waugh what he "did for the college." Waugh answered that he "drank for it" (*ALL* 164).

Hertford influenced Waugh's writing in many ways. In "The Balance" (1926), Ernest Vaughan resides in the "front quadrangle of one of the uglier and less renowned colleges."[21] In *Decline and Fall*, Paul Pennyfeather's friend Stubbs resides in Hertford. Paul goes there to eat "honey buns and anchovy toast," and he likes the "ugly, subdued little College" (*D&F* 286). Paul's college is Scone, but Waugh used many other names from Hertford. Mr. Postlethwaite, the domestic bursar, is taken from one of Waugh's servants.[22] Arthur Potts is derived from R. J. R. Potts, who took his degree in 1925. Toby Cruttwell, a notorious criminal, is the first of several ridiculous characters named after the dean in Waugh's early novels and stories. In *Labels* (1930), the cathedral at Malaga reminds Waugh of the "chapel at Hertford College" and the "venerable figure of my history tutor, ill at ease in his starched white surplice, biting his nails and brooding, I have no doubt, on all the good he intended for each one of us."[23] M. E. Hardcastle took a third-class degree in 1924; in *Work Suspended* (1942), Alfred Hardcastle chairs a dodgy development company (*CSS* 267–69); in *Brideshead Revisited*, Hardcastle lends his car to Sebastian Flyte (23). Charles Ryder resides in an unspecified college, but he lives in "ground-floor rooms in the front quadrangle" (*BR* 24). Sebastian vomits into these rooms, and something similar happened to Waugh himself.[24] Lady Marchmain's brothers, Simon and Ned, were at the same college, and "Ned had rooms on the garden front" (*BR* 141). Waugh described Hertford and Oxford in *A Little Learning* (*ALL*, 1964), his autobiography, where Cruttwell is said to have been a "wreck of the war in which he had served gallantly" (174). Cruttwell became principal of Hertford in 1930, published the acclaimed *History of the Great War* (1934), and persuaded the university "to give geography a better standing by establishing both a Chair and an Honour School in the subject."[25] Greenidge thought Waugh's portrait was "a little unjust,"[26] and Eric Whelpton, a veteran, as was Cruttwell, "wrote a letter of protest to *The Times*." Cruttwell dismissed Waugh as a "silly little suburban sod with an inferiority complex and no palate."[27]

Hertford College was rebuilt in the late nineteenth and early twentieth centuries. Sir Thomas Graham Jackson (1835–1924), R.A., designed the hall, the chapel, the north range of old buildings, almost all of new buildings, and the bridge.[28] In 1922, Waugh thought the buildings were "pretty beastly" (*LEW* 7). To bathe, Waugh "had to cross the 'Bridge of Sighs' and penetrate the steamy cellars of the new buildings" (*ALL* 165). While some worried about preserving Oxford, Waugh recommended "judicious destruction." Demolition should include "the whole of Hertford [and the adjacent Indian Institute, now occupied by the Modern History Faculty], thus changing Oxford from a comparatively ugly city to a comparatively beautiful one" (*LEW* 49). Waugh wrote that Hertford's buildings are "nondescript, befitting their history," and he concurred with the judgment that the front on Catte Street "looks like a bank" (*ALL* 164–65). One critic describes Jackson's "extensive work at Hertford College" as a "fussy and indigestible design."[29]

At New College, Arthur Waugh took a double third in Mods and Greats in 1890 (*ALL* 169).[30] Hertford was earnest, but New College was "posh."[31] Founded in 1379, New College is one of Oxford's oldest colleges. Arthur's cousin warned him to "beware of Oxford women" and never to leave his college on Sunday without "a top-hat and morning-coat."[32] Charles Ryder's father received similar advice in *Brideshead Revisited*, and Charles himself is advised by his cousin Jasper (25–27). Maurice Bowra took a double first at New College,[33] and he was appointed lecturer and dean of Wadham College in Waugh's first year. Waugh thought he "could not be happy outside New College" (*LEW* 7), but he was probably right to choose the Hertford scholarship. His schoolmate from Lancing, Hugh (later Baron) Molson, tried for a scholarship at New College at the same time and failed,[34] though he won one at the next opportunity (*ALL* 165). Waugh had other friends from Lancing at New College, Rupert Fremlin and Max Mallowan, and he spent time with them in his first terms (*LEW* 6; *ALL* 165). He met Viscount Sudley, who wrote *William, or More Loved Than Loving* (1933), republished by Chapman & Hall in 1956 with a preface by Waugh. David Plunket Greene was at New College, along with Basil Murray, one of the models for Basil Seal. Waugh saw the names of two undergraduates, Best and Chetwynd, at the foot of a New College staircase adjoining the back wall of Hertford, and he combined them to create Margot Beste-Chetwynde in *Decline and Fall*.[35] In *Work Suspended*, Roger Simmonds went to New College (*CSS* 275–76). A. A. Carmichael, one of the masters in "Charles Ryder's Schooldays" (1982), also was there. In *Love among the Ruins* (1953), Waugh observes that the money spent to raise Miles Plastic could have sent "whole quiversful of boys to . . . New College and established them in the learned professions" (*CSS* 448). In *The End of the Battle* (a.k.a. *Unconditional Surrender*, 1961), Guy Crouchback's father has a "tobacco-jar bearing the arms of New College, bought by Mr. Crouchback when he was a freshman."[36]

Waugh wrote very little about the Bodleian Library. In *Decline and Fall*, Pennyfeather and Stubbs disagree with Mr. Sniggs, the junior dean, regarding plans to rebuild the Bodleian (*D&F* 285–86). A new library was built in the late 1930s, and Waugh declared that the "new Bodleian outrages one of the finest streets in Europe" (*EAR* 252). For Nancy Mitford's "list of modern buildings spoiling old," Waugh thought she would "surely have mentioned" the new Bodleian Library (*LEW* 369). Prior to construction of the new Bodleian, Dr. Herbert E. Counsell practiced surgery at 37 Broad Street from 1903 to 1934.[37] Friends took Waugh to Dr. Counsell in 1925, after he had injured himself climbing out the window of the Clarendon Hotel bar, and the doctor pronounced Waugh's ankle broken (*DEW* 232–33). According to Waugh, Dr. Counsell "ran his own welfare service for undergraduates in the Broad, wore the tweed cloaks and rough silk shirts and ties of Hall Bros, and was permanent prompter at all O.U.D.S. [Oxford University Dramatic Society] performances" (*ALL* 196).

Waugh's program of judicious destruction also included "the Holywell front of New College" (*LEW* 49). East on Holywell Street is the direction Charles Ryder walked with Lady Marchmain in *Brideshead Revisited*, as they discussed Sebastian and turned north "to the Parks, through Mesopotamia, and over the ferry to North Oxford," the middle-class residential part of the city. There Lady Marchmain has a "houseful of nuns . . . under her protection" (142),[38] but North Oxford is otherwise dubious in Waugh's fiction. In "Edward of Unique Achievement" (1923), an "aged and dissolute doctor" earns an "irregular livelihood by performing operations in North Oxford" (*CSS* 577). In *Decline and Fall*, the dons go to North Oxford to escape the Bollinger Club (*D&F* 1). In *Brideshead Revisited*, Charles Ryder joins the "daughters of North Oxford" in the Ruskin School of Art (106). In the same direction, Pennyfeather and Stubbs "took to going for walks together, over Mesopotamia to Old Marston and Beckley" (*D&F* 286). Waugh himself visited Francis Crease in Marston, "a village, then secluded, on the other side of Mesopotamia from Oxford" (*ALL* 155).

North on Parks Road lies Wadham College, where Maurice Bowra became warden. As did Cyril Connolly, Bowra became a friend only after Waugh had "attracted some attention as a novelist" (*ALL* 204). Mr. Samgrass in *Brideshead Revisited* is supposed to be a portrait of Bowra.[39] When Bowra was knighted in 1951, Waugh found it "really very odd as he has done nothing to deserve it except be head of the worst College at Oxford and publish a few books no one has ever read" (*LEW* 344). Maxwell Fleming, a friend from Waugh's childhood, was also at Wadham.[40] Farther north is Keble College, where Waugh's cousin Claud Cockburn was a scholar. Dick Young, the model for Captain Grimes in *Decline and Fall*, was also at Keble,[41] and Sebastian Flyte supposes that he might mend his ways by going to lectures there (*BR* 105). Sebastian is Roman Catholic, but Keble is Anglican, "opened in 1870 to buttress the Tractarian movement." Until about 1950, Keble "produced more students reading for degrees in theology than any other college."[42] Waugh noted that Cockburn "came up, most inappropriately, to Keble" (*ALL* 200).

At the corner of Broad Street is the Clarendon Building, named for Edward Hyde, first Earl of Clarendon, a member of Magdalen Hall. He wrote the *History of the Rebellion and Civil Wars in England* (1702–04) and devoted the royalties to the Clarendon Building to house Oxford University Press.[43] The press moved to Walton Street in 1830 and later rejected Scott-King's translation of Bellorius (*CSS* 355). The Sheldonian Theatre was built by Christopher Wren, and there, on his first visit to Oxford, Waugh saw the rostrum where his father had won the Newdigate Prize and had recited his poem in 1888.[44] The Newdigate was the most important award for an aspiring writer. Waugh also wrote a poem for the Newdigate in early days at Oxford, but it turned out to be "pretty bloody rot" (*LEW* 6). In *Decline and Fall*, the Bollinger Club finds Mr. Sanders's manuscript for the Newdigate and has "great fun" with it (4).

Across the street is Blackwell's Book Shop, where in *Decline and Fall* Paul Pennyfeather finds a copy of Augustus Fagan's *Mother Wales* (287). Charles Ryder meets Mr. Samgrass buying a "little heap" of "recent German books" in Blackwell's (*BR* 140).

Next is Trinity College. On that first visit in 1920, Waugh saw the gate scaled by his great-uncle at 2:00 a.m. (*DEW* 101). John Sutro was a scholar of Trinity, and Sutro revived the *Cherwell* (*ALL* 189), the undergraduate magazine that published Waugh's early stories and drawings. Waugh first ate plovers' eggs at Sutro's house in St John's Wood, "not as described in *Brideshead Revisited*" (*ALL* 194). Waugh also remembered that "Trinity hearties broke up a party," but Brian Howard boasted that the aesthetes would "tell our fathers to raise your rents and evict you" (*ALL* 205). In *Brideshead*, Charles Ryder walks down "the empty Broad to breakfast," enters a tea shop, and sees "a few solitary men from Balliol and Trinity, in bedroom slippers." They pay their bills and shuffle away, "slip-slop, across the street to their colleges" (58–59). Ronald Knox was appointed a fellow of Trinity in 1911, as emphasized in Waugh's biography, and in 1959 Waugh spoke at the "unveiling of Ronald's bust at Trinity." He "slept in college & had quite forgotten the horror of Oxford bed rooms" (*LEW* 518–19).

Balliol College was founded in 1263. In 1922, Waugh joined "a jolly Problem Club run by some men at Balliol" (*LEW* 10).[45] Waugh met Richard Pares, his "first homosexual love" (*LEW* 435), but Pares disliked alcohol,

withdrew from Waugh, earned a first-class degree, and became a professor
of history at the University of Edinburgh. Pares appears in Waugh's report
for the *Oxford Fortnightly Review*, where he is described as "too clever . . .
and too scholarly, for the Union" (*EAR* 12). In "Portrait of Young Man with
Career" (1923), published in the *Isis*, a character named Jeremy wants to
meet Pares because "he is a man to know," though Evelyn describes Pares
as an "amiable rogue" (*CSS* 562). Pares contributed to the characters of
Collins, an "embryo don" in *Brideshead Revisited* (27), and Joe Cattermole
in *The End of the Battle*.[46] Cattermole reminds Guy Crouchback that they
were at "Balliol 1921–1924" (*EB* 210). In *A Little Learning*, Waugh wrote
that Pares had an "appealing pale face and a mop of fair hair, blank blue
eyes and the Lear-Carroll-like fantasies of many Balliol Wykehamists"
(191). In 1923, Pares wrote a mock-scholarly explication of Edward Lear's
"The Pobble Who Has No Toes" for Sutro's *Cherwell*; in his last work of
fiction, *Basil Seal Rides Again* (1963), Waugh wrote that his hero is known
as "old Pobble," since he lost his toes in a training accident in the Second
World War. If he had not been "tragically struck down by creeping paraly-
sis," Waugh speculated, Pares would "probably have been elected Master
of Balliol" (*ALL* 192).

Waugh met many other Balliol men who became important later in
life. They included Cyril Connolly, the man of letters who was one of
Waugh's favorite targets; Alfred Duggan, the historical novelist; Graham
Greene, the Catholic novelist who remained "aloof" at Oxford (*ALL* 200);
Christopher Hollis, who published one of the first critical studies of Waugh
in 1954; Matthew Ponsonby, who was arrested with Waugh in London in
1925; Anthony Powell, the novelist who commissioned Waugh's first book
in 1927; Peter Quennell, the poet and critic; John Heygate, whose relation-
ship with She-Evelyn destroyed Waugh's first marriage in 1929; and Peter
Rodd, who married Nancy Mitford and contributed to the character of
Basil Seal. Returning from Balliol, Waugh walked along Broad Street with
Maurice Bowra (*LEW* 625). After he had finished his final examinations,
Waugh spent the evening in Balliol. Patrick Balfour, later known as a journalist and the 3rd Baron Kinross, let him out of Richard Pares's "window
by a string at a little before 1 o'clock" (*DEW* 163).

Waugh made enemies at Balliol as well. He repeated the nickname
"Philbrick the Flagellant" (*ALL* 177) and received a beating from Philbrick
and Basil Murray.[47] Philbrick is the enigmatic butler in *Decline and Fall*
and the art school's secretary in "The Balance," and "Phillrick" [*sic*] is the
tailor in "A House of Gentlefolks" (1927). V. J. R. D. Prendergast, also at
Balliol, once characterized Waugh as "undesirable bohemian company,"[48]

and he gave his name to the doubting clergyman in *Decline and Fall*. Waugh's greatest rival was, however, F. F. "Sligger" Urquhart, the dean of Balliol. Urquhart presided over a "sober salon" of good-looking intellectuals (*ALL* 180), and he recruited Pares. Waugh resented it, and Quennell remembered his shouting "The Dean of Balliol sleeps with men!"[49] Cyril Connolly encountered Waugh "making an abominable row outside the gate of Balliol College." When Connolly asked why, Waugh answered that he was "poor."[50] Urquhart's rooms were "on the first floor over the Balliol back gate, overlooking the Martyrs' Memorial,"[51] so Waugh may have been trying to annoy the dean. In 1924, Urquhart was suspected of having helped to close the Hypocrites' Club,[52] which Waugh described as the "stamping-ground of half my Oxford life" (*ALL* 181). In *The Scarlet Woman* (1925), a film made with Greenidge, Waugh played the dean of Balliol, who pets the Prince of Wales and tries to convert England to Roman Catholicism. By the time he wrote *Ronald Knox* (1959), Waugh's views had changed: Urquhart was "the first Roman Catholic since the Reformation to be elected Fellow of an Oxford college." Sligger attracted people with "simple, unselfish affection," though "there were always people outside his circle who derided what they took to be its cosiness and softness."[53] In *The End of the Battle*, Guy Crouchback is said to have been a "friend of Sligger's" (211).

Ronald Knox had also been at Balliol, and the college before the First World War became an irrecoverable ideal. Despite the "most joyless architecture in the University," Waugh wrote in his biography of Knox, Balliol "still professed a 'tranquil consciousness of effortless superiority' which Ronald's generation was the last to justify" (*TL* 192). Many of Waugh's fictional characters were at Balliol, though he often suggests that they did not belong. In "The Balance," Adam Doure takes Ernest Vaughan to a party in Balliol, but Ernest is sick in the quad (*CSS* 28). In *Black Mischief*, Basil Seal and Seth were at Balliol, but Basil used to go away for "weekends without leave" and to climb "into College over the tiles at night."[54] Seth, the emperor of Azania, was an "undergraduate of no account in his College" (146). In *A Handful of Dust* (1934), Tony Last was at Balliol, and in *Brideshead Revisited*, "four Indians from the gates of Balliol" head for the river on Sunday morning with the "Unpleasant Plays of Bernard Shaw" (58).[55] Others scramble to get in. In "Charles Ryder's Schooldays," the boy Symonds studies for the Balliol scholarship (*CSS* 337), and in *Scott-King's Modern Europe*, Lockwood tried for the same scholarship but "had to go into the army" instead (*CSS* 402).

Adjacent to Balliol is St John's College, where Edmund Campion was a fellow. Waugh's biography opens with a description of St John's in 1566, the year of Queen Elizabeth's visit. Waugh suggested that Oxford should have ignored the Reformation and remained in the "spacious, luminous world of Catholic humanism." Instead, the university became "provincial, phlegmatic, and exclusive" (*TL* 13–14).[56] Campion Hall used to be north of St John's, at 11 St. Giles, from 1919 to 1935,[57] when a new building became available. Initially, Campion Hall was one of Waugh's targets. In *Labels*, he jokes that the Jesuits "directly employed" a pilot who took passengers to fly stunts. Waugh also jokes that Christopher Hollis converted after such a flight (*Labels* 9–10). In 1924, Father C. C. Martindale instructed Waugh's friend Alastair Graham in the faith.[58] Father Martindale asked to see *The Scarlet Woman*. Waugh was reluctant, but the film was shown at Campion Hall in 1925, Martindale laughed, and Greenidge's brother John added a "*Nihil Obstat*" over Martindale's signature, a humorous claim that the Roman Catholic Church approved of the film.[59] The Martyrs' Memorial commemorates Archbishop Cranmer and Bishops Latimer and Ridley, executed as Protestants by the Catholic Queen Mary in 1555 and 1556. Latimer said, "Be of good cheer, Master Ridley, and play the man. We shall this day light such a candle, by God's grace, in England, as I trust shall never be put out." Scott-King parodies the famous statement in his tribute to Bellorius (*CSS* 390), and Ian Kilbannock does so for Trimmer in *Officers and Gentlemen* (1955),[60] perhaps because Waugh doubted the authenticity of Latimer's epitaph.[61] Waugh asked Maurice Bowra what would happen if "all the governing body of . . . a mediaeval college like New College were to be converted to Roman Catholicism." Was there "any legal impediment to their turning over the chapel to popish worship"? (*LEW* 531)

St. Giles leads to the Woodstock Road and Somerville College, attended by Waugh's eldest daughter, Teresa. In 1955, Waugh found Somerville to be "a handsome building" (*DEW* 748). Somerville is adjacent to Wellington Square, where "proletarian scholars" scramble fiercely for facts in *Brideshead Revisited* (27). The Woodstock Road is also the site of "the first Oxford Playhouse located in the former big-game museum opposite Somerville."[62] As an undergraduate, Waugh designed programs for the Oxford University Dramatic Society (OUDS) (*ALL* 189). The OUDS also hosted the "glorious First Night" of *The Scarlet Woman* in 1926.[63] Part of the film was made on the Woodstock Road in 1925. After an hour, Waugh grew weary of acting, and when one scene called for a taxi, he "got into it and drove away, rather to everyone's annoyance" (*DEW* 232). The founder of the Oxford Playhouse, James Fagan, may have lent his name to Augustus Fagan in *Decline and Fall*.[64] On Sunday morning in *Brideshead*, some churchgoers head to St Aloysius, a Catholic church beside Somerville and perhaps the source of the name for Sebastian's teddy bear. Others go to Blackfriars (*BR* 59): established in 1921 in St. Giles, Blackfriars "became an important centre of Roman Catholic preaching and scholarship."[65] Book 1 of *Brideshead* is set in the mid-1920s. Other churchgoers are bound for Pusey House (*BR* 59), "a major centre for high-church apologetics," founded in 1884. From 1910 to 1926, "Pusey House constructed new buildings on St Giles', including a new chapel which soon functioned as an Anglican alternative to the college chapels."[66] Waugh attended Mass there in 1924 (*DEW* 188).

After he left the university, Waugh floundered for a few years, he kept going back to Oxford and attributed his decline to luncheon in John Sutro's lodgings in Beaumont Street on November 12, 1924 (*ALL* 212). In December, Waugh "moved to 40 Beaumont Street and began a vastly expensive career of alcohol" (*DEW* 189). In "The Balance," Swithin Lang lives in fashionable lodgings in Beaumont Street. Also in Beaumont Street is the Ashmolean, the oldest museum in England. In *Brideshead*, Charles Ryder meets students from the Ruskin School of Art "two or three mornings a week . . . among the casts from the antique at the Ashmolean Museum" (106). At a dinner in 1953, Waugh and Bowra praised the Ashmolean (*LEW* 415). When Dick Young died in 1972, he left a "collection of German and Chelsea porcelain to the Ashmolean Museum" (*LEW* 616n). At the western end of Beaumont Street is Worcester College; Roger Fulford from Lancing was there, and Waugh visited. In 1924, after heavy drinking, Waugh was carried to Worcester, where he "relapsed into unconsciousness punctuated with severe but well-directed vomitings" (*DEW* 190). A month later, Waugh noted that Fulford's "hearties object to me for some reason" (*DEW* 198). Waugh occasionally used the Randolph Hotel on Beaumont Street: he stayed there in 1926 (*DEW* 271), lunched in 1937 (*DEW* 425), found the place full in 1945 (*DEW* 634), and lunched again in 1955 (*DEW* 748).

George Street was important to Waugh for two reasons, both now gone. The Oxford Carlton Club and the George, a restaurant and bar, were at the corner of George Street and the Cornmarket. The Carlton was conservative, though Waugh specified that "more than party loyalty was required for membership" (*ALL* 183). Edward of Unique Achievement is a member, and Jasper advises Charles to join in *Brideshead Revisited* (26). The George was popular with undergraduates known as the "Georgeoisie," though Waugh thought he had "wasted much money" on its "inferior cuisine" (*ALL* 166). In *Brideshead*, Sebastian dines at the George "in false whiskers" (29), and Anthony Blanche consumes four Alexander cocktails at the George bar before taking Charles to dinner at Thame (47). Edward of Unique Achievement dines at the George before murdering his history tutor, and he goes down George Street to dispose of the dagger in the canal (*CSS* 574). Edward would have passed the New Theatre, where Waugh saw *Iolanthe* in 1922.[67] A performance at the New Theatre to benefit the preservation of Oxford prompted Waugh to propose judicious destruction in 1930 (*LEW* 49). George Street leads to Hythe Bridge Street, where Charles and Sebastian go to the Nag's Head in *Brideshead* (108), and the towpath, where Adam walks away from Oxford in "The Balance" (*CSS* 34). With "Hamish Lennox," his pseudonym for Alastair Graham, Waugh visited the Nag's Head in the 1920s, along with other "Oxford inns frequented by townees" (*ALL* 193), though pubs were out of bounds for undergraduates. Waugh and friends also "walked up the tow-path and practised sortilege at Binsey" (*ALL* 168). To the west lies the Rail Station, where the Oxford Railway Club departed in 1923 (*ALL* 195). On the run into Oxford, Waugh notes in "The Balance," the London train offers views of the "reservoir, gas works and part of the prison" (*CSS* 21). Some churchgoers in *Brideshead* are going to St. Barnabas (59), in the area known as Jericho. The church was "popular with ritualist undergraduates," and the area became "known as S Barnabas Junction—All Change for Rome."[68]

In St. Michael Street is the Oxford Union. In *Rossetti* (1928), Waugh wrote that the Union Debating Hall is an "ugly enough building," designed by Benjamin Woodward (1815–61), the "arch-fiend of Oxford architecture."[69] Waugh visited the Union in 1921, but he found the debates not "much better than Lancing" (*DEW* 151). Nevertheless, he had longed to participate since his first visit to Oxford in 1920 (*DEW* 101), and he made his "unremarkable maiden speech" on February 8, 1922 (*ALL* 166),[70] early in his first term. Waugh had "no success as a speaker," but he did his best as a Conservative, when Richard Pares and "many of the best brains" were Labour (*ALL* 182–83). In the election for president of the Union in June 1923, Waugh garnered only 25 votes; Christopher Hollis won with 309.[71] Still, the Union provided plenty of material for writing. Throughout his three years in Oxford, Waugh reported debates for three undergraduate publications, the *Isis*, the *Cherwell*, and the *Oxford Fortnightly Review*. In "Portrait of Young Man with Career," Jeremy is to speak at the Union on the "Near East. Macedonia. Oil, you know" (*CSS* 562). Having murdered his history tutor, Edward of Unique Achievement gives a speech "more successful as an alibi than as a piece of oratory" (*CSS* 573). Waugh wrote part of his first book, *Rossetti*, at the Union Library in August 1927 (*DEW* 287). In *Labels*, Waugh claimed that life membership in the Oxford Union entitled him to temporary membership in the Sporting Club, Monte Carlo (28–29). In *Black Mischief*, Seth claims to represent "the New Age" because he has been to the Oxford Union (22). In *Brideshead*, during Eights Week in May, women are greeted in the Union "by a sudden display of peculiar, facetious, wholly distressing Gilbert-and-Sullivan badinage" (21–22). Waugh participated in the Eights Week Debate of 1946, but he was disappointed to see "the audience falling off their benches at the most banal jokes" (*LEW* 229). In *The End of the Battle*, Joe Cattermole says he spoke at the Union, though he "wasn't any good" (211).

Across the street from the Union are Maltby and Son, the binders Waugh employed for years after leaving Oxford. In "The Balance," Adam attends the "Maltby School of Art," operated by old Mr. Maltby and young Mr. Maltby (*CSS* 8).

The Cornmarket, or the Corn, was home to another club, the New Reform, "subsidised by Lloyd George in the belief that it would be a nursery for earnest young Liberals" (*EAR* 610). Waugh belonged "impartially" to the liberal New Reform and the conservative Carlton Clubs (*ALL* 183). He remembered that the New Reform stood "at the corner of the Cornmarket on Ship Street" (*EAR* 610), but Greenidge thought it was in Market Street.[72] When the Hypocrites closed, there was a "mass migration" to the New Reform (*ALL* 183). Waugh and friends "drank a good deal of champagne in mid-morning . . . and scoffed from the windows at the gowned figures hurrying from lecture to lecture" (*EAR* 610). Some suggested that the club was a "meeting-place of homosexuals," but Waugh assured two visiting politicians that every member had a "complete orgasm" every time he passed a woman in the street.[73] Waugh also "joined the White Rose, an occasional dining-club devoted to the Stuart cause." They had "dinners at the Golden Cross, which were regularly raided by the proctors" (*ALL* 183). In *Brideshead Revisited*, Charles Ryder greets undergraduates from his college in the yard of the Golden Cross, as he makes his way to Sebastian (59). With the Ruskin School of Art, Waugh and Peter Quennell met once a week "to draw from the nude in a studio over a teashop in the Corn" (*ALL* 190). The Clarendon Hotel once stood in the Corn. On November 6, 1925, Waugh avoided friends by hiding in the Clarendon bar; when they followed, he climbed out of the window and fell on his ankle. Laid up for three days, he studied the Pre-Raphaelites and decided to write about them (*DEW* 232–33). In *Brideshead*, Charles notices tourists "on the steps of the Clarendon Hotel discussing a road map with their chauffeur" (59). Waugh wrote that one of Harold Macmillan's "gravest crimes" was "destroying the Clarendon Hotel to build a Woolworth stores in the Corn." The change symbolized Macmillan's "break with his undergraduate life–the Clarendon was the meeting-place of his friends" (*LEW* 610). Both the City of

Oxford and the university agreed with Waugh: the Clarendon Hotel was "the only secular building of architectural merit in the Cornmarket and one of the few surviving relics of Oxford's earlier existence as a country market town."[74] It was torn down in 1954, on the site of what is now the Clarendon Centre.[75]

Carfax is mentioned three times in *Brideshead Revisited*. First, Charles and Sebastian cross it in Hardcastle's car to leave Oxford, heading west (23). Second, Charles meets "the Mayor and corporation, in scarlet gowns and gold chains, preceded by wand bearers and followed by no curious glances, in procession to the preaching at the City Church" (59–60). After 1896, the City Church was All Saints in the High Street. Declared redundant in 1971, the church became the library of Lincoln College in 1976.[76] Third, Charles takes the bus back to Carfax after escorting Lady Marchmain to North Oxford (*BR* 144). Waugh included the "clock tower at Carfax" in his program of judicious destruction, along with the Town Hall on St. Aldate's (*LEW* 49).

In 1924, Waugh went to a dance at the Town Hall (*DEW* 190), probably the inspiration for the dance in "The Balance." Ernest Vaughan leaves the dance and crashes a car into a shop window "halfway down St Aldate's" (*CSS* 29). In St. Aldate's is Alice's Shop, otherwise known as the Sheep Shop in *Through the Looking-Glass* (1871). Lewis Carroll's real name was *Charles Lutwidge Dodgson*; Dodgson was an undergraduate and then don at Christ Church across the street. Waugh read *Alice in Wonderland* after his first term in 1922 (*LEW* 9). His many allusions to Carroll include the "low door in the wall . . . which opened on an enclosed and enchanted garden" in *Brideshead* (31). Lady Marchmain refers to the "Alice-in-Wonderland side of religion" (*BR* 127). In "Unacademic Exercise" (1923), published in the *Cherwell*, undergraduates take Billy Donne "down St Aldate's" to turn him into a werewolf (*CSS* 586). John Donne was an undergraduate at Hart Hall in the 1580s,[77] and the *Cherwell* had a "gloomy" office in St. Aldate's.[78] In the same street lived the "chief shareholder" in the *Isis*, an "alcoholic figure named Gull." The *Isis* was "primarily a newspaper giving many pages to athletics," and it was "greatly looked down on by aesthetes and intellectuals." For Waugh, the "sole . . . attraction of the *Isis* was that it paid its contributors." A regular column, Isis Idol, was devoted to "a prominent undergraduate" (*ALL* 188). Waugh's contributions were both unconventional: Cruttwell, a don, and Harold Acton, the aesthete par excellence.[79] Acton created the *Oxford Broom*, a magazine to sweep moribund traditions out of Oxford. Waugh designed the cover and supplied a story, "Antony, Who Sought Things That Were Lost," in June 1923.

Also in St. Aldate's stood the Hypocrites' Club, the name from the club's motto, the first line of Pindar's *Olympian Odes*, "Water is best," though the members drank beer.[80] In 1963, Waugh wrote that the club's rooms had been "demolished" (*EAR* 610).[81] Waugh consistently gives the address as 31 St Aldate's, but Stannard and Carpenter refer to "34 St Aldate's,"[82] Hastings to "131 St Aldate's."[83] All authorities agree that the club was over a bicycle shop; Greenidge remembered that it was a few doors down from the Sheep Shop,[84] but No. 31 would have been on the opposite side, between the Christ Church Memorial Garden and Folly Bridge. The site has been extensively rebuilt, now occupied by the police station and student housing.[85] Waugh remembered the Hypocrites in the "process of invasion and occupation by a group of wanton Etonians who brought it to speedy dissolution." The club became "notorious not only for drunkenness but for flamboyance of dress and manner which was in some cases patently homosexual" (*ALL* 179–80). Loveday served as secretary (*ALL* 180), and Waugh used the name in "Mr Loveday's Little Outing" (1936), the story about a homicidal lunatic originally named Cruttwell. When the club was closed in 1924, Richard Plunket Greene took over the lease (*ALL* 217). Just before Alastair Graham left England, Waugh and Graham revisited the Hypocrites, but Waugh "hated 31 St Aldate's for its discomfort and its associations" (*DEW* 178–79). In his autobiography, however, Waugh wrote that the club had been the "source of friendships still warm today" (*ALL* 181).

On the west side of St Aldate's, tucked into Rose Place, is the Old Palace, a half-timbered building of three stories, home of the Catholic Chaplaincy and the Newman Rooms. The Old Palace was the residence of the first and last Catholic bishop of Oxford, Robert King, who conformed to Catholicism during the reign of Mary I (1553–58). As an undergraduate, Waugh went to listen to G. K. Chesterton's lecture to the Newman Society and met Harold Acton (*ALL* 197–98). As an eminent writer, Waugh returned to the Newman in 1936 to give "as bad a lecture" as he had ever heard (*LEW* 107), and in 1951 to attend a meeting "dead drunk" (*LEW* 361). He stayed with Ronald Knox, chaplain to Catholic undergraduates at Oxford from 1926 to 1939 (*EAR* 353). Waugh was shown into an "infamous bedroom" and served "repulsive food" (*LEW* 106). In 1952, Knox published a volume of Oxford conferences entitled *The Hidden Stream*. In his biography of Knox, Waugh notes that "the Twill mill-stream . . . runs under Rose Place and emerges prettily into the Christ Church Memorial Garden" (*TL* 307). One section of the Knox biography is also entitled "The Hidden Stream." At the Old Palace in 1959, Waugh attended an "absolutely ghastly vin d'honneur" (*LEW*

530); his son Auberon called it a "launch party" for Evelyn's biography of Knox.[86] The party was "black with clergymen," and Evelyn was "deafened & asphyxiated" (*LEW* 530). In *Brideshead Revisited*, Sebastian Flyte attends Mass at the Old Palace and shouts the Hail Marys (60). Lady Marchmain hears that Sebastian "never goes to the Newman," however, and he is ordered to live at the Old Palace with Monsignor Bell. Sebastian prefers not to be known as the "rather embarrassing local inebriate" (*BR* 143–44).

West on Brewer Street is Campion Hall, opposite Pembroke College, which "harboured Hugh Lygon and certain other aristocratic refugees from the examination system" (*ALL* 167). Beyond both is St Ebbe's, where Charles and Sebastian frequent "Hogarthian little inns" in *Brideshead* (108). Waugh converted to Roman Catholicism in 1930, and in 1934 he started a biography of Edmund Campion (*TL* 5). The book ends with the martyrdom of Campion, who was canonized in 1970, a few years after Waugh's death. *Edmund Campion* refers to the martyrdom of Alexander Briant, a member of Hart Hall, canonized in 1975. Royalties were devoted to a new building for Campion Hall,[87] which Waugh described as "one of [Sir Edwin] Lutyens's cleverest constructions" (*TL* 335). Father Martin D'Arcy, who instructed Waugh, became master of Campion Hall in 1933 (*TL* 335). In *The Tablet* in 1946, Waugh praised Campion Hall's hospitality, its "air of a private house" (*EAR* 317). Waugh's visits were not always agreeable, however. In 1936, he saw "D'Arcy's latest *bric-à-brac*" (*DEW* 412), and in 1955 the master, Father Corbishley, failed to make him welcome. Father Corbishley did take him to the Ashmolean the next day, but Waugh resolved to "break the habit of going up for what each year becomes a less cordial celebration" (*DEW* 747).

In *Brideshead Revisited*, Charles Ryder encounters a "crocodile of choir-boys, in starched collars and peculiar caps, on their way to Tom Gate and the Cathedral" (60). Tom Gate leads to Christ Church and the college chapel, also the cathedral for the City of Oxford. Above the gate is Tom Tower (1681–82), built by Sir Christopher Wren. The tower houses "Great Tom," the bell that is rung 101 times each evening at 9:05 p.m., once for every scholar in the foundation. At the beginning of *Brideshead*, one of Sebastian's companions says that they have "till Tom stops ringing" to get back to the House, the nickname for Christ Church (29). Sebastian is "found by the junior dean at one o'clock, wandering round Tom Quad hopelessly drunk" (*BR* 141). In the middle of the quad is Mercury, the statue and its pool. Waugh remembered that Edward, 6th Earl of Longford, supported Irish home rule and was thrown into Mercury after the Irish Republican Army assassinated Sir Henry Wilson in 1922 (*EAR* 556). In *Brideshead*, "twenty terrible young men" want to put Anthony Blanche in Mercury. He decides to jump in and to strike "some attitudes" (*BR* 48–50). Blanche lives in Peckwater Quad, an attractive setting, always dubious in Waugh's fiction. In "The Balance," Adam seeks two undergraduates in Peckwater: Mr Egerton-Verschoyle is incoherent after "entertaining to luncheon," and "Mr Furness has been sent down" (*CSS* 23). In "Winner Takes All" (1936), Gervase Kent-Cumberland is at Christ Church, but his younger brother Tom is "sombrely sick in a corner of Peckwater Quad" (*CSS* 188). Waugh may have associated the quad with Harold Acton's younger brother, William, who fell from a window in Peckwater in 1926.[88]

Founded by Cardinal Wolsey in 1546, Christ Church has a distinguished history that is reflected in Waugh's fiction. John Plant's great-grandfather was a canon of Christ Church (*CSS* 235), Lord Marchmain was there, and he sent his son Sebastian to the same college (*BR* 141). Undergraduates in the 1920s included Hubert Duggan, whose deathbed Act of Contrition Waugh witnessed in 1943 (*DEW* 552–53). *Labels* and *Vile Bodies* (1930) are both dedicated to another House man, Bryan Guinness, along with his wife, Diana, later Lady Mosley.[89] Waugh knew Tom Driberg, who had been at Lancing and went up to Christ Church as a scholar in 1924. Driberg was debagged, or had his trousers stripped, in Tom Quad, and he wrote that *Decline and Fall* offers only a "mild account of the night of any Bullingdon Club dinner in Christ Church."[90] The Bullingdon becomes the Bollinger Club in *Decline and Fall*, but Tom Watch in "Love in the Slump" (1932) and Gervase Kent-Cumberland in "Winner Takes All" both belong to the Bullingdon. In *Brideshead*, Anthony Blanche takes Charles to a "delightful hotel" at Thame (47), the Spread Eagle, where Waugh dined at least twice in 1926 (*DEW* 245, 267). Anthony observes that the Spread Eagle "luckily doesn't appeal to the Bullingdon" (*BR* 47). The club was devoted to sports, especially riding and hunting. Brian Howard, more aesthete than athlete, "never got into the Bullingdon, but he charged gallantly at the fences in the Grind" (*ALL* 205), or steeplechase. Tom Watch finished "second on a borrowed hunter in the Christ Church 'grind'" (*CSS* 58), and in *Put Out More Flags* (1942), Ambrose Silk remembers that he rode "ridiculously and ignominiously in the Christ Church Grind."[91]

Harold Acton lived in Meadow Buildings (*ALL* 198), a Victorian structure once thought ugly. In Christ Church between the world wars, "Tom, Canterbury and Peckwater quadrangles were respectable, but not the Meadow Buildings,"[92] a significant detail in *Brideshead*. Sebastian lives "high in Meadow Buildings" (*BR* 31), and Charles goes there to a luncheon of plovers' eggs. Acton recited poems through a megaphone to anyone who happened to be in Christ Church Meadow.[93] In *Brideshead*, Anthony Blanche stands "on the balcony with a megaphone," and in "languishing, sobbing tones" he recites "passages from *The Waste Land* to the sweatered and muffled throng that was on its way to the river" (33). Blanche is an "aesthetic bugger," like Ambrose Silk, and the two characters consist of "1/3 Brian [Howard] 2/3 Harold Acton" (*LEW* 506). In *Labels*, Waugh meets a Greek who had been at the House and regrets that "he had not found any 'aestheticism' in his day" (121). With Hugh Trevor-Roper, the Christ Church history don, Waugh engaged in public debate about Catholic recusants (*LEW* 641–47). In 1957, the prime minister appointed Trevor-Roper the Regius Professor of Modern History at Oxford, and Waugh thought it "funny to hold up Trevor-Roper as Macmillan's great folly instead of Suez or Cyprus" (*LEW* 527). Waugh's son Auberon won an exhibition to Christ Church, but his father advised him to abandon the study of English. Auberon switched to philosophy, politics, and economics (PPE); lost interest; and left after a year.[94] Waugh thought that his son had never been "captivated by Oxford," that he had "used the House simply as a place from which to sally out to London."[95] Folly Bridge, south of Christ Church, was another candidate for destruction, Waugh thought, "to isolate [Oxford] from through traffic" (*LEW* 49).

After luncheon, Sebastian and Charles walk "under the walls of Merton" to the Botanical Gardens, so that Sebastian can "see the ivy" (*BR* 33–34). Beyond the Botanical Gardens is Magdalen Bridge, where Waugh was photographed on a motorcycle in 1925. In *Brideshead*, Charles and Anthony Blanche return from Thame over Magdalen Bridge (57). Waugh described the bridge as a "pretty structure," so "its total demolition is unnecessary; one arch would be enough" to prevent traffic from entering Oxford (*LEW* 49). Waugh had few friends at Magdalen College, founded in 1458, but he knew Viscount Elmley, later the 8th Earl Beauchamp, and the eldest brother of Hugh Lygon. Elmley served as secretary of the Hypocrites' Club and appeared in *The Scarlet Woman* under a stage name, to avoid upsetting his father. Elmley is thought to be the model for Lord Brideshead, or Bridey, who was also at Magdalen (*BR* 92), as were Henry Yorke, the novelist who wrote under the name of Henry Green, and John Betjeman, the poet laureate. Mr. Macassor, the predatory bookseller in "The Balance," has a son at Magdalen, who is "able to keep his rooms full of flowers and, during the season, to hunt two days a week" (*CSS* 20). Another undergraduate, Henry Quest, belongs to the Bullingdon and lives in "the uglier part of Magdalen." Adam Doure is in love with Henry's sister Imogen and "cannot stand" her brother (*CSS* 22–23).

Waugh's predecessor as editor of the Lancing College magazine and president of the debating society, James Lewis Hill, took bachelor's and master's degrees at St Edmund Hall,[96] founded in 1238. The church of St Peter in the East, now the hall's library, once had a supper party on the roof (*ALL* 195). The church used to stand outside Oxford's city wall, but the Dreamer misunderstands in *The Loved One* (1948). He appropriates the name "St Peter-without-the-walls" and proclaims that his church has no walls.

Waugh and Hugh Lygon took "digs together in Merton Street next door to the tennis-court" (*ALL* 207). That was for the autumn of 1924, when Waugh would have fulfilled his residence requirement. The final examinations had been a disaster, however, and Waugh's "father decided that a Third Class B.A. was not worth the time and expense of going up for a further term" (*ALL* 208). Waugh and Lygon went on the Oxford University Arctic Expedition to Spitsbergen in 1934 (*EAR* 144), but in 1936 Lygon died after an accident in Germany. He is thought to have influenced the character of Sebastian.[97] In *Brideshead*, Charles and Sebastian plan to take lodgings in Merton Street, "in a secluded, expensive little house near the tennis court" (140). Merton College, founded in 1264, housed a few of Waugh's friends, notably Billy Clonmore, later 8th Earl of Wicklow, and Robert Byron, who edited the *Cherwell* (*ALL* 189).[98] At a party at Merton in 1924, Waugh noticed that "everyone was wearing a new sort of jumper with a high collar rather becoming and most convenient for lechery because it dispenses with all unromantic gadgets like studs and ties" (*DEW* 188). "The Balance" is subtitled "A Yarn of the Good Old Days of Broad Trousers and High-Necked Jumpers." Harold Acton was known for wearing broad trousers, or "Oxford bags." In "The Balance," Adam seeks an aesthetic friend named Mr. Sayle at Merton, but he is busy "playing 'L'Après midi d'un Faun' on the gramophone to an American aunt" (*CSS* 22). At the end of Merton Street are Oriel Square and Canterbury Gate to Christ Church. A cabman returns the teddy bear Aloysius to Sebastian at Canterbury Gate (*BR* 87). Charles sees Sebastian "driving in a hansom cab" (*BR* 29), and Waugh recalled that hansom cabs could be hired at Canterbury Gate in the 1920s (*ALL* 168).

Harold Acton moved from Meadow Buildings to 10 Oriel Street (*DEW* 210), and he and Waugh recited Edith Sitwell "to the chimneys" there.[99] In *Decline and Fall*, as Pennyfeather and Stubbs bicycle down the High Street from one lecture to another, they almost run into "an open Rolls Royce that swung out of Oriel Street at a dangerous speed." In the back sits Philbrick (*D&F* 287). Waugh gave a party in King Edward Street, attended by his brother Alec and Joyce Fagan dressed as a man. When the proctors arrived, Joyce claimed to be Terence Greenidge and fooled them.[100] In "The Balance," Lord Basingstoke toils over a history paper in his rooms in King Edward Street (*CSS* 21–22). In *Brideshead*, Charles first sees Sebastian at Germer's, the hairdresser at 3–4 King Edward Street. Sebastian buys an ivory-backed hairbrush to threaten Aloysius "with a spanking when he was sulky" (*BR* 28).

At the corner of King Edward Street and High Street, or "the High," is No. 108, the site of Dolbear and Goodall, Chemists, from 1906 to 1937.[101] The day after vomiting into Charles's rooms in *Brideshead*, Sebastian puts himself "unreservedly in the hands of Dolbear and Goodall" (31). To the west are Alfred Street and St Columba, the destination of some churchgoers in *Brideshead* (59). St Columba was the Presbyterian chaplaincy to the university, dedicated in 1915. Farther west on the High Street is No. 131, Payne and Son, Goldsmiths, still in business. There in 1924, just before his viva voce, Waugh bought "a very beautiful cameo" and "a little 1800 mourning ring" for Alastair Graham, who was leaving England for Africa (*DEW* 171–72). Just past Payne's is the passage to the Chequers, one of the pubs frequented by Waugh and Graham. On the north side of the High Street is the Mitre, where Waugh stayed during his scholarship examination in 1921, the first time he stayed in a hotel on his own (*ALL* 138). Property of Lincoln College, the Mitre probably derived its name from the bishop of Lincoln's miter on the college's coat of arms. When his son Auberon went up in 1959, Waugh invited Maurice Bowra and John Sparrow to luncheon at the Mitre. Sparrow, the warden of All Souls, showed a "kindly, avuncular interest" in Auberon, but Bron "never saw Bowra again after that day."[102] In Turl Street in 1946, Waugh "bought a nice copy of Edmund Evans *Chronicle of England* [1864] for 3/6 at the Turl Bookshop" (*LEW* 230). In 1925, Ducker of the Turl made some "very lovely" shoes for Waugh (*DEW* 203), who continued to use Ducker's services until 1952. Then, in "one of those upsetting changes of middle life," Waugh learned that Ducker had "fallen into sloth & gone out of business," and he had to go to Cambridge for shoes (*LEW* 380).[103] To the east is No. 104, Sanders of Oxford, where Waugh searched for rare books. Brian Aldiss worked there from 1947 to 1955,[104] and he found Waugh to be a "minor devil" and a "bad payer."[105] A little farther is the Rhodes Building of Oriel College, built in 1911, which Waugh thought should be destroyed (*LEW* 49). Across Magpie Lane is No. 94, the site of Hall Bros. Tailors from 1909 to 1931.[106] Waugh was a regular customer. He paid his bills in Oxford in 1926, "marching from shop to shop in dragging overalls with pocket book full of £5-pound notes." Most shops seemed glad to get Waugh off their books, "except Hall's," who seemed to have "some real personal feeling" for him (*DEW* 266). Next door, Nos. 92 and 93, is the Old Bank Hotel, formerly the Old Bank. As undergraduates, Greenidge once lent Waugh one hundred pounds, and Waugh carried the single note "rejoicing down the High" (*ALL* 207). He kept an account at the Old Bank for the rest of his life.[107]

The Examination Schools were built by Sir T. G. Jackson between 1876 and 1882.[108] Waugh took his final examinations here in June 1924. He studied at the last minute and hoped for a second-class degree, but he was "uneasily aware . . . that the questions had been rather inconvenient." Cruttwell hosted a party for the history candidates, but Waugh "arrived tipsy and further alienated their sympathies by attempting, later, to sing a Negro spiritual" (*ALL* 207–08). His viva voce was scheduled for July 29, and Waugh stayed with Alastair Graham at the Abingdon Arms in Beckley. Wearing the required "subfusc suit and white tie," he walked into Oxford (*ALL* 208), a distance of five miles. Fortified with a "large whisky," supplied by his "kindly wine merchant," Waugh answered questions that were "purely formal" and wired his parents with news of a "certain third" (*DEW* 171–72). He never received a degree because he failed to fulfill the requirement of nine terms' residence.[109] In May 1928, however, Oxford's registrar issued a certificate stating that Waugh had "satisfied the Examiners in the Final Honour School of Modern History in Trinity Term, 1924, and was placed by them in the Third Class."[110] The certificate was one tactic in Waugh's campaign to marry Evelyn Gardner. Her mother, Lady Burghclere, interviewed Cruttwell in Oxford, also in May 1928, and heard about Waugh's drunkenness and homosexuality. Influenced by her fiancé's view of his former tutor, Evelyn Gardner reported that her mother had found Cruttwell "palpitating with perverse vices."[111] Lady Burghclere opposed the wedding, but He-Evelyn and She-Evelyn married on June 27, 1928 and informed her mother in mid-July (*DEW* 295). Among Waugh's friends, Robert Byron, Cyril Connolly, Christopher Hollis, and Anthony Powell also got thirds. Harold Acton got a fourth in modern languages. Claud Cockburn, Graham Greene, and Terence Greenidge managed seconds,[112] and Hugh Molson took a first in jurisprudence (*LEW* 9). Among Waugh's fictional characters, Tom Watch in "Love in the Slump" takes a third in history, as Waugh did (*CSS* 58). John Plant in *Work Suspended* gets "a second in Mods and a first in Greats" (*CSS* 235), and Ryder's cousin Jasper in *Brideshead* earns a first in Greats (106). In 1925, Waugh went to a "pathetic party" at "69 the High where all the people who felt they should have been asked to Christ Church were drowning their chagrin" (*DEW* 229). In "Love in the Slump," Tom

Watch shares "dingy but expensive lodgings in the High with young men richer than himself" (*CSS* 59), and in "Winner Takes All," Gervase Kent-Cumberland has "fashionable lodgings in the High Street" (*CSS* 189).

Waugh had slight connections to Brasenose College, founded in 1509. In his first year, he went to Brasenose and listened to an "American revivalist of great transatlantic fame" (*LEW* 11), perhaps a source for Mrs. Melrose Ape in *Vile Bodies*. Brasenose was also the college of Alastair Graham,[113] whom Waugh described as Pares's "successor as the friend of my heart." Graham soon left the university, but for two or three years he and Waugh were "inseparable" (*ALL* 192), and Graham printed *P.R.B.* (1926), Waugh's essay on the Pre-Raphaelite Brotherhood. Graham is believed to be the main model for Sebastian Flyte in *Brideshead*, and "pub-crawling hearties from BNC" sometimes spoil Charles and Sebastian's evenings in the Turf in Hell Passage (*BR* 108–109), adjacent to Hertford College. As *Brideshead* indicates, "sport was an important part of Brasenose life."[114] Explaining terms for the French translator of *Brideshead*, Waugh wrote that BNC was "one of the older but less reputable colleges."[115]

The bells of St Mary the Virgin strike nine as Charles and Sebastian start driving to Brideshead; they avoid "collision with a clergyman, black-straw-hatted, white-bearded, pedalling quietly down the wrong side of the High Street," then cross Carfax and pass the station (*BR* 23). St Mary's strikes seven in "The Balance," when Adam thinks of visiting Ernest Vaughan (*CSS* 24), and it strikes half past twelve as Edward of Unique Achievement falls asleep after murdering his tutor (*CSS* 575). After dinner with Anthony Blanche, Charles thinks he hears "St Mary's strike each quarter till dawn" (*BR* 58), and Sebastian sings, "'Green arse, Samgrass–Samgrass, green arse,' . . . to the tune of St Mary's chime" (*BR* 128). On Sunday, some churchgoers head to St. Mary's (*BR* 59). Evelyn's great-grandfather, James Hay Waugh, preached at St. Mary's in 1854 (*ALL* 17–18), and Evelyn heard Dean Inge preach there in 1922 (*LEW* 7).

Radcliffe Camera appears in the background in "The Balance" (*CSS* 21). Waugh remembered that whenever Cruttwell dined outside Hertford, he "got grossly drunk . . . and was sometimes to be seen as St Mary's struck midnight, feeling his way blindly round the railings of Radcliffe Camera believing them to be those of the college" (*ALL* 174). Nicholas Hawksmoor suggested the idea of Radcliffe Camera, James Gibbs designed it, and the building was completed in 1749. With Radcliffe Camera in mind, Waugh referred to the "great continuous process of building which extended from the fourteenth to the middle of the eighteenth century. . . . Nothing erected since deserves artistic consideration,"[116] not even Campion Hall.

All Souls has no undergraduates, only fellows who pursue research instead of teaching. Fellows of All Souls should be, Henry James supposed, the happiest people in the world.[117] Founded in 1438, the college commemorates "All Souls of the Faithful Departed" in the Hundred Years' War. As an undergraduate, Waugh used All Souls to climb into Hertford after hours (*ALL* 176). In 1924, Waugh noted that Richard Pares had become a fellow of All Souls (*DEW* 185). In *Brideshead Revisited*, Charles Ryder's father "sat for All Souls and, in a year of hot competition, failed," so Charles "came up with an ill-considered sense that there lay the proper and natural goal of the life of reason" (44). Scott-King also failed to obtain a fellowship (*CSS* 353), but Mr. Samgrass is a fellow of All Souls in *Brideshead* (105), as is Joe Cattermole in *The End of the Battle* (216). Waugh wrote that novel, his last, after visiting Pares at All Souls in 1954. Suffering from muscular sclerosis, Pares was "quite paralysed except his mind & voice and awaiting deterioration and death," with "no Christian faith to support him" (*LEW* 435).[118] Pares died in 1958, and the character of Joe Cattermole may be a tribute to an old friend. Pares was Labour in the 1920s, and Cattermole admires Tito's partisans; the portrait is affectionate, but Waugh had found something lacking in Pares, and in Oxford.

Waugh spent only eight terms in Oxford, but he exploited that time throughout forty years of writing. In his autobiography, near the end of his life, Waugh wrote that Oxford had been "a Kingdom of Cokayne" (*ALL* 169), and that he had "wanted to taste everything Oxford could offer" (*ALL* 171). Freed from Lancing, Waugh was "reborn in full youth," and he "regarded Oxford as a place to be inhabited and enjoyed for itself, not as the preparation for anywhere else" (*ALL* 171). He estimated that "at least half of the undergraduates were sent to Oxford simply as a place to grow up in" (*ALL* 172). In Waugh's fiction as in his life, Oxford prepares undergraduates for civilized society, not only introducing them to the arts, clubs, and alcohol, but also serving as a point of reference for all subsequent experience.

Waugh mentions "a quintessential Oxford" that he "knew and loved from afar and intended to find" (*ALL* 167). He never explains what he means; nor does he say whether or not he found what he was looking for. "Quintessential Oxford" is sought in the work of other writers, but their definitions are equally vague.[119] Waugh had been contemplating this subject at least five years before publication of his autobiography: his speech dedicating his friend's bust at Trinity College in 1959 is entitled "Ronald Knox: The Quintessence of Oxford." In all of his "social and intellectual habits," Waugh claims, Knox was "the quintessence of Oxford; or, at least, of one precious part of her richly diverse tradition." Knox's part of the tradition includes writing, as in *Let Dons Delight* (1939). The book "has been regarded by many as a rather chilly leave-taking; as the repudiation, even, of the whole academic world," but Waugh's "more sympathetic reading reveals a wistful and tender affection." According to Waugh, "friendship was the most important thing in Ronald's life," second only to "his religion, and closely knit with it."[120] In Waugh's view, Knox embodied the quintessence of Oxford for four reasons: his intellect, his friendships, his writing, and his Catholicism.

Unlike Knox, Waugh never found quintessential Oxford in studies, and his "lessons were in no curriculum of scholarship or morals" (*ALL* 191). He used his intellect by criticizing Oxford, and he enjoyed undercutting Oxford's academic eminence. As did Knox, Waugh found part of the quintessence in the "catalogue of friendships" he compiled at Oxford (*ALL* 190). Also as did Knox, Waugh wrote about Oxford. His early works, "The Balance" and *Decline and Fall*, are satirical, but no one has ever written more beautifully about Oxford than Waugh did in *Brideshead Revisited* and *A Little Learning*. "Architecture" is a term Waugh applied to both writing and buildings, and his appreciation of Oxford is more comprehensive, more aesthetic, than Knox's. Because of the buildings erected prior to 1750, Waugh wrote, Oxford is "a city of peculiar grace and magnificence" (*EAR* 83), but he dismissed Victorian and modern architecture as blots upon earlier, superior work. Architectural distinction reflected spirituality, the fifth element of Waugh's quintessential Oxford, and the most crucial. Oxford was Catholic in origin, but that faith had been superseded by Anglicanism, new colleges such as Hertford, and scientific inquiry. Through composition of *Edmund Campion*, and perhaps through friendship with Ronald Knox, Waugh began to appreciate the Catholic conception of Oxford's medieval colleges. Troubled by the transience of pleasure and the suppression of Catholicism, and compelled to write about them, Waugh found himself revisiting Oxford, in person and in his imagination. Familiarity with Oxford is taken for granted in Waugh's writing, and anyone who does not know the city is lost in parts of *Brideshead*. Seeing these places helps one to visualize scenes in Waugh's fiction, but it also enables one to appreciate Waugh's critique of Oxford, to judge its validity, and to grasp its aesthetic and theological dimensions.

NOTES

1. Andrew Goudie, ed., *Seven Hundred Years of an Oxford College: Hertford College, 1284–1984* (1984; rep., Oxford: Hertford College, 1999), 7–9.

2. Ibid., 41–44.

3. M. C. Curthoys, "The Colleges in the New Era," in *The History of the University of Oxford,* Vol. 7, *Nineteenth-Century Oxford, Part 2,* ed. M. G. Brock and M. C. Curthoys (New York: Oxford University Press, 2000), 117.

4. Goudie, *Hertford College,* 62.

5. Curthoys, "Colleges in the New Era," 117.

6. Ibid., 118.

7. Goudie, *Hertford College,* 57–58. Waugh wrote that the college was "endowed by the first Lord Revelstoke in 1874." See *A Little Learning: The First Volume of an Autobiography* (Boston: Little, Brown, 1964), 165. Hereafter cited as *ALL.* He was mistaken. Edward Charles Baring (1828–97) was created the first Baron Revelstoke in 1885. His first cousin once removed, Thomas Charles Baring (1831–91), endowed Hertford. Waugh later became friends with the first baron's fifth son and the younger brother of the second and third barons, Maurice Baring (1874–1945).

8. Curthoys, "Colleges in the New Era," 117.

9. Goudie and Curthoys differ on the details: Goudie mentions only twelve fellowships, whereas Curthoys mentions eighteen; Goudie gives figures that total £229,000, whereas Curthoys says that by 1881 "batches of stock amounting to over £100,000 [were] transferred by Baring." See Goudie, *Hertford College,* 67–68, and Curthoys, "Colleges in the New Era," 118.

10. *ALL* 137.

11. John Howard Wilson, "Lancing College, the Woodard Schools, Evelyn Waugh, and Middle-Class Education," *Nassau Review* 8, no. 1 (2000): 85, 87.

12. Evelyn Waugh, *The Letters of Evelyn Waugh,* ed. Mark Amory (1980; rep., New York: Penguin, 1982), 11. Hereafter cited as *LEW.*

13. Terence Greenidge, *Evelyn Waugh in Letters,* ed. Charles Linck (Commerce, Tex.: Cow Hill Press, 1994), 14.

14. Evelyn Waugh, *Decline and Fall* (1928; rep., Boston: Little, Brown, 1956), 5. Hereafter cited as *D&F.*

15. Evelyn Waugh, *Brideshead Revisited* (Boston: Little, Brown, 1945), 105. Hereafter cited as *BR.*

16. Evelyn Waugh, *The Essays, Articles and Reviews of Evelyn Waugh,* ed. Donat Gallagher (Boston: Little, Brown, 1983), 609–10. Hereafter cited as *EAR.*

17. Evelyn Waugh, *The Ordeal of Gilbert Pinfold* (1957; rep., Boston: Little, Brown, 1979), 98.

18. Greenidge, *Evelyn Waugh,* 15.

19. Goudie, *Hertford College,* 79.

20. Ibid., 79.

21. Evelyn Waugh, *The Complete Short Stories and Selected Drawings,* ed. Ann Pasternak Slater (London: Everyman's Library, 1998), 24. Hereafter cited as *CSS.*

22. Goudie, *Hertford College,* 83.

23. Evelyn Waugh, *Labels: A Mediterranean Journal* (1930; rep., London: Penguin, 1985), 156. Hereafter cited as *Labels.*

24. Selina Hastings, *Evelyn Waugh: A Biography* (Boston: Houghton Mifflin, 1994), 83.

25. Goudie, *Hertford College,* 94–98.

26. Greenidge, *Evelyn Waugh,* 116.

27. Goudie, *Hertford College*, 96.

28. Ibid., 68.

29. Peter Howell, "Oxford Architecture, 1800–1914," in *History of the University of Oxford*, Vol. 7, 753.

30. For an explanation of Oxford degrees and terms such as *Mods and Greats*, see John Dougill, *Oxford in English Literature: The Making, and Undoing, of "The English Athens"* (Ann Arbor: University of Michigan Press, 1998), 265–67.

31. Greenidge, *Evelyn Waugh*, 14.

32. Arthur Waugh, *One Man's Road* (London: Chapman & Hall, 1931), 112.

33. Humphrey Carpenter, *The Brideshead Generation: Evelyn Waugh and His Friends* (Boston: Houghton Mifflin, 1990), 94.

34. Christopher Sykes, *Evelyn Waugh: A Biography* (1975; rep., New York: Penguin, 1977), 60.

35. E. H. Hanson, letter to Christopher Sykes, June 6, 1976, Sykes Papers, box 25, folder 11, Special Collections Division, Georgetown University Library. I am grateful to Donat Gallagher for this reference.

36. Evelyn Waugh, *The End of the Battle* (Boston: Little, Brown, 1961), 87–88. Hereafter cited as *EB*.

37. Stephanie Jenkins, *Broad Street, Oxford*, 2006, http://www.headington.org.uk/oxon /broad/buildings/north/new_bodleian/37.htm

38. Presumably based on a real order: "The Vatican gave approval in 1907 for Roman Catholic women to study at Oxford, living in the hostel at Cherwell Edge run by nuns of the Order of the Holy Child Jesus." See Janet Howarth, "'In Oxford but . . . not of Oxford': The Women's Colleges," in *History of the University of Oxford*, Vol. 7, 288.

39. Sykes, *Evelyn Waugh*, 345.

40. Hastings, *Evelyn Waugh*, 84.

41. Carpenter, *Brideshead Generation*, 141.

42. F. M. Turner, "Religion," in *The History of the University of Oxford*, Vol. 8: *The Twentieth Century*, ed. Brian Harrison (New York: Oxford University Press, 1994), 303.

43. Goudie, *Hertford College*, 36.

44. Evelyn Waugh, *The Diaries of Evelyn Waugh*, ed. Michael Davie (Boston: Little, Brown, 1976), 100–1. Hereafter abbreviated *DEW*. For the Newdigate Prize Poem, see Dougill, *Oxford in English Literature*, 267–68.

45. Martin Stannard places the Problem Club at Brasenose College, but he seems to have confused "Problem Club . . . at Balliol" and "coffee with some men in BNC." See *LEW*, 10–11, and Stannard, *Evelyn Waugh: The Early Years 1903–1939* (New York: Norton, 1987), 68.

46. Donat Gallagher believes that Cattermole is very like James Klugman, a much-loved, gentle, tireless, and effective communist who, working within the Special Operations Executive and its successors, promoted Tito and undermined Mihailovic in Yugoslavia during the Second World War.

47. Christopher Hollis, *Oxford in the Twenties: Recollections of Five Friends* (London: Heinemann, 1976), 88.

48. Ibid.

49. Peter Quennell, "A Kingdom of Cokayne," in *Evelyn Waugh and His World*, ed. David Pryce-Jones (Boston: Little, Brown, 1973), 37.

50. Sykes, *Evelyn Waugh*, 79.

51. Carpenter, *Brideshead Generation*, 90.

52. Sykes, *Evelyn Waugh*, 88.

53. Evelyn Waugh, *Two Lives: Edmund Campion—Ronald Knox* (New York: Continuum, 2001), 196. Hereafter abbreviated *TL*.

54. Evelyn Waugh, *Black Mischief* (New York: Farrar & Rinehart, 1932), 147. Hereafter abbreviated *BM*.

55. As usual in Waugh's fiction, incidental details reflect reality: "Undergraduates of the 1930s frequently recall the response of cinema audiences, 'well rowed, Balliol!', when black men paddled a canoe in the film *Sanders of the River*." See Brian Harrison, "College Life, 1918–1939," in *History of the University of Oxford*, Vol. 8, 97.

56. By no means an eccentric judgment: J. G. Darwin concludes that Oxford in 1914 was "curiously underdeveloped and almost parochial." See "A World University," *History of the University of Oxford*, Vol. 8, 636.

57. Stephanie Jenkins, *St Giles' Street, Oxford*, 2006, http://www.headington.org.uk/oxon/stgiles/tour/east/11.htm

58. Carpenter, *Brideshead Generation*, 139.

59. Greenidge, *Evelyn Waugh*, 2.

60. Evelyn Waugh, *Officers and Gentlemen* (1955; rep., Boston: Little, Brown, 1979), 201.

61. Evelyn Waugh, "A Poet of the Counter-Reformation," *Spectator* 197 (July 13, 1956): 63. I am grateful to Donat Gallagher for this reference.

62. Valentine Cunningham, "Literary Culture," in *History of the University of Oxford*, Vol. 8, 447. The Oxford Playhouse has been in Beaumont Street since 1938. See Richard Whiting, "University and Locality," in *History of the University of Oxford*, Vol. 8, 559.

63. Greenidge, *Evelyn Waugh*, 2.

64. Sykes, *Evelyn Waugh*, 129.

65. Turner, "Religion," in *History of the University of Oxford*, Vol. 8, 298–99.

66. Ibid., 303.

67. Greenidge, *Evelyn Waugh*, 101–102.

68. Ibid., 37.

69. Evelyn Waugh, *Rossetti: His Life and Works* (New York: Dodd, Mead, 1928), 85. Woodward built the University Museum on Parks Road. His next project was "the debating hall of the Union Society (1856–7). Built of brick, notched in the same way as the woodwork, and with a steep-pitched roof, its plan is an elongated octagon. The sheer wall-surfaces, with the windows punched into them, again show the influence of Ruskin." Woodward also designed "additions to Dr Acland's house at 40–41 Broad Street, and to Professor B. Price's house, Middleton Hall, in St Giles (both in 1857), and a new east window for the Latin Chapel of Christ Church (1860)." See Howell, "Oxford Architecture, 1800–1914," in *History of the University of Oxford*, Vol. 7, 741 and note. Middleton Hall, 11 St Giles Street, was the site of Campion Hall from 1919 to 1935.

70. Martin Stannard, *Evelyn Waugh: The Early Years 1903–1939* (New York: Norton, 1987), 68.

71. Ibid., 76.

72. Greenidge, *Evelyn Waugh*, 33.

73. Claud Cockburn, "Evelyn Waugh's Lost Rabbit," *Atlantic*, December 1973, 57.

74. Richard Whiting, "University and Locality," in *History of the University of Oxford*, Vol. 8, 565.

75. Stephanie Jenkins, *Cornmarket, Oxford*, 2006, http://www.headington.org.uk/oxon/cornmarket/clarendon.htm

76. Stephanie Jenkins, *The Mayors of Oxford*, 2006, http://www.headington.org.uk/oxon/mayors/city_church/allsaints.htm

77. Goudie, *Hertford College*, 24–25.

78. Greenidge, *Evelyn Waugh*, 102.

79. Stannard, *Early Years*, 78.

80. Hastings, *Evelyn Waugh*, 90.

81. The American edition of *A Little Learning* states that the Hypocrites' Club "still stands at No. 31 and is preserved as an Historic Monument" (*ALL* 180).

82. Stannard, *Early Years*, 83; Carpenter, *Brideshead Generation*, 74.

83. Hastings, *Evelyn Waugh*, 90.

84. Greenidge, *Evelyn Waugh*, 33.

85. I am grateful to Ann Pasternak Slater for having investigated this site on "the second hottest afternoon in England in the last hundred years." E-mail to author, July 18, 2006.

86. Auberon Waugh, *Will This Do? The First Fifty Years of Auberon Waugh: An Autobiography* (1991; rep., New York: Carroll and Graf, 1998), 125.

87. Stannard, *Early Years*, 388.

88. Ibid., 124.

89. "Vile Bodies" is also the name of a jazz band organized in 1983 by Humphrey Carpenter, author of *The Brideshead Generation*, among other books.

90. Carpenter, *Brideshead Generation*, 42.

91. Evelyn Waugh, *Put Out More Flags* (Boston: Little, Brown, 1942), 37.

92. Harrison, "College Life, 1918–1939," in *History of the University of Oxford,* Vol. 8, 94.

93. Carpenter, *Brideshead Generation*, 44.

94. Auberon Waugh, *Will This Do?,* 127–28.

95. Evelyn Waugh, letter to Roy Harrod, July 21, 1960, British Library.

96. Wilson, "Lancing College," 87.

97. Sykes, *Evelyn Waugh*, 343.

98. Carpenter, *Brideshead Generation*, 35, 39.

99. Ibid., 143–44.

100. Hastings, *Evelyn Waugh*, 99.

101. Stephanie Jenkins, *The High, Oxford*, 2006, http://www.headington.org.uk/oxon/high/tour/south/108.htm

102. Auberon Waugh, *Will This Do?,* 126.

103. Waugh tells three different versions of this experience: the others are in *DEW*, 781, and Charlotte Mosley, ed., *The Letters of Nancy Mitford and Evelyn Waugh* (New York: Houghton, 1996), 287.

104. Jenkins, *The High, Oxford*, http://www.headington.org.uk/oxon/high/tour/south/104.htm

105. Cunningham, "Literary Culture," in *History of the University of Oxford,* Vol. 8, 420–21.

106. Jenkins, *The High, Oxford*, http://www.headington.org.uk/oxon/high/tour/south/092_094.htm

107. Greenidge, *Evelyn Waugh*, 135.

108. Howell, "Oxford Architecture, 1800–1914," in *History of the University of Oxford,* Vol. 7, 749.

109. Stannard, *Early Years,* 94.

110. *Waviana* Vol. 16, Waugh Collection, Milverton, Somerset, UK.

111. Hastings, *Evelyn Waugh,* 165.

112. Carpenter, *Brideshead Generation,* 126.

113. Ibid., 84.

114. D. J. Wenden, "Sport," in *History of the University of Oxford,* Vol. 8, 528.

115. Evelyn Waugh, letter to W. N. Roughead, January 10, [1946], box 142, A. D. Peters Collection, Harry Ransom Center, University of Texas at Austin.

116. Evelyn Waugh, *"Dominus Illuminatio Mea,"* Evelyn Waugh Manuscript Collection, Harry Ransom Center, University of Texas at Austin.

117. Dougill, *Oxford in English Literature,* 5.

118. Isaiah Berlin wrote that Pares had died "a believing Christian." See "Richard Pares (1902–1958)," *Balliol College Record,* July 1958. I am grateful to Donat Gallagher for this reference.

119. Dougill, *Oxford in English Literature,* 247–58.

120. Evelyn Waugh, "Ronald Knox: The Quintessence of Oxford," *Tablet,* May 2, 1959, 419. Waugh sent a copy of his speech to Lady Diana Cooper and wrote that it "drew tears from many old eyes." See Cooper, *Letters of Waugh and Cooper,* 268. To Ann Fleming, Waugh wrote that his speech "made Tommy Lascelles blub" (*LEW* 518).

"A Later Development":
Evelyn Waugh and Conversion

John W. Mahon

Two of the most decisive developments in Evelyn Waugh's life were the collapse of his first marriage and his conversion to Roman Catholicism, which occurred within a year of each other. As with marriage and divorce, conversion appears throughout Waugh's novels, biographies, and occasional writings. Indeed, a pattern emerges in the fiction: conversion functions as a structuring device that often conveys thematic points relating to vocation, nowhere more clearly than in *Helena* (1950), his favorite novel. In Waugh's work, conversion has a dual meaning. On the one hand it suggests turning toward God and entering a religious community at a particular time, as Helena and Waugh did. On the other hand it can refer to a person who already belongs to a religious community and, as Guy Crouchback does, learns to conform more closely to the will of God.

Waugh's entry into the Roman Catholic Church in 1930 presents an interesting study in what he was reluctant to call "conversion." In *The Ordeal of Gilbert Pinfold* (1957), Waugh writes that "the Pinfolds were Roman Catholic, Mrs Pinfold by upbringing, Mr Pinfold by a later development. He had been received into the Church—'conversion' suggests an event more sudden and emotional than his calm acceptance of the propositions of his faith—in early manhood."[1] Pinfold/Waugh went through an intellectual exercise, although Waugh reveals that he converted because he began to see life as "unintelligible and unendurable without God."[2] As Joseph Pearce suggests, Waugh's conversion was partly "a matter for the emotions."[3] Moreover, it is significant that Waugh uses the term *conversion* as though it were restricted to a sudden, emotional event, resembling St. Paul's experience on the road to Damascus, an irruption of eternity into time and a radical change in direction.[4] Although few people experience conversion as dramatically as St. Paul did, converts often recognize a specific moment as decisive in coming to belief. Waugh does not mention a specific or decisive moment in his own conversion, but his first wife suddenly betrayed him within a year of their marriage, and pain and bewilderment appear to have prompted his inquiries into Catholicism. As do most converts then and now, Waugh underwent the required set of instructions leading to entry into the Catholic Church.

What we know of Waugh's conversion is gained from his diaries, a few letters, and brief accounts published over the years. After his wife's adultery in summer 1929, Waugh felt "lost, isolated, and wholly without purpose. More and more he found himself drawn towards a contemplation of the Christian faith he had superficially abandoned. . . . But now his inspiration was not the Anglican Church in which he had been brought up, but the Church of Rome."[5] In spring 1930, he asked Olivia Plunket Greene to find a Jesuit who might instruct him, and she recommended Father Martin D'Arcy, SJ, a philosopher at Oxford who was living temporarily at Farm Street in London. D'Arcy seems to have been the perfect instructor, and he reinforces the view that Waugh's conversion was primarily, but not entirely, intellectual: "Evelyn . . . never spoke of experience or feelings. . . . I have never myself met a convert who so strongly based his assents on truth. . . . Nor, though he writes about 'little emotion,' was his conversion so very matter of fact, because it proved to be an illumination and an inspiration. Hard, clear thinking had with the help of grace given him the answer for which he had been searching, and one can see its effect in his subsequent writings."[6] Suitably for Waugh, D'Arcy "was strikingly good at listening to other people and apprehending their viewpoint . . . and he was especially sympathetic to those who came to the Catholic Church seeking order in a world that had lost its values." D'Arcy had another "essential qualification for dealing with Waugh, a sense of humour."[7] Waugh first visited D'Arcy on July 8, 1930, and several more meetings took place in the following months. He entered the church on Michaelmas, September 29, 1930.

There is a frustrating lack of detail in this crucial period of three months when Waugh moved from interest in Catholicism to embracing it. The diaries are superficial, and few relevant letters seem to have survived. In his diary for July 8th, Waugh wrote: "Went to Father D'Arcy at 11. Blue chin and fine, slippery mind. The clergy house at Mount Street superbly ill-furnished. Anglicans can never achieve this ruthless absence of 'good taste.' We talked about verbal inspiration and Noah's Ark."[8] On July 9th, Waugh spent "a morning with D'Arcy" (*DEW* 321). They met again on July 11th and discussed infallibility and indulgences, then at least three more times before July 19th, when Waugh dined with Gwen and Olivia Plunket

Greene and talked about religion. During August, he visited the Lambs' home in Coombe Bissett and conversed with Douglas Woodruff, a cradle Catholic, and Christopher Hollis, a convert. Waugh also had a long conversation with Olivia. Before leaving for Ireland to visit the Pakenhams on August 21st, Waugh wrote to D'Arcy to express certain reservations:

> As I said when we first met, I realize that the Roman Catholic Church is the only genuine form of Christianity. Also that Christianity is the essential and formative constituent of western culture. In our conversations and in what I have read or heard since, I have been able to understand a great deal of the dogma and discipline which seemed odd to me before. But the trouble is that I don't feel Christian in the absolute sense. The question seems to be must I wait until I do feel this—which I suppose is a gift from God which no amount of instruction can give one, or can I become a Catholic when I am in such an incomplete state—and so get the benefit of the sacraments and receive faith afterwards?[9]

Almost twenty years later, Waugh wrote to Penelope Betjeman (a model for Helena and herself a convert): "With me, [D'Arcy] saw it was no good hoping for much & the thing to do was just to get the seed in anyhow & hope some of it would come up."[10] In "Come Inside," he wrote: "I look back aghast at the presumption with which I thought myself suitable for reception and with wonder at the trust of the priest who saw the possibility of growth in such a dry soul" (*EAR* 368).

A cleaning woman and Waugh's Lancing friend Tom Driberg witnessed the reception. As David Wykes observes, Waugh saw human life "as frantic aimlessness in comparison with the certainty and stability of the eternal order," a view "implicit in his earliest writings and in his two published novels. Catholicism added an alternative existence to the one depicted in his work." Wykes adds that "Driberg's column in the *Daily Express* announcing Waugh's conversion had described him at a society gathering, 'watching critically from the balcony.' Conversion meant that in one way Waugh had withdrawn from the world of meaninglessness, godlessness, and chaos, yet he remained passionately interested in it . . . if not spiritually or intellectually of it."[11]

Several of Waugh's novels and biographies feature conversion, but, as in his own case, he provides surprisingly few details of his subjects' change of heart and formal reception. Absence of detail is most striking in *Helena*, as Waugh passes up the opportunity to describe his heroine's conversion. According to David Wykes, Waugh "should have been able to bring autobiographical experience to bear" but instead "gives no explanation of what led Helena to become a Christian."[12] Helena's conversion "occurs midway through the novel and is the key to her later behavior," but Waugh "alludes to it casually" and "the reader [misses] a climax."[13] In a lyrical chapter anachronistically entitled "The Second Spring," Waugh evokes the Roman world after the Edict of Milan established toleration of the church. Constantine is triumphant on all fronts, his son Crispus prospers in his military career, and Helena becomes a Christian:

> Reports of [Crispus] came to Helena, as once of his father, and were as fondly welcomed. His name was remembered always at her palace Mass. For Helena had been baptized.
>
> None knows when or where. No record was made. Nothing was built or founded. There was no public holiday. Privately and humbly, like thousands of others, she stepped down into the font and emerged a new woman. Were there regrets for her earlier loyalty? Was she persuaded point by point? Did she merely conform to the prevailing fashion, lie open unresisting to Divine Grace and so without design become its brimming vehicle? We do not know. She was one seed in a vast germination.[14]

Why did Waugh not invent a conversion and reception for the Dowager Empress based on contemporary accounts of catechumens in those early centuries of Christianity? One answer might be the strategic and artistic reasons that inform Waugh's fiction and nonfiction: in order to focus attention on Helena's discovery of the true cross, the fulfillment of her vocation, Waugh, as did some other biographers of Helena, avoided details of the actual conversion.[15] Waugh nevertheless conveys the importance of the conversion through the dramatic contrast between Helena's pagan and Christian lives, for in the chapter announcing her conversion the tenor of the novel changes. Moreover, while neither *Helena* nor *Brideshead Revisited* describes the central characters' instruction and reception, both novels set out the events that precede and explain the conversions and, in the case of *Helena*, how conversion affects behavior.

Douglas Lane Patey suggests a different explanation: "A deliberate reticence shrouds the conversions of the central characters of *Brideshead* and *Helena*: both events pointedly occur offstage, implying that as works of grace, comings-to-faith are not finally explicable in psychological terms (i.e., through narrative) at all."[16] This argument has considerable weight because similar reticence shrouds Waugh's accounts of his own conversion and that of Ronald Knox.[17] Unlike most biographers, Waugh felt that "close investigation of motives in the lives of real people was an impertinence," and he was wary of "revealing too much about himself."[18] Yet in each case

Waugh provides enough background information to allow readers to infer the reasons for conversion.

In *Helena,* for example, the heroine asks for specific facts about the tale of Mithras recounted by her husband, Constantius: where did these events occur, and when? Dissatisfied with the vagueness of Mithraism, she skeptically turns to gnosticism, as championed by her old tutor Marcias. When Helena asks "how he knows" that gnosticism is true, Marcias answers that "these things are beyond time and space" (*Helena* 84). Their conversation covers ground familiar to Christians and prepares Helena for conversion. Helena tells Marcias that his religion "would never do" for her: "If I ever found a teacher it would have to be one who called little children to him." Marcias replies that such is not the "spirit of the time . . . we should have to forget everything and be born again to answer your questions" (*Helena* 85). Helena then sends for Lactantius, a Christian, who gives her "a straight answer" to questions about "when and where [this God of yours] could be seen." Lactantius states: "As a man [Christ] died two hundred and seventy-eight years ago in the town now called Aelia Capitolina in Palestine" (*Helena* 86). Helena's conversion follows this exchange.

Helena's becoming a Christian was part of the "Second Spring," the mass movement toward Christianity that followed Constantine's muddled acceptance of the new religion. Knowing nothing about the conversion, Waugh wisely leaves all possibilities open.

While Helena's conversion proves energizing, sending her in pursuit of the true cross, her husband's conversion to Mithraism renders him passive. Constantius has been initiated into the cult, but the initiation has made "no deep impression" (*Helena* 64). Eighteen years later, "nearing middle-age" (*Helena* 65), Constantius's career seems stalled and his life aimless. Regular visits from the local priest seek to stimulate interest, but Constantius is satisfied with the early stages in the path to enlightenment. After Constantius had joined the congregation in the local cave, "he fasted and bathed; he accepted the veil of Cryphius and the Soldier's Brand. And there he stopped short. The priest urged him to prepare for the honey and ashes." Unlike Helena, who embarks on her journey of discovery, Constantius remains passive, because he is "content": he "had found what he wanted" (*Helena* 66).

In *Sword of Honour* (1965), Guy Crouchback is a born Catholic, and Guy routinely accepts faith early in life. Faith becomes a matter of "urgent personal importance" only later (*EAR* 371), and he turns seriously to God.[19]

Since the failure of his marriage, Guy has persisted in a dry spiritual state, a loveless, ambitionless "apathy." He hopes to change this condition by joining the war but finds that motive misconceived. After several painful and disillusioning experiences, he develops from deluded idealist to experienced realist, from routine worshipper to sensitive believer, from priggish husband to sympathetic widower, and from self-centered loner to self-giving lover. Two crucial events relevant to Guy's conversion occur in the third volume of the trilogy, *The End of the Battle* (1961). The first is Guy's meditation at the funeral Mass for his father, when he sheds his "apathy," however tentatively. He succeeds in praying for some "function" in life, for a task to perform and the help to perform it: "God required more than that. He had commanded all men to *ask*. . . . Even he must have his function in the divine plan. He did not expect a heroic destiny. Quantitative judgments did not apply. All that mattered was to recognize the chance when it offered. Perhaps his father was at that moment clearing the way for him. 'Show me what to do and help me to do it,' he prayed."[20] When Virginia, alone and penniless, becomes pregnant by Trimmer, Guy recognizes that "this is just one case where I can help" (*EB* 190) and, conforming to God's will, selflessly marries her. The second development occurs when Guy listens to Mme Kanyi's searing indictment of war makers and recognizes the falsity of his own hopes for redemption through war. She descries "a will to war, a death wish, everywhere. Even good men thought their private honor would be satisfied by war." Guy acknowledges that he was "one of them" and asks God for forgiveness (*EB* 297).

Guy's slow and painful return to spiritual health sharply contrasts with Virginia Troy's lighthearted acceptance of Catholicism. When Virginia tells Guy's uncle Peregrine that she is converting to Catholicism, he is not impressed: Virginia needs a husband, so the conversion seems too convenient. Nevertheless, Virginia becomes a Catholic and makes her first Confession at the same time as Guy, in Italy, confesses his wish to die. In Westminster Cathedral, Virginia tells "everything; fully, accurately, without extenuation or elaboration. The recital of half a lifetime's mischief took less than five minutes. 'Thank God for your good and humble confession,' the priest said. She was shriven. The same words were said to her as were said to Guy. The same grace was offered." Later she asks, "Why do people make such a *fuss?* It's all so easy. But it is rather satisfactory to feel that I shall never again have anything to confess as long as I live" (*EB* 215). Virginia deludes herself, but her words are prophetic. She is killed by a bomb, and, according to the Roman Catholic "machinery of salvation," is "saved."

The conversion of Charles Ryder in *Brideshead Revisited* has led to an interesting controversy. According to Laura Mooneyham, Charles is

converted shortly after Lord Marchmain's death, but the prologue shows
his conversion has failed. Only after narrating his memories is Charles
taken to the second, genuine conversion of the epilogue.[21] Jeffrey Heath is
more persuasive. Lord Marchmain's deathbed repentance starts a *process*
of conversion leading to Charles's reception into the church. At the moment
of death, Charles Ryder, despite his earlier resistance, finds himself praying
with Julia "for a sign," for Lord Marchmain's "acceptance of forgiveness."
When that "sign" is given, his own conversion becomes inevitable. The
avalanche of belief has swept away everything, including plans for life with
Julia. For Heath, the theme of conversion is closely allied to the theme of
vocation. Charles's "maturation depends upon his acceptance of his unique
purpose in God's design," and though he initially refuses "to conform to
the plan God has for him . . . his resistance is in vain." In Heath's interpretation, the "central conflict in *Brideshead* . . . is between the will of man and
the will of God."[22] Charles "has wished for inspiration, and for a wife and
a family and a home; the grace of conversion destroys his hopes for these
and gives him the Holy Spirit and the Bride of Christ and the Household of
the Faith and the City of God."[23]

As with Guy and Virginia, Charles Ryder's momentous and tortuous
experience of coming to the faith is matched by a minor character's conversion, in this case Rex Mottram's attempt to enter the church. Possibly
"based on Waugh's uncomfortable recollection of his own instruction,"[24]
Rex's lessons parody Waugh's. In his letter to D'Arcy, Waugh says he
understands dogma that had seemed odd. Waugh wanted to understand
Catholicism, but Rex seeks instruction merely to facilitate a church wedding to Julia Flyte. He agrees to anything and asks simply to "sign on the
dotted line." Trying to explain the doctrine of infallibility (which Waugh
discussed with D'Arcy), Father Mowbray asks whether rain is bound to fall
once the pope sees a cloud and says, "It's going to rain." Rex replies: "Oh,
yes, Father." Father Mowbray sadly reports that Rex is "the most difficult
convert I have ever met" (*BR* 192). Father D'Arcy found Waugh to be a very
different kind of convert, who based his decision on rational acceptance of
what he firmly held to be truth.

In two of his three biographies, Waugh deals with conversion of a special kind, from clergyman within the Church of England to priest within
the Church of Rome.

Born in 1540, Edmund Campion was probably baptized a Catholic, but
when he accepted ordination as a deacon in the Church of England, Waugh
reports in his biography *Edmund Campion* (1935), "by canon law he had
put himself in a state of excommunication."[25] Campion seems to have rec-

onciled with the Catholic Church in 1569, a few months after his formal apostasy.[26] Early lives of the martyred Jesuit testify that he sought reconciliation before departing for Ireland, thus exposing himself to arrest and imprisonment as a Catholic. In Waugh's view, "it is highly unlikely that, placed as he was [at Oxford], he could get in touch with anyone possessed of the necessary faculties to absolve him" (*Campion* 36). Preferring an alternative tradition, Waugh proposes that Campion was reconciled after he reached Douai in Belgium in 1572: "From then onwards he was admitted to the sacraments without which he had spent the past ten or twelve years of his life. From then onwards, for the first time in adult life, he found himself living in a completely Catholic community, and, perhaps, for the first time, began to have some sense of the size and power of the world he had entered" (*Campion* 65). Waugh described his own life after conversion as an "endless delighted tour of discovery in the huge territory of which I was made free" (*EAR* 368).[27] Although Campion's conversion leads to martyrdom, Waugh places his decision, like that of Helena, in a context larger than the individual, a Catholic milieu described in loving detail. In different ways, Helena and Campion become saints because they do God's will within the community of faith. After he was condemned to a horrible death as a traitor, Campion defended this community in ringing words:

> In condemning us you condemn all your own ancestors—all the ancient priests, bishops and kings—all that was once the glory of England, the island of saints, and the most devoted child of the See of Peter.
>
> For what have we taught, however you may qualify it with the odious name of treason, that they did not uniformly teach? To be condemned with these lights—not of England only, but of the world—by their degenerate descendants, is both gladness and glory to us. (*Campion* 222)

In *Monsignor Ronald Knox* (1959), Waugh explains that Knox began to doubt his Anglican faith on St. Augustine's Day, May 26, 1915.[28] Knox was twenty-seven years old, an Anglican priest with a brilliant career ahead at Oxford; as an undergraduate he had won virtually every academic distinction. By the time Knox began to doubt, many of his friends had already "poped" or "verted," including his best friend, Guy Lawrence, who was received at Farm Street on May 24th: "It was all done in under one hour" (*Knox* 139). Knox was a leading light in Anglo-Catholicism: he and his friends considered themselves neither Church of England nor Roman Catholic but simply Catholic. For two years Knox remained undecided and was close to losing his faith. He left Oxford, allowed his fellowship at Trinity College to lapse, and taught at Shrewsbury School.

In *A Spiritual Aeneid,* Knox provides details about these difficult years, which included extensive reading in theology. Henry Hart Milman's multi-volume *History of Latin Christianity* provided Knox with his "only sudden access of illumination" at this time. Milman noted that the popes always seemed to be on the winning side in early controversies, and Knox realized "that *what we mean when we talk of the Catholic party is the party in which the Bishop of Rome was, and nothing else"* (Knox's emphasis). Knox "could have laughed aloud."[29] Confronted by a choice between Catholicism and atheism, Knox felt "a strong desire to laugh" as soon as he decided to convert.[30] None of these details appears in Waugh's biography, though Waugh devotes more than twenty pages to circumstances leading to Knox's reception. Waugh also avoids details of Knox's reception, merely quoting from the diary of the guest master at Farnborough Abbey, where Knox was making a retreat: "Sept. 22nd—Mr. Knox was received into the Church by Fr. Abbot after the Conventual Mass" (*Knox* 158). Knox's own account includes a description of reading on retreat (Robert Hugh Benson's *Come Rack! Come Rope!* and other novels) and a conversation with one of the monks to make certain that he had not "underestimated one or two claims of the Catholic religion."[31] He reports enthusiastic congratulations bestowed by monks at the abbey and many friends, especially those who "could rejoice at whatever light had been given me in relief of my darkness. In return, what can I wish them but the greatest of God's earthly blessings—the consciousness of doing his will?"[32]

Central to Waugh's faith was the quest to do God's will: "He believed that God had assigned a task to every human soul, and that to live in harmony with God's will meant identifying correctly the task assigned and doing it to the best of one's ability. In his own case, the task was to be a writer."[33] The biographies of Campion and Knox describe callings fulfilled. Vocation is also important in Waugh's treatments of Helena, Charles Ryder, and Guy Crouchback. When Helena succeeds in finding the true cross, Waugh writes: "Her work was finished. She had done what only the saints succeed in doing; what indeed constitutes their patent of sanctity. She had completely conformed to the will of God" (*Helena* 157). Charles has only begun to identify his vocation at the end of *Brideshead Revisited,* and *Helena* completes his story by showing the effects of conversion. Helena achieves sainthood by doing the one thing God created her to do, but she also gains a new understanding of the City that has fascinated her from the beginning. She had hoped to go to Troy, the city of her namesake, to see its ruins, and she succeeds in reaching the most important city of the day, Rome. As a new Christian visiting Rome, she realizes that the City, God's

Church, must break out of the walls that confine it. Helena realizes her destiny in Jerusalem, not Troy or Rome. In a passage from the *Iliad* that Marcias quotes early in the novel, Aphrodite calls Helen to Troy where "Paris is waiting on his carved bed" (*Helena* 22). Helena receives instead "the mystical call of God, quiet and serene," and her response is an "act of heroic virtue."[34] Her "supreme moment is at once the recovery of the muddy wood from total extinction and . . . the discovery of her true self."[35]

In Rome, Helena's new understanding of Christianity enriches worship at the Lateran basilica, where she is just another member of the congregation and recognizes their connection: "The intimate family circle of which she was a member bore no mark of kinship. The barrow-man . . . the fuller . . . the lawyer or the lawyer's clerk might each and all be one with the Empress Dowager in the Mystical Body" (*Helena* 94). Helena's prayer in Bethlehem at the Epiphany expresses Waugh's own experience of conversion: she identifies with the Magi, who also "were late in coming." After considering the delays they encountered, Helena notes that the Magi nevertheless "came, and were not turned away. You too found room before the manger. Your gifts were not needed, but they were accepted and put carefully by, for they were brought with love." For Helena, the Magi are her "especial patrons . . . and patrons of all late-comers, of all who have a tedious journey to make to the truth." She concludes: "For His sake who did not reject your curious gifts, pray always for all the learned, the oblique, the delicate. Let them not be quite forgotten at the Throne of God when the simple come into their kingdom" (*Helena* 145–46). According to Laura Waugh, her husband "thought that prayer one of the best passages that he ever wrote."[36] In a letter to Laura from Dubrovnik in January 1945, Waugh pointed out that "the Epiphany is the feast of artists. . . . After St. Joseph and the angels and the shepherds and even the ox and the ass have had their share of the crib, twelve days later appears an exotic caravan. . . . They have come an enormous journey across a desert and the splendid gifts look much less splendid than they did when they were being packed in Babylon. The wise men committed every sort of bêtise—even asking the way of Herod & provoking the massacre of the innocents—but they got there in the end and their gifts *were* accepted" (*LEW* 197). Prayers in Waugh's fiction help characters to recognize their mission in life. Charles Ryder gains new hope in the chapel at Brideshead, and Helena's prayer to the Magi strengthens her resolve. In prayer during his father's funeral Guy Crouchback realizes that he must invite God's direction, not just nurse his hurts.

Sainthood is found in complete conformity to the will of God. Waugh's dry soul of 1930 became fruitful in writing *Campion* and the works that followed. He insists on the uniqueness of each person in God's plan, as in a brief, moving portrait of Edith Stein, murdered by Nazis: "The aimless, impersonal wickedness which could drag a victim from the holy silence of Carmel and drive her, stripped and crowded, to the gas chamber and the furnace, still lurks in the darkness. But Edith's death is perhaps an irrelevant horror. Her life was completed in Carmel. She did not sit, waiting on God. She went out alone and by the God-given light of her intelligence and strength of purpose, she found Him" (*EAR* 435). Led to conversion through intellect, Waugh admires others' use of intelligence in the spiritual quest.

In *The Use of Memory*, Tom Burns reports that "it must have been in the autumn of 1930 when I first met Evelyn Waugh. The occasion was a dinner *à trois*, with Douglas Woodruff." Burns continues: "For Evelyn it was the beginning of an exploration that was to end seven years later with marriage in the glades of the Catholic aristocracy. . . . There is a certain skepticism, tolerance and familiarity with sacred things which the Church inculcates in those who have been nourished by her teaching from the cradle. Latecomers often have a different response. Evelyn saw himself as a man who had joined a regiment with traditions and rules which he never questioned."[37] Burns and Waugh both recognized that their religion was "more than a defiance of fashion, something other than aestheticism. Religion was a matter of putting roots into reality. Nothing else. This was our tacit bond." Years later, in 1948, this bond prompted Burns to ask Waugh to prepare a British edition of Thomas Merton's *The Seven Storey Mountain*: "Evelyn instantly saw the value of the book, cut it down and edited it with great sensitivity (he calls it an 'enthralling task' in his *Diaries*). We produced a best-seller under the Hopkins title of *Elected Silence*."[38]

Robert Murray Davis notes that "Waugh cut over one-fifth of the original text, occasionally in blocks of paragraphs but more frequently a sentence here, a phrase there in order to make the narrative move more rapidly, to give it point and emphasis, and to focus it, as the new title implies, upon the central issue of the book: Merton's movement from the secular world to the life of contemplation."[39] Waugh leaves untouched Merton's description of his decision to convert. This moment did not occur in prayer but while reading a life of Gerard Manley Hopkins:

> [Hopkins] was thinking of becoming a Catholic. He was writing letters to Cardinal Newman (not yet a Cardinal) about becoming a Catholic.
>
> All of a sudden, something began to stir within me, something began to push me, to prompt me. It was a movement that spoke like a voice.
>
> "What are you waiting for?" it said. "Why are you sitting here? Why do you still hesitate? You know what you ought to do? Why don't you do it?"

The voice urges him to "get up and go." He seeks a priest and says, "Father, I want to become a Catholic."[40]

Waugh also leaves untouched Merton's narrative of his reception on November 16, 1938 at Corpus Christi Church in Manhattan. It is a detailed description, more complete than anything in Waugh's own work. Editing the work of another writer who is comfortable telling his story, Waugh was freed from the reticence and respect for privacy that prevented him from portraying details about similar moments in his own life and in the lives of the characters in his fiction and biography.[41]

NOTES

1. Evelyn Waugh, *The Ordeal of Gilbert Pinfold* (Boston: Little, Brown, 1957), 9.

2. Evelyn Waugh, *The Essays, Articles and Reviews of Evelyn Waugh*, ed. Donat Gallagher (London: Methuen, 1983), 367. Hereafter cited as *EAR*.

3. Joseph Pearce, *Literary Converts* (San Francisco: Ignatius Press, 2000), 163.

4. One of Waugh's earliest works was a play entitled *Conversion*, performed on June 19, 1921 at Lancing College and subtitled *The Tragedy of Youth in Three Burlesques*. Each of three short acts parodies school life, and conversion occurs abruptly in each act. In act 1 ("School, as maiden Aunts think it is"), a bully is converted by a "good boy," who suggests asking, "What would Auntie say?" In act 2 ("School, as modern authors say it is"), Collier is expelled for stealing spoons but changes his ways when confronted by one of the masters, Mr. Tadema, who overhears Collier's quoting Ernest Dowson. Tadema asks "How, after that, can you descend to stealing? . . . Live portentously. Whenever you are going to do a mean thing, think of a chorus from Atalanta." Collier agrees that "it's a glorious thing to be a pagan. Wine and roses and desire." Stage direction: "*Exeunt quoting.*" Most interesting is act 3 ("School, as we all know it is"): a prefect, Maine, chides Townsend, who disturbs chapel services, for "deliberate opposition to a definite fact of the School System." Townsend is accused of having "decided that the Chapel services are a farce and that the Christian religion is built on a lie." Townsend protests that he is only combating the boredom of school life, and when he refuses to "adopt a sane attitude," Maine threatens to make his life miserable. Maine holds "all the cards," so Townsend submits. In an epilogue, the performers apologize if they have offended and beg forgiveness for the author:

> So for indulgence on his faults we pray;
> We stand converted, and so end our play.

See Evelyn Waugh, *Conversion*, in *Evelyn Waugh, Apprentice: The Early Writings, 1910–1927*, ed. Robert Murray Davis (Norman, OK: Pilgrim, 1985), 94–115. The conversions are not religious.

5. Selina Hastings, *Evelyn Waugh: A Biography* (Boston: Houghton Mifflin, 1994), 223.

6. Martin D'Arcy, "The Religion of Evelyn Waugh," in *Evelyn Waugh and His World*, ed. David Pryce-Jones (Boston: Little, Brown, 1973), 64.

7. Humphrey Carpenter, *The Brideshead Generation: Evelyn Waugh and His Friends* (Boston: Houghton Mifflin, 1990), 221–22.

8. Evelyn Waugh, *The Diaries of Evelyn Waugh*, ed. Michael Davie (London: Weidenfeld & Nicolson, 1976), 320. Hereafter cited as *DEW*.

9. Qtd. in Gene D. Phillips, *Evelyn Waugh's Officers, Gentlemen, and Rogues* (Chicago: Nelson-Hall, 1975), 53–54.

10. Evelyn Waugh, *The Letters of Evelyn Waugh*, ed. Mark Amory (New York: Ticknor & Fields, 1980), 269. Hereafter cited as *LEW*.

11. David Wykes, *Evelyn Waugh: A Literary Life* (Houndsmill, UK: Macmillan, 1999), 76.

12. Ibid., 160.

13. Phillips, *Evelyn Waugh's Officers,* 92.

14. Evelyn Waugh, *Helena* (1950; rep., New York: Doubleday Image, 1967), 90–91. Hereafter cited as *Helena*.

15. Antonia Harbus, *Helena of Britain in Medieval Legend* (Cambridge: D. S. Brewer, 2002), 137. Helena's visit to Rome and its aftermath occupy only 14 percent of Waugh's narrative, compared with 84 percent in the medieval poem *Elene*. In *The Living Wood,* his 1947 novel about Helena, Louis de Wohl also skips details of Helena's reception into the church. Deserted by Constantius, Helena lives in retirement in Britain, surrounded by Christians but not yet converted. The most prominent Christian, Albanus, visits her and discusses his belief. One of her servants, Hilary, admits that he has become a priest, and, though the religion is illegal, Helena accompanies Hilary to a Mass in a private home, where Albanus presides. As he reads the Sermon on the Mount from a scroll, soldiers burst into the room and begin arresting everyone, but Hilary helps Helena to escape. He carries a gold vessel entrusted to him by Albanus, who is executed after the raid (and who, as a Christian martyr, gave his name to the English city of St. Albans). Hilary and Helena are waylaid by a looter who tries to grab the goblet, but Hilary will not surrender it. Hilary is mortally wounded and entrusts the goblet to Helena. The novel later refers to Helena as a Christian, so the reader infers that this incident has been decisive in Helena's conversion. In a longer novel, De Wohl devotes less space to the discovery of the true cross than Waugh does. See De Wohl, *The Living Wood* (Philadelphia: Lippincott, 1947). In her 1951 play *The Emperor Constantine,* Dorothy Sayers assumes that Helena was born a Christian. The play focuses on Constantine and his grandfather, King Coel, and the cross figures only briefly. In the final scene, set in Rome in AD 326, Helena asks for a ship to go to Jerusalem—she has had a dream directing her there. In the epilogue, set in 337, the dying Constantine is baptized as Helena appears carrying the cross. See Sayers, *The Emperor Constantine: A Chronicle* (London: Victor Gollancz, 1951). Cynewulf's Old English poem *Elene* begins with Constantine's victory at the Milvian Bridge. After his conversion, "he bade his mother fare unto the Jews upon a journey." Helena's Christianity is assumed. The poem focuses on the ultimately successful pilgrimage to Jerusalem.

16. Douglas Lane Patey, *The Life of Evelyn Waugh: A Critical Biography* (Oxford: Blackwell, 1998), 36.

17. In "Converted to Rome: Why It Has Happened to Me," published in the *Daily Express* three weeks after conversion, Waugh is impersonal about his experience and emphasizes the "essential issue" (*EAR* 103), the choice between Christianity and chaos. In the nineteenth and twentieth centuries, some of the best and the brightest in Europe and the United States converted to Catholicism. The First World War, fascism, and communism

drove many to the church. Joseph Pearce's *Literary Converts* suggests the extent: Waugh, Graham Greene, Muriel Spark, Edith Sitwell, David Jones, Ronald Knox, Malcolm Muggeridge, David Thomas, Roy Campbell, Alfred Noyes, Christopher Dawson, Alec Guinness, Avery Dulles, Clare Boothe Luce, Thomas Merton, and Dorothy Day.

18. Carpenter, *Brideshead Generation*, 273.

19. Sincere adult conversion is always more than "reception" into a Christian community; it is the beginning of a lifelong endeavor to grow in understanding and holiness. Lady Marchmain and her children in *Brideshead Revisited* are all cradle Catholics. She, her son Bridey, and her daughter Cordelia have a devout faith that appears unshaken. Nanny Hawkins is similar. Both Sebastian and Julia encounter moments of urgent personal importance in religious experience. The injured Kurt draws Sebastian toward genuine engagement with faith. Her father's deathbed conversion forces Julia to realize "what I didn't know till to-day . . . that there was one thing unforgivable . . . to set up a rival good to God's." See Evelyn Waugh, *Brideshead Revisited* (Boston: Little, Brown, 1945), 340. Joseph Pearce suggests that "the simple unaffected faith of cradle Catholics like [Hilaire] Belloc, as distinct from the comparative zeal of converts . . . shaped the characterization of the Flytes." See *Literary Converts*, 236. Some cradle Christians in Waugh's work go through the motions but have no faith. Tony Last worships in the parish church but remains indifferent to religion. See Evelyn Waugh, *A Handful of Dust* (1934; rep., Boston: Little, Brown, 1962). In early years, Charles Ryder is indifferent to the Anglicanism of his baptism: "He had been confirmed the term before, incuriously, without expectation or disappointment. When, later in life, he read accounts of the emotional disturbances caused in other boys by the ceremony he found them unintelligible; to Charles it was one of the rites of adolescence." See Evelyn Waugh, "Charles Ryder's Schooldays," in *The Complete Stories of Evelyn Waugh* (Boston: Little, Brown, 1999), 317.

20. Evelyn Waugh, *The End of the Battle* (1961; rep., New York: Dell Delta, 1964), 75. Hereafter cited as *EB*.

21. Laura Mooneyham, "The Triple Conversions of *Brideshead Revisited*," *Renascence* 45; no. 4 (Summer 1993): 225–35.

22. Jeffrey Heath, *The Picturesque Prison: Evelyn Waugh and His Writing* (Montreal: McGill-Queen's University Press, 1982), 161.

23. Ibid., 182.

24. Carpenter, *Brideshead Generation*, 223.

25. Evelyn Waugh, *Edmund Campion* (1935; rep., Boston: Little, Brown, 1946), 36. Hereafter cited as *Campion*.

26. A. F. Vossen, ed., *Two Bokes of the Histories of Ireland Compiled by Edmund Campion* (Assen: Van Gorcum, 1963), 7.

27. Waugh's enthusiasm for his faith is evident in his encouragement of others. Tactless efforts to convert John Betjeman from Anglo-Catholicism to Roman Catholicism led Penelope Betjeman to warn Waugh that her husband resented the pressure and threatened to leave her if she converted (as she eventually did). Waugh responded, "Please tell John I am sincerely sorry for persecuting him and won't again." See Pearce, *Literary Converts*, 242. Waugh was one of Edith Sitwell's godparents at a ceremony attended by her friends, including Alec Guinness. As does Waugh, Guinness speaks of "no emotional upheaval, no great insight" leading to conversion, but "the whole world, however poverty-stricken, seemed a wide-open bright and sunlit place, 'where all contraries are reconciled.'" See Pearce, *Literary Converts*, 311.

28. Evelyn Waugh, *Monsignor Ronald Knox: Fellow of Trinity College, Oxford and Protonotary Apostolic to His Holiness Pope Pius XII* (Boston: Little, Brown, 1959), 141. Hereafter cited as *Knox*.

29. Ronald Knox, *A Spiritual Aeneid* (1918; rep., New York: Sheed & Ward, 1958), 193–94.

30. Ibid., 215.

31. Ibid.

32. Ibid., 217.

33. Wykes, *Evelyn Waugh*, 76.

34. A. Clement, *The Novels of Evelyn Waugh: A Study in the Quest-Motif* (New Delhi: Prestige, 1994), 162.

35. Ibid., 154.

36. Phillips, *Evelyn Waugh's Officers*, 95.

37. Tom Burns, *The Use of Memory* (London: Sheed & Ward, 1993), 61–62.

38. Ibid., 63–64.

39. Robert Murray Davis, "How Waugh Cut Merton," *Month*, April 1973, 150.

40. Thomas Merton, *Elected Silence* (London: Burns & Oates, 1949), 236–37.

41. Merton makes three references to Waugh himself, and Waugh deleted two of them. Describing school holidays in London in 1930, Merton recalls breakfast in bed: "I knew I would have to wait a little to get a bath, so I would stay in bed for an hour or so more reading a novel by Evelyn Waugh or somebody like that." See Merton, *The Seven Storey Mountain* (1948; rep., New York: Harcourt, Brace, 1998), 86. Waugh cuts this sentence but retains one where Merton explains that he discovered "all the names that people most talked about in modern writing: Hemingway, Joyce, D. H. Lawrence, Evelyn Waugh, Céline" (88). Most interesting is Waugh's deletion of Merton's third and longest reference to him. Describing conversion, Merton states that his reading "became more and more Catholic. I became absorbed in the poetry of Hopkins and in his notebooks. . . . I was deeply interested in Hopkins' life as a Jesuit." Merton also read Joyce and Crashaw, and he "began to be surrounded, interiorly, by Jesuits. . . . Perhaps, in the back of my mind, was my greatest Jesuit hero: the glorious Father Rothschild of Evelyn Waugh's *Vile Bodies*, who plotted with all the diplomats, and rode away into the night on a motorcycle when everybody else was exhausted." See Merton, *Seven Storey Mountain*, 231–32. Waugh's reason for cutting this reference is unclear. The passage praises Father Rothschild, otherwise a benign version of the stereotypical scheming Jesuit. Rothschild has said that young people hunger for permanence and that another war is inevitable, and his comments represent the center of value in the novel. See Evelyn Waugh, *Vile Bodies* (1930; rep., Boston: Little, Brown, 1958), 182–86.

"That Glittering, Intangible Western Culture": "Civilizing" Missions and the Crisis of Tradition in Evelyn Waugh's *Black Mischief*

Lewis MacLeod

TOWARD THE MIDPOINT OF *BLACK MISCHIEF* (1932), AS BASIL SEAL AND SETH forcibly modernize the imaginary African nation of Azania, their Ministry of Modernization is deserted except for "a small cluster of puzzled blacks" and "a single dog who gnawed her hindquarters in the patch of shadow cast by two corpses, which rotated slowly face to face, half circle East, a half circle West."[1] This image, with its dead faces mirroring each other, its confused orientation (not east, not west), and its incomplete revolutions, is a sobering but probably apt encapsulation of many of the novel's major issues. The bodies dangle aimlessly beside the manic, self-important energy of the self-consciously "civilizing" effort to modernize; they drift sometimes east and sometimes west, providing shelter for pest-ridden beasts and provoking the confusion of the native population.

This sometimes east,[2] sometimes west drift is central to *Black Mischief*'s affect and complicates the idea that Waugh is a uniformly Eurocentric writer. While Waugh's depictions of Africa often take the form of grotesque (and probably racist) caricatures, the novel simultaneously amounts to a stinging rebuke of European norms, and Azania's manifold problems arise from European notions of modernity as well as "native ignorance." Despite his often reactionary politics, Waugh ultimately refuses to uphold the notion of a universalized European humanism and to make categorical distinctions between the worlds (and the worldviews) of "enlightened" European modernity and "benighted" African primitiveness. Instead, he shows that wholesale renunciation of traditions, even African traditions, leads to chaos and destruction. Perhaps unintentionally, Waugh makes a remarkably pluralist gesture and puts the African "native" and the English gentleman of his later novels on very similar cultural footing: both deal with fallout from an underconsidered effort to "modernize" the cultural and physical spaces they once considered their own.

Black Mischief is less about the "native problem" than the "European problem," or, more specifically, the problems associated with the haphazard effort to remake Africa with European templates. Like the bodies that twist directionless in the air, Azania is subject to forces that twist in upon themselves rather than move onward to some brighter future. At different times, Azania seems to be moving both "West" and "East," moving rapidly toward a specifically Western modernity, while willfully, or at least emphatically, turning away from it. Even as Seth's victory is heralded as an advance for "soldiers of progress and the new age," tribal drums are heard "throbbing in sunless, forbidden places" (*BM* 117), emphasizing the survival of cultural practices that cannot be reconciled with Seth's ad hoc agenda.

Throughout *Black Mischief,* the encounter between West and East, between Europe and Africa, is configured in terms of European notions of progress, of the new age, and Africa's comparative primitiveness, its benighted, sunless darkness. A too-ready belief in the superiority of all things European underscores most of the novel's major action, as Eurocentric notions of "value" seek to displace local practices and procedures. Such attitudes underscore most colonial and imperial encounters and act as cultural justification for the imperial presence; the civilizing mission of Western modernity serves as cover story for the economic and military motivations that actually fuel the urge to empire. In *Black Mischief,* this is obvious from the outset as "the European powers" eagerly await "their opportunity to proclaim a Protectorate" (*BM* 10), to get what they want under the guise of paternalistic protection.

The importation of modernity is, in fact, the importation of the Western worldview, since the West has a monopoly on the modern.[3] Many theorists believe that the entire notion of the "'modern' is not separable from empire,"[4] that the notion of the barbaric, primitive "other" is the necessary foil to civilized "progress." In *The Great Arch: English State Formation as Cultural Revolution*, Philip Corrigan and Derek Sayer maintain that "cultural images provided the moral energy of English imperialism." In their view, "it took a national culture of extraordinary self-confidence and moral rectitude to construe . . . imperialism as a 'civilizing mission.'" Perhaps more importantly, this self-assurance was able "to bedazzle the domestically subordinated with the spectacle of empire," the ostentatious display of cultural supremacy.[5] In *Black Mischief,* Seth is awed by the "glittering, intangible Western culture" he sees in Basil (*BM* 113), and he doubts whether his nation will ever be modern and cultured enough to "get the full respect of the [European] powers" (*BM* 128).

For Seth, modernity and civilization are the same. To civilize is to modernize, yet, as the romantic poets recognized at the start of the industrial revolution, modernization is not always the friend of culture, and often it is hostile to local, small-scale cultures in particular. In England, the move toward industrialization was first experienced in terms of cultural erasure, destruction of an ancient way of life, and the onslaught of technological barbarism, a vacuous, mechanized noncivilization obliterating redemptive, pastoral culture. Post-Enlightenment notions of "progress" (in its eighteenth- and twenty-first-century guises) are usually universalist in nature, the stuff of McDonald's, Coca-Cola, and Walmart, not craft stores and boutiques. To modernize is to delocalize, to departicularize minority cultural practice and dissolve it into the one-size-fits-all framework of "progress."

Laments for a preindustrial, pastoral England continued throughout the imperialist period and fueled preoccupation with the noble savage and desire to "reracinate" the English character.[6] Such laments usually ignore premodern Africa, because European modernity signals not the end of "traditional culture," but rather the beginning of "culture proper" in Africa. *Inside* the framework of European culture, there is room for debate about the relative merits of traditional and contemporary approaches, but this debate concerns only the most valuable *version* of Western culture; the assumption of superiority always remains intact. Faced by Blake's "dark, satanic mills," the romantic poet turns away, looking nostalgically backward to a previous and in his view superior civilization, but when Seth looks at a railroad, he sees the *beginning* of civilization. He sees "barbarism" retreat "step by step," "the seeds of progress [taking] root" (*BM* 11). If Wordsworth's complaint is that the world is too much with him, Seth's fear is that the world has never been with him at all, that he and his country do not and cannot really exist except in the terms Western culture provides. His desperate attempt to be "in accordance with modern thought" (*BM* 126) is, in fact, a self-loathing desire for reinvention, an urge to remake himself and his country according to the "proper" template. For Seth, the more Azania remains Azanian, the more primitive its character. The more it conforms to the universalist dimensions of modern thought, the more civilized the country becomes.

Seth's desire to reorganize the country according to geometric principles, to construct a city "with ruler and pencil" (*BM* 127) and "by the points of the compass" (*BM* 128), is, in essence, a desire to reconstruct Azania in terms of rationalist, universalist principles; to connect with principles that apply everywhere, for everyone, at all times, principles that render all participants equal, all geometric cities the same, and by extension make Matodi and Debra Dowa equal to Paris, London, and Berlin. Not surprisingly, such efforts are at the expense of tradition; Seth's great northern thoroughfare, as relentlessly straight and unyielding as the points of the compass, must pass directly through the Anglican Cathedral, and, as "modernity" arrives in Azania, the nation's shaky sense of identity is further eroded. In earlier generations, Matodi was characterized by a steady stream of "detribalized natives, drawn from their traditional grounds by the glamour of city life" (*BM* 15), but the city's future seems increasingly fragmented and disjointed. Debra Dowa "lost all evidence of national character" during the reign of Amaruth (*BM* 15), but the reign of Seth seeks "Western character" that creates a Frankenstein's monster of national culture: it has a lot of the right pieces but none of the desired effects. Even before Basil arrives, the local people look at the city's disjointed features and wonder whether they "might as well be in a British Colony" (*BM* 95).

Despite its claims to universal applicability and absolute superiority, Western modernity has not always succeeded in creating the homogeneous, "rational" world it claims to represent. In Africa, Neil Lazarus reminds us, "pre-colonial social, cultural, and ideological forms survived the colonial era meaningfully";[7] the European steamroller did not smooth and straighten everything out, and remnants of "premodern" worldviews remain. Seth's plan to dismantle historic buildings meets considerable and sustained resistance from citizens who remain skeptical of his notions of progress, and, after the war, his "soldiers of progress" are "homeward bound to the [traditional] villages" (*BM* 116). Like the half-rotating corpses outside the Ministry of Modernization, the movement to modernity is incomplete and prone to shifts in direction. The result is neither a thoroughly modern nor a traditional country, but a fractured hybrid with a bizarre configuration of largely incompatible features. Seth's palace, unlike the plan of his arrow-straight thoroughfare, is framed by "an irregular fortified stockade" and is "far from orderly or harmonious." Its small "nucleus . . . of French design" is surrounded by "scattered sheds of various sizes" (*BM* 14). While Seth envisions gleaming highways and public transit, a journey through his city is still an erratic obstacle course, as William Bland is directed "behind the Baptist school and the Jewish abattoirs, then past the Parsee death-house and the fever hospital," then on through "the Arab cemetery" (*BM* 140).

This type of contrast prompts Albert Memmi, in his influential book *The Colonizer and the Colonized*, to describe Africa as a "profitable purgatory" in the eyes of the West.[8] The African colony, a nonculture with an *über*-culture grafted onto it, is neither "here" nor "there." In Mrinalini Sinha's terms, the colony has borne the "uneven and contradictory impact of the intersection between metropolitan and colonial histories."[9] In *Black Mischief*, this contradictory intersection of forces is most apparent in Seth, at once emperor of Azania, lord of Wanda, tyrant of the seas, and, very recently, "an undergraduate of no account" at Oxford (*BM* 112). Seth has a divided, hybrid sensibility derived from his exalted status in Africa and his "no account" obscurity in European thought and culture. While his power derives from the fact that he is "Seth, grandson of Amurath" (*BM* 16), he sees himself as an agent of progress, a harbinger of "modern" life. At least in his own view, Seth represents "Light and Speed and Strength, Steel and Steam, Youth, Today and Tomorrow" (*BM* 40). He has been to Europe and "the whole might of Evolution rides behind him" (*BM* 17).

Much as Seth struggles to maintain a kingdom "in accordance with modern thought" (*BM* 126), his modernity is naïve and not fully digested. It does not make him smooth, urbane, and sophisticated; it makes him "capricious and volatile" (*BM* 148). He overloads his bookshelves and his brain with the contradictory impulses of European modernity to such a degree that "ideas bubbled up within him, bearing to the surface a confused sediment of phrase and theory, scraps of learning half understood and fantastically translated" (*BM* 148).

Seth's country bears the mark of this confused sediment, and most of his major setbacks stem from his overestimation of modernity's transformative power and his underestimation of the value and force behind existing customs. Seth's victory medals may bear "the figure of Progress" with an airplane in one hand and a telephone in the other (*BM* 18), but a look at his streets shows "a gang of convicts, chained neck to neck . . . struggling to shift a rusty motor-car which lay on its side blocking the road" (*BM* 93). Seth is convinced that "tanks and aeroplanes" (*BM* 16) have sealed his victory because he has accepted the universality of Western "progress," failing to understand that progress might be case and site specific, that the "patents of modernity inspired by the European illustrated papers" (*BM* 190) might not be the stuff of African salvation.

Indeed, some of General Connolly's early comments to Seth highlight the problems with the emperor's faith in all things modern and prefigure the fate of his aspirations. Insisting on the explicitly antimodern source of his military victory, Connolly reminds Seth that the war "was won . . . by two very ancient weapons—lies and the long spear" (*BM* 40). Tellingly, he warns Seth about the pitfalls of assuming the universality of Western conditions. Of Seth's beloved tank, he says, "My dear boy, you can't take a machine like that over this country under this sun. The whole thing was red hot after five miles" (*BM* 41). The breakdown of the tank foreshadows the breakdown of the entire Western apparatus Basil and Seth try to import. Overlooking ground-level conditions and relying on the theoretical supremacy of Western models, Seth's One Year Plan never acknowledges the resilience of specifically Azanian conditions and traditions it intends to remake. The birth-control pageant, for example, operates under a banner saying, "Through Sterility to Culture" (*BM* 190), without recognizing that "progeny [is] a favourite boast" in *existing* Azanian culture; for many influential Azanians, fertility is a source of pride and prestige that lies "at the very roots of sport and decency" (*BM* 143). The spectacular failure of the birth-control pageant is simply a large-scale version of the earlier problem with the tank. Both are destroyed by a specifically Azanian climate that overwhelms European concepts. Both demonstrate that "you can't take a machine like that [into] this country" without unforeseen consequences.

Like the country he attempts to govern, Seth himself is subject to constant rumblings of internal strife, and civil war is finally inevitable. Divided against himself, one part African dictator, one part desperate colonial mimic, Seth remains a paranoid and mercurial insomniac, "awake and alone, his eyes wild with the inherited terror of the jungle, desperate with the acquired loneliness of civilization" (*BM* 26).

In contrast to Seth and his schizoid sense of doubt, his partner Basil Seal is characterized by a remarkable sense of self-possession and self-confidence. Basil is not constantly worried about what other people think: he does not even care whether anyone else is present. Almost absurdly comfortable with his own position in the world, Basil speaks half a dozen languages, calls dons by their Christian names, and borrows large amounts of money with only personal charm for collateral. To Seth, Basil is "the personification of all that glittering, intangible Western culture to which he aspired" (*BM* 113). A young man who had "a reputation of peculiar brilliance among his contemporaries" at Oxford (*BM* 112), Basil outshines Seth in the eyes of the European cultural elite, though Seth longs for acceptance. In the encounter between African and European, as Leela Gandhi notes, "one of the participants invariably 'knows better' than the other, whose world view . . . must be modified or 'improved.'"[10] Relations between the tyrant of the seas and his untitled employee are frequently inverted, with Seth's tentatively seeking the approval of Basil, rather than Basil's deferring to an emperor. Bluntly, Basil's cultural clout trumps Seth's military and political power. In this way, they participate in a quintessentially colonial power structure: primary movers are rendered secondary, while secondary presences assume authority. Basil's mystique translates into a great deal of cultural capital, even if he is low on actual capital.

In *Orientalism*, Edward Said describes this lopsided relationship in terms of what different individuals and groups "can afford to ignore." While the West can afford to overlook the non-Western world, Said says, "the converse is not true." Non-Westerners possess knowledge, but it lacks cultural capital, so they "still want to come and sit at the feet" of the Western academy. In relation to European and American "superiors," Said says, the third world thinker "will remain only a 'native informant,'" a secondary figure in terms of his own primary identity.[11] In *Black Mischief*, Connolly and Youkoumian are subject to Basil's judgments despite their objections and their much more reliable, if less glittering, understanding of local customs. Indeed, in the conflict between Connolly and Basil over the boots, "the native" refuses to sit at the feet of his supposed cultural superior.[12] Connolly's understanding of Azanian topography and the Azanian people conflicts with the all-encompassing mandate of Basil's Ministry of Modernization, designed to "promote the adoption of modern organization and habits of life throughout the Azanian Empire" (*BM* 120). Because almost anything can fall under "habits of life," Basil's jurisdiction is both mammoth and undefined. While most government offices "acquired the habit of relegating all decisions to Basil" (*BM* 121), he is simultaneously "the Minister of Damn All" to Connolly (*BM* 122). Basil is minister of everything cultural but nothing practical, and while Connolly appeals to common sense, Basil effuses an abstracted, urbane sophistication. Antiintellectual but astute, Connolly fears that Basil will "lame the whole army in a day" if he tries to make them wear boots (*BM* 131). Basil's complaint is that Connolly's "a decent soldier" but "*not quite modern*" (*BM* 127): the general is fit for elemental, primitive matters of combat, but unfit for the more rarefied exercise of modern, civilized thought.

Seth of course sides with Basil and initiates another of the novel's major fiascos, but Basil's influence and authority, while European in origin, derive primarily from his presence in Africa. Despite his undergraduate promise, Basil flees England because of escalating debts and disintegrating prospects. He is an intolerable bore to his friends, a chronic disappointment to his mother, and a disgrace to the legacy of his well-respected father. Azania restores him to cultural legitimacy. In this way, Basil follows a well-established pattern for young European men. For Memmi (and several other postcolonial thinkers), the colony is, almost by definition, a receptacle for redundant Europeans, a place where "jobs are guaranteed, wages high, careers more rapid and business more profitable."[13] Basil goes from petty thief to first minister in a fortnight, a rapid career indeed. In fact, Basil's whole enterprise anticipates Memmi on the characteristic work of colonial administrations: "In organizing their daily habits in the colonial community, they imported and imposed the way of life of their own country . . . from which they draw their administrative, political and cultural inspiration, and on which their eyes are constantly fixed."[14] According to his mother, Basil is not "the kind of man who would do in Kenya" (*BM* 81), but Basil does some slick business for a reasonable stretch of time in Azania. With Seth as buyer, Basil is, essentially, in the import business: his commodity is his own civilization and culture.[15]

Black Mischief draws a great deal of comic energy and dramatic tension from sharp juxtapositions not just between the modern and the primitive, but also between similar but not synonymous notions of the civilized and the barbaric. Most of the novel's best moments rest on a kind of switch that Waugh pulls on Seth, substituting modernity for civilization when Seth least suspects it. For Seth, "to civilize" is "to modernize," yet so much of Waugh's work suggests just the opposite: modernity is a threat to civilization, a form of vulgar degeneration, not cultural advancement. Waugh is clearly (and sometimes disturbingly) gleeful in his cartoonish descriptions of "jungle" ignorance and savagery, and he will never be mistaken for a cultural pluralist, but his depictions of the "native" reaction to Basil's modernity are sympathetic and instructive insofar as they prefigure a number of concerns in his later novels.

For Waugh, the most important parts of culture and civilization are their valuable traditions, not any kind of unconsidered modernity, and even when those traditions are not his own, he extends his singularly elegiac sensibility, his sense of loss and nostalgia, to include foreign but established cultures in decline. His sympathy for the "grave, impoverished [Arab] men whose genealogies extended to the time of the Prophet" (*BM* 14) is essentially the same he would later express for more familiar figures in *A Handful of Dust* (1934), *Brideshead Revisited* (1945), and *Sword of Honour* (1965). *Black Mischief* includes the "frail descendent of the oldest family in Matodi," who "sat among his kinsmen, moodily browsing over his lapful of khat," lamenting that "there [is] no room for a gentleman in Matodi nowadays" and bemoaning the fact that the city has yielded to the "vulgar display" of "upstarts" (*BM* 94). Bluntly, Waugh's quintessentially English fin-de-siècle figures are transplanted to a new continent with their values and their grievances intact; a declining group of once-respected figures have suffered serious setbacks yet stubbornly refuse to abandon their traditions and will not "start decking themselves out in coat and trousers and topee like a lot of half-caste bank clerks" (*BM* 95). Tradition, even African tradition, earns Waugh's respect; modernity arouses his suspicion.

In *A Tourist in Africa* (1960), Waugh writes that African self-determination is "the debate that occupies all the colonial territories, in which a stranger would be absurd to join,"[16] yet he had long ago joined that debate in a surprisingly subtle way. Less a send-up of barbarian customs than an investigation into cultural instability, *Black Mischief* spoofs African primitiveness but also ridicules Western modernity. As he compares the reciprocal chaos of untamed jungle and modern city, Waugh seems frequently to be criticizing his *own* society by tracing its gestation and semiaborted birth in Africa. The chaos modernity imports to Africa implicitly points to the instability modernity has imposed on the West. The world of Waugh's fiction is more subtle than his politics suggest, and *Black Mischief* is not quite the smug, Eurocentric, right-wing book it has sometimes been taken to be.

In *Remote People* (1931), Waugh travels through Africa and acknowledges "how wrong I was . . . in all my preconceived notions about this journey."[17] The same might well be said for the various journeys (east and west, up and down, back and forth) that mark our movement through the surprising land- and cityscapes of *Black Mischief.*

Notes

1. Evelyn Waugh, *Black Mischief* (1932; rep., Harmondsworth, UK: Penguin, 1962), 118. Hereafter cited as *BM.*

2. I speak of the East not so much in terms of geographic placement as in terms of binary oppositions. The "East" is conceived as the opposite of the West, as margin, not center; orient, not occident.

3. Even highly advanced nations, like the Japanese, have their alterity from Western standards measured by the residual effects of "traditions," which compromise any claim to thoroughgoing modernity.

4. C. J. Wan-Ling Wee, *Culture, Empire, and the Question of Being Modern* (Lanham, MD: Lexington Books, 2003), 4.

5. Philip Corrigan and Derek Sayer, *The Great Arch: English State Formation as Cultural Revolution* (Oxford: Blackwell, 1985), 193–94.

6. Just as the imperial enterprise was conceived as a civilizing mission, the untamed colony was viewed as robust and masculine. As an alternative "to effete and supposedly advanced metropolitan life," the colony could "displace overly refined concepts of 'feminine,' aestheticized English high culture." See Wee, *Culture, Empire, and Being Modern*, 5, 9. Waugh locates this effete sensibility in Basil, a grown man, who meets resistance with his eyes "clouded in an expression characteristic to him, insolent, sulky and curiously childish" (*BM* 122).

7. Neil Lazarus, *Nationalism and Cultural Practice in the Postcolonial World* (Cambridge: Cambridge University Press, 1999), 88–89.

8. Albert Memmi, *The Colonizer and the Colonized* (Boston: Beacon Press, 1965), 5.

9. Mrinalini Sinha, *Colonial Masculinity: The "Manly Englishman" and the "Effeminate Bengali" in the Late Nineteenth Century* (Manchester: Manchester University Press, 1995), 10.

10. Leela Gandhi, *Postcolonial Theory: A Critical Introduction* (New York: Columbia University Press, 1998), 28.

11. Edward Said, *Orientalism* (New York: Vintage, 1979), 324.

12. Obviously, Connolly is not a true native of Azania, yet his detailed understanding of the country and his marriage to a local woman make him less uniformly European, and more functionally African, than Basil. Basil and to a lesser degree Seth treat him as a primitive rather than a modern man.

13. Memmi, *Colonizer and Colonized*, 4.

14. Ibid., 5.

15. In *A Tourist in Africa*, Waugh recognizes this type of cultural commerce at the end of the imperial era: "The British Empire is being dissolved on the alien principles which we ourselves imported, of nineteenth-century Liberalism." See Waugh, *A Tourist in Africa* (London: Chapman & Hall, 1960), 164. The British were forced to buy back the concepts they had once sold, but, as Basil and Seth's experiment indicates, the offerings in Africa reflected the ugliness and absurdity of Western culture.

16. Waugh, *Tourist in Africa,* 111.

17. Evelyn Waugh, *Remote People* (1931; rep., London: Duckworth, 1985), 97.

Sovereign Power in Evelyn Waugh's
Edmund Campion and *Helena*

Irina Kabanova

E*DMUND* C*AMPION* (1935) AND *HELENA* (1950) ARE THE TWO MOST OVERTLY RE-
ligious works by Evelyn Waugh. They also describe traditional societies
where the central institution of power was sovereignty. Waugh does not use
the term "sovereignty" in any of his texts, but whenever words like *emperor*, *king*, and *queen* appear, the text deals with the problem of sovereign
power. The concept of sovereignty is of late origin. The sixteenth-century
French political theologian Jean Bodin defined sovereignty as supreme
perpetual absolute power, the power to institute laws and to take life.[1]
Bodin and Thomas Hobbes, as did all social-contract theorists, placed sovereignty in the person of the king.[2] The eighteenth century saw the rise of
the concept of popular sovereignty, which places sovereignty exclusively
in the nation. In the twentieth century the term was used to describe the attributes of a state rather than a person and was largely limited to the sphere
of international law. Today the concept continues to be the focus of politico-philosophical discussions. In their reflections upon modern situations,
Carl Schmitt, Michel Foucault, Giorgio Agamben, and Jacques Derrida,
to name a few, return to the origins of sovereignty and rethink its aporia.[3]
They distinguish among three types of sovereignty—political, social, and
psychological. I share their view that philosophy does not offer the closest
studies of power and sovereignty: works of art and literature do.

The disciplining, normalizing, coercive practices of modern democra-
cies were identified by Foucault, but Waugh was naturally more interested in power embodied in a person. Waugh's artistic instincts react most
strongly when dealing with the sovereign figure. In both his biography of
Edmund Campion and his novel about St. Helena, Waugh uses the con-
ventions of traditional historiography in differing degrees. He gives general overviews of historical periods and evaluates political, social, and

economic aspects of life in Tudor England and the Roman Empire at the end of the third and the beginning of the fourth century. In *Campion*, he takes a European perspective on the power mechanisms of the Reformation and Counter-Reformation: he writes about the political aspirations of the Holy See and the inept bureaucracy of the Spanish Empire under Philip II; within Great Britain he shows the interaction of different government bodies (the Privy Council, the Court, Parliament) and the mechanisms of the legal system. He thus masters what in *Helena* he would summarily name "the tiny mechanisms of Power that regularly revolve, like a watch still ticking on the wrist of a dead man,"[4] or, in another metaphor expressing the author's disdain, "the foetid termitary of power" (*Helena* 70). Waugh allows his reader many glimpses into this termitary and its secret passages, but in the center he puts the characters who either are true sovereigns (Queen Elizabeth I and Emperor Constantine) or have achieved psychological sovereignty through their faith (Campion and Helena). Definitely preferring psychological sovereignty, Waugh also offers subtle studies of political sovereignty.

Challenging sovereign power, Campion chose martyrdom, a decision that determined the plot of the biography. Sovereign power is indivisible; challengers must be punished. Catholics under Elizabeth were regarded as a source of potential civil disobedience. By staying loyal to the old church, they claimed rights as believers beyond those the state afforded to its citizens. They thus became agents of depoliticization and threatened politics grounded on territory, nation-state, and sovereign. What is at stake here is the theological concept of sovereignty: God in neoclassical thought, in Hobbes and Bodin, is considered to be the sovereign of the sovereign (the prince or the king), and claiming that God is one's direct sovereign subverts the prince's power. God is excluded from the contract that establishes sovereignty in human society, so Catholics' direct tie to God rather than the state was a real danger to Elizabeth's rule. Waugh never tires of stressing the apolitical, purely religious character of Campion's mission, refusing to see it as an attempt to undermine the sovereign, but that is—by implication if not by intent—precisely what it was. Waugh veils the fact in legal arguments, emphasizing that Campion was sentenced to death on forged accusations, since he did not plot to murder the queen. Executing him at Tyburn, his prosecutors committed a *legal and ethical* mistake, but by defending the principle of sovereignty they did not err *politically*.

In the biography, the two types of sovereignty are in direct conflict. In *Campion*, Waugh glorifies the hero of "the gallant company of English counter-Reformation": fiery, eloquent, chivalrous.[5] Campion progresses, as the titles of the four parts of the book indicate, from gentle scholar to priest, hero, and martyr. Through reason, the author attempts to explain the mystery of Campion's transition from the world of "the pulpit and the lecture-room" (*Campion* 65) to the world of violence and torture, where he nobly acquits himself. Waugh emphasizes the importance of "the precise discipline of the Ignatian *Exercises*" (*Campion* 65), including prayer and mortification. The object of this discipline is to renounce the world, the flesh, and the devil, to increase the mastery of the individual over the body. Campion is shown to triumph "by the supernatural grace that was in him" (*Campion* 65), through "the love of holiness, the need to sacrifice" (*Campion* 28). The author accepts the claim of *Campion's Brag* (1580), "which lies at the root of all Catholic apologetics, that the Faith is absolutely satisfactory to the mind, enlisting all knowledge and all reason to its cause; that it is absolutely compelling" (*Campion* 101).

Søren Kierkegaard distinguishes among three levels of human experience, each level higher than its predecessor. The first is the aesthetic level, based on individual sensual perception; the second is ethical, the level of the generality of law; finally on the third, the religious level, the Knight of Faith goes beyond generality. Campion reaches the highest possible level of human experience, thus achieving psychological sovereignty, which explains his transformation.

Another character treated in depth in *Edmund Campion* is Queen Elizabeth. There are only two scenes where she and Campion meet face to face, but their lives are entwined in the narrative in ways that reflect the connections among different types of sovereignty. Campion's imagined conspiracy against the queen shows the closest link between them. The king or queen embodies political sovereignty. She has her own body, which is born and dies; however, according to juridical theology of the Middle Ages, the sovereign's body is also invested with never-dying spiritual function, the physical yet intangible and unchangeable bulwark of the kingdom. When condemned for plotting to murder the sovereign, a rebel requires special ceremonies and special discourse designed, in Foucault's words, "to code the 'lack of power' with which those subjected to punishment are marked. In the darkest region of the political field, the condemned man represents the symmetrical, inverted figure of the king."[6] Agamben concurs: "At two extreme limits of the order, the sovereign and *homo sacer* present two symmetrical figures that have the same structure and are correlative."[7] This idea is indicated in Waugh's biography by symmetry of plot: the opening and closing scenes focus on Elizabeth's and Campion's deaths, and the author makes them die thinking of each other. In Campion's last words in the biography, he prays on the gallows "for Elizabeth your Queen and my Queen, unto whom I wish a long quiet reign with all prosperity" (*Campion* 166).

The political sovereign, Queen Elizabeth, is ubiquitous in the narrative, to the extent that it almost becomes her biography as well. The opening scene of her agony can be interpreted medically and psychologically, but it also illustrates crucial aspects of sovereignty. Power operates through fear induced by unpredictability, and there is irresponsibility as well as irrationality inherent in sovereignty. Elizabeth is a true sovereign to the last: whatever her former accomplishments, in this scene she is frightful in person, unpredictable in her furies, and irresponsible in her refusal to recognize her successor, to dispose of her property, and to repent. She is irrational to believe that while she wears a pagan talisman she cannot die. A sovereign is always a monster, if we understand by monstrosity a departure from normality, and Elizabeth is monstrous. She denies herself the human faculty of speech: "There was always company in the little withdrawing room waiting for her to speak, but she sighed and sipped and kept her silence" (*Campion* 9). Silence is a weapon of the sovereign to frighten her subjects. As a sovereign, she has been outside the system of law since her coronation. Set apart from humanity, the monstrosity of the sovereign finds expression in the very appropriate metaphor of the marionette or dummy. This is the first impression of the old woman in whom little life is left: "She sat on the floor, propped up with cushions, sleepless and silent, her eyes constantly open, fixed on the ground, oblivious to the coming and going of her councillors and attendants" (*Campion* 9). She is virtually a dummy, more and more "lapsing into stupor" (*Campion* 10).

The metaphor is developed in the scene of Campion's interview with the queen after his arrest. The portrait of the queen is based on metonymy, as she is reduced to the appearance of a marionette: "The vast red wig nodded acknowledgement; the jewels and braid and gold lace glittered and the sunken, painted face smiled in recognition" (*Campion* 133). If Campion publicly abjures his faith, the queen proposes, there will be "no limit to the heights he might reach" (*Campion* 134). But what communication can there be between the marionette and the man who has fully realized his humanity? The two sovereigns of different kinds, Elizabeth and Campion, are face to face, and Waugh openly contrasts two types of power, the queen's power based on force, her right to dispose of men, and Campion's power of spiritual conviction: "They had no desire to kill the virtuous and gifted man who had once been their friend, a man, moreover, who could still be of good service to them. . . . They had been used to the spectacle of men who would risk their lives for power, but to die deliberately, without hope of release, for an idea, was something beyond their comprehension" (*Campion* 134).

The marionette is often used in the politico-philosophical discourse of sovereignty, though I doubt that Waugh consciously borrowed the metaphor. On the other hand, the dummy differs from many standard satirical devices whose function is to reduce characters to talking flesh, to shallow surface, to eliminate psychological dimension and thus to cut off readers' sympathy. Starting with *Decline and Fall* (1928), Waugh's works abound in all kinds of "shadows" (Paul Pennyfeather), human automata, and incomplete human beings "unnaturally developed," such as Rex Mottram in *Brideshead Revisited* (1945).[8] Waugh's repertoire of dehumanizing metaphors stretches from machine to animal. The persistence of the dummy metaphor applied to sovereigns proper in Waugh's texts cannot be accidental; it catches some basic properties of sovereignty.

Campion is twice compared with early Christian martyrs, an anticipation of the novel written fifteen years later. *Helena*, the work of Waugh's maturity, is less the life of the title character than the panorama of her epoch.

If political sovereignty is a human artifact, a historical phenomenon taking different forms and guises, known under different names, then it can either prosper or fall, and it can be deconstructed. *Campion* is set in the period when personal sovereignty is on the rise; in *Helena*, Waugh turns to the decline of the Roman Empire, manifested in a quick succession of feeble emperors. In this crisis of sovereignty, true power belongs to the army. Very early in the novel, Helena's husband, Constantius, rides "at the head of battle-worn, victorious legions, at the heart of power . . . in his service uniform into a conquered and anxious world" (*Helena* 26). Mostly the short-lived emperors of the Flavian dynasty do not appear in the novel, and the reader gets only a record of their violent deaths: "murdered by his staff at the shores of the Bosphorus" (*Helena* 36); "dead, burned in his tent, by an assassin, by a thunderbolt, none knew how" (*Helena* 61); "dead, stabbed by a cuckold Tribune" (*Helena* 62). All these deaths contribute to the devaluation of power, grabbed by the military and handed on to a succession of undeserving favorites. The ruling Flavians are strictly speaking not Roman–they are from Illyria, or Dalmatia. Waging permanent wars on the borders of the empire, they go to Rome only to celebrate triumphs and jubilees. They see Rome as a dangerously sophisticated city and sense that the Romans regard them as exotic animals. They are coarse soldiers speaking broken Latin; Helena's in-laws "were a prosaic race; some farmed their ancestral holdings; some had profited by their high connections to the extent of small trade monopolies and sinecures; many of them had not yet troubled to adopt the fanciful new patronymic of 'Flavius'" (*Helena* 50).

A whole parade of dummy emperors marches through the pages of *Helena*. The reader learns the sensation of AD 260, the news spreading across the Roman Empire as a good joke: "They have him [the Immortal Valerian] on show in Persia, *stuffed*" (*Helena* 16). The officers stationed in Britain give more details about the shocking desecration of the emperor's body–"First a mounting-block, then a footstool, now a dummy, skinned, tanned, stuffed full of straw, swinging from the rafters for the Persians to poke fun at" (*Helena* 17)–and speculate about its disastrous effect on the prestige of the empire. The cruel anecdote serves a double purpose: it conveys the crisis of Roman power and introduces the dummy as the leitmotif connected with the emperor, the sovereign.

The dummy emperor functions also to accentuate the pagan, barbarous element in the late Roman Empire. The queen of Palmyra, Zenobia, is led in Aurelian's triumph and "comes down on her hands and knees from the sheer weight of jewellery" (*Helena* 55). As the emperors' court moves farther east, it becomes more oriental in politics and luxury. In Nicomedia, where Diocletian and Maximian jointly hold court, they "rather overdo things." We see "old Maximian holding a golden pineapple in a suit so stiff with gold lace and jewels that he can hardly move," and the slave-born "Diocletian just stood there looking stuffed–like Valerian" (*Helena* 68). Emperors become dummies in their official function and when represented in art. Constantine criticizes the sculptor working on his arch: "Your figures are lifeless and expressionless as dummies. . . . I've seen better work done by savages. Why, damn it, there's something there that looks like a doll that's supposed to be *Me*." Fortified by the sovereignty of art, the sculptor explains that he was "not aiming at exact portraiture" (*Helena* 106–07).

Helena tells the eternal story of how power corrupts, how a man becomes a dummy, through Constantine, who changes from a lively and lovable boy into a frightening and frightened figure, cut off from his family and the real world. The turning point is evident in Constantine's words when he flees from his rival: "When the historians write of me they will say that if I wish to live, I must determine to rule." Constantine is determined to rule, to hold the world together, to restore "the sanctity of the name of Rome" (*Helena* 75). Self-preservation and the noble wish to make Rome holy again, to put new life in the empire, are the bases of his first successes, but by the time he celebrates his twentieth jubilee in AD 326, the experience of sovereignty has wrought a characteristic change in him.

In the brilliant chapter entitled "Constantine's Great Treat," Helena goes to Rome to the jubilee. She is basically a decent private person, a sensible, open-minded woman, shying away from any exercise of power, but after long delays, she has to resort to the authority of her title as the empress dowager to obtain an interview with her son. These delays introduce the court atmosphere of informers, intrigues, murders, and magnificent ceremonies hiding dark secrets; psychologically they prepare the reader for meeting the divine Constantine. After three weeks' waiting, he grants access, and his mother sees a dummy: "From the neck down he was all upholstery. A surcoat of imperial purple, laced with floriations of gold wire and studded with amorphous pearls, hung stiff as a carpet to the carpeted floor. . . . Above the surcoat was a wide collar of gold and enamel, a massive thing suited to the bull-neck. . . . Above the collar rose the face . . . ; he was rouged but purely for ornament. . . . The surface of the face was in some sort of motion. The Emperor was trying to smile" (*Helena* 104). The parallels with the portrait of Elizabeth in *Edmund Campion* are evident, and Waugh makes exuberant use of historically recorded detail. Both sovereigns are fond of wigs of outrageous colors, but surely a wig is less striking on a queen than on the head of the emperor, a Roman soldier:

> But it was none of these things which first caught the notice of Helena.
> "My dear boy, what on earth have you got on your head?"
> The face above the collar assumed an expression of alarm.
> "On my head?" he put up a hand as though to dislodge some bird which might inadvertently have perched there. "Is there anything on my head?"
> Two courtiers danced forward. They were shorter than Constantine and made little jumps to see what was amiss. . . . The courtiers craned and peered; one raised a finger and touched. They looked at the Empress Dowager in abject consternation.
> "That green wig," said Helena.
> Constantine straightened. The courtiers relaxed.
> "Oh," he said, "dearest mother. How you frightened me! It's just a little thing I popped on this morning. I have quite a collection. You must ask to see them. Some are *very* pretty. Today I was in such a hurry to see you, I took the first that came to hand. Don't you like it?" he asked anxiously. "Do you think it makes me look pale?" (*Helena* 104)

Nothing, with the possible exception of faith, stands up against the attack of Waugh's comedy.

Constantine's moods and his periodic refusals to see anybody are the standard techniques of sovereign power designed to inspire awe in subjects. They increase the value of the sovereign's public appearances, just as silence increases the value of the sovereign's words. Absence correlates with the sovereign's unique status, since absence and exception are properties of God. Political sovereignty at the time was firmly based on theological and religious grounds, so it is natural that Constantine starts to see himself as God. He seriously believes that he has assumed God's cares and functions, so it is logical for him to suppose that he has assumed God's attributes as well. He doubts in earnest that he is going to die in the ordinary way and fantasizes about immediate, triumphal transportation to heaven; the author refers to his "disordered mind" (*Helena* 114). Madness goes well with the delusions of temporal sovereignty.

Constantine's character is convincing because it is drawn from at least two perspectives. He breaks with humanity, whose laws and moral norms do not apply to a sovereign. On the other hand, moral standards keep being applied to Constantine, and the resulting tension creates the depth and ambiguity of his character. In his private interview with Helena after murdering his son and wife, Constantine is a monster crying for sympathy. Because he is in a spiritual desert, people seem "scarcely human beings; just things, in the way, in the wrong place, that have to be moved and put to use or thrown away. Nero thought he was God. A most blasphemous and improper idea. I know I am human. In fact I often feel that I am the only real human being in the whole of creation. And that's not pleasant at all, I can assure you. Do you understand at all, mother?" (*Helena* 122). Waugh catches the paradox of what Derrida calls the "absolute master, all-powerful and powerless, powerless in his sovereign omnipotence."[9] Helena diagnoses her only son's condition as "Power without Grace" (*Helena* 122), the author's verdict on the institution of political sovereignty from the point of view of psychological sovereignty. Her next words are Waugh's comment on the democratic conditions of our time: "Sometimes," Helena continued, "I have a terrible dream of the future. Not now, but presently, people may forget their loyalty to their kings and emperors and take power for themselves. Instead of letting one victim bear this frightful curse they will take it all on themselves, each one of them. Think of the misery of the whole world possessed of Power without Grace" (*Helena* 122). Helena's prophecy informs the whole of Waugh's fictional world.

Waugh touched on sovereignty in several other ways at different times. For example, he used idiosyncratic animal metaphors to deal with some problems of sovereignty, although these differ from the typical animal metaphors abounding in European discourses. In presenting female sovereigns, he raised questions about the exercise of sovereignty by a woman in traditional societies. His ambiguities include depictions of the productive, positive aspects of power. Moreover, a study of his reading might reveal what, if anything, he owed to theoretical texts. Suffice to say that Waugh's studies of sovereign figures expose the drives inherent in human nature, including the pleasure principle, the power drive, and the death wish. The topic held an additional, irresistible appeal for Waugh's imagination because sovereignty led him outside the mundane world and into the realm of extravaganza.

NOTES

Research for the essay was supported by the INO-Center, the Russian Ministry of Education, the Kennan Institute, the Carnegie Corporation, the John D. and Catherine T. MacArthur Foundation, and the Open Society Institute (Soros Foundation).

1. Jean Bodin, *The Six Books of the Commonwealth* (1583; rep., New York: Arno, 1979).

2. Thomas Hobbes, *Leviathan* (1651), ed. R. Tuck (Cambridge: Cambridge University Press, 1991).

3. See Carl Schmitt, *Political Theology: Four Chapters on the Concept of Sovereignty* (Cambridge, MA: MIT Press, 1985); Michel Foucault, *History of Sexuality*, Vol. I: *An Introduction* (New York: Random House, 1978); Giorgio Agamben, *Homo Sacer: Sovereign Power and Bare Life* (Stanford, CA: Stanford University Press, 1998); and Jacques Derrida, "Psychoanalysis Searches the States of Its Soul: The Impossible beyond a Sovereign Cruelty," in *Without Alibi* (Stanford, CA: Stanford University Press, 2002), 238–80.

4. Evelyn Waugh, *Helena* (1950; rep., Harmondsworth, UK: Penguin, 1979), 89. Hereafter cited as *Helena*.

5. Evelyn Waugh, *Edmund Campion* (1935; rep., Harmondsworth, UK: Penguin, 1954), 160. Hereafter cited as *Campion*.

6. Paul Rabinow, ed., *The Foucault Reader* (New York: Pantheon Books, 1984), 176.

7. Agamben, *Homo Sacer*, 84.

8. Evelyn Waugh, *Brideshead Revisited* (Boston: Little, Brown, 1945), 200.

9. Derrida, "Psychoanalysis," 261.

Waffle Scramble:
Waugh's Art in *Scoop*

Ann Pasternak Slater

Waugh cared deeply about his craft as a novelist. His skill is routinely praised. I do not believe it has yet been properly analyzed and understood.[1] However, anatomization carries its own risks—as the pattern is identified, comedy is diminished. In all his novels, Waugh organizes his fantastical raw materials according to a covert formal schema. Analysis is likely to lose the fantastical and leave only the schema: this is the danger of criticism. One justification for scrutiny is that Waugh himself sought understanding of his craft.

Numerous passages in Waugh's critical and fictional writings suggest, by implication, the criteria by which he wished his own work to be judged. The most pained in expression, and the closest in time to *Scoop* (1938), occurs in his review of Cyril Connolly's *Enemies of Promise*. Connolly, Waugh suggests, is a failed aspirant to that rare thing, the Art of Criticism. Why? Not for the expected reason, a lack of "creative" ability: "A better word, except that it would always involve explanation, would be 'architectural.' I believe that what makes a good writer, as distinct from a clever and cultured man who can write, is an added energy and breadth of vision which enables him to complete a structure."[2] However, *Enemies of Promise* is "structurally jerry-built." Its three parts have nothing to do with each other, and Connolly "comes very near to dishonesty in the way in which he fakes the transitions between these elements and attempts to pass them off as the expansion of a single theme." Waugh continues with remorseless lucidity: "Nor does he seem to be fully aware of this defect in either his own work or in those he examines; on page nine he recommends the habit of examining isolated passages as a wine taster judges a vintage by rinsing a spoonful round his mouth; thus, says Mr Connolly, the style may be separated from the impure considerations of subject matter. But the style is the whole." Waugh lays out his own alternative credo with characteristically oblique self-deprecation, and open disdain for Connolly's cultural snobbery: "Writing is an art which exists in a time sequence; each sentence and each page is dependent on its predecessors and successors; a sentence which he admires may owe its significance to another fifty pages distant. I beg Mr Connolly to believe that even quite popular writers take great trouble sometimes in this matter" (*EAR* 238–39). Precisely what Waugh meant can be illustrated by a much later diary entry during the composition of *Helena* (1950):

> *Saturday 12 January 1946*
>
> Yesterday I had to mention the fall of Palmyra. Longinus was executed there. I brought this in as decoration and made Helena have heard of him. Today I rewrote a paragraph of the first chapter making the tutor mention him. Then, because Mr Hodges, my nurse's father, was a fabulous figure to me, I gave Helena two fables: first of the nursery, the exemplary soldier; secondly of the schoolroom, the stupendous pundit. Then I introduced to the Longinus paragraph the fact that Helena felt his death as a bereavement, the final end of her education. Then I introduced into the passage about Tetricus's betrayal the sense that Helena thought the grave of her nurse's father dishonoured. So the book prospers.[3]

In just this way one sentence owes its significance to another, fifty pages distant.[4]

The unexpected influence of Mr. Hodges, father of Waugh's nurse, in a novel set in the remote Roman Empire raises another aspect of Waugh's art—the ineradicable centrality of his own experience. Most of his fiction derives from the events of his own life, ingeniously transfigured and transposed. An early admission of this abiding tactic was prompted by the popular reception of *Vile Bodies* (1930) as a decipherable roman à clef: "Obviously," Waugh conceded, "there must be a connection of some kind between a writer's work and his life," but "nothing is more insulting to a novelist than to assume that he is incapable of anything except the mere transcription of what he observes." The closing peroration of this important essay stresses both the ramshackle nature of Waugh's raw materials and the skill with which they must be transformed.

> One has for one's raw material every single thing one has ever seen or heard or felt, and one has to go over that vast, smouldering rubbish-heap of experience, half stifled by the fumes and dust, scraping and delving until one finds a few discarded valuables.
>
> Then one has to assemble these tarnished and dented fragments, polish them, set them in order, and try to make a coherent and significant arrange-

ment of them. ("People Who Want to Sue Me," *Daily Mail*, May 31, 1930,
in *EAR* 72–73)

Throughout Waugh's writing life, his method is both clear and consistent.
He rummages in the smoking rubbish tip of experience and seizes on its
grimy *trouvailles*. Some are identified in his diaries and letters. Some he
explores in his journalism. He plays with some in his correspondence. He
sets them in rough order in his travel books. Finally the polished artifacts
are transformed into the elegantly sustained, elaborately camouflaged leit-
motifs of his fiction. Much of Waugh's appeal lies in his novels' apparent
anarchic disorder. Yet the illusory chaos is coherently and significantly
arranged. Every disorderly element has its appointed place.

Scoop offers an outstanding illustration of these techniques. Out of the
inconsequential details salvaged from his own life, Waugh completes a
structure as bizarre and enduring as the architecture of Antoni Gaudí he
once admired in Barcelona.

The key to *Scoop*'s structure hides in an inconspicuous parenthetic
clause, ingeniously camouflaged with trivia:

> At the back of the paper, ignominiously sandwiched between Pip and Pop,
> the Bedtime Pets, and the recipe for a dish named "Waffle Scramble," lay
> the bi-weekly half-column devoted to Nature:
>   LUSH PLACES, *edited by William Boot, Countryman*.[5]

At this early point in *Scoop*, William's column seems the paragraph's climactic main subject. Later, architectonically, Waffle Scramble and the semiiden-
tical alliterating alternatives of Pip and Pop will trump it in importance.

Scoop was published in 1938. Its genesis began in 1934.

After the breakdown of his first marriage and conversion to Catholicism Waugh assumed he could neither marry nor have children. It was only
by chance that he heard of a similar case where an annulment had been
granted. In autumn 1933 he applied to the Westminster Diocesan Court
for an annulment of his own. While waiting for a response, he proposed
to Teresa Jungman, whom he had pursued for two years without success,
and was rejected. He spent the winter in Morocco writing *A Handful
of Dust*, completing it in England in late spring 1934. That summer he
must have felt at a loose end. At three days' notice he agreed to join an
old friend, Hugh Lygon, on a three-man expedition to Spitsbergen in the
Arctic.

Waugh was still in love with Teresa. He met Hugh by chance on Thursday, July 6th. Friday was spent at Lillywhite's purchasing skis, ice axes, and balaclavas. Wind-proof clothes and a sleeping bag were from an unduly respectful shop in Holborn: "when I arrived the salesman said, 'The Spitzbergen Expedition'" (*DEW* 386). Equipment began to collect at the Savile Club: "A billiard cue came for another member and it was put with my luggage" (*DEW* 387). By Monday they were in Norway, and Waugh was writing in his diary, a little pathetically, "It is Teresa's birthday. She ought now to be receiving a series of parcels from me with no name attached. It is more fun for her that way" (*DEW* 388). Few of Waugh's travels failed to provide him with raw material. The 1934 trip to the Arctic is an oddity because it was potentially the most dangerous, and yet, in fictional terms, apparently unproductive. In Waugh's view it was a fiasco. Through freak floods the group was separated. They nearly drowned and were marooned with injuries and inadequate rations. Nothing of these grim experiences survives in Waugh's fiction. But two mundane details from the preparations did germinate. The misplaced pomp of the Holborn outfitters welcoming the Spitsbergen Expedition resurfaces in William Boot's grand reception at a London emporium to buy kit for his assignment as war correspondent in Ishmaelia: "It was General Cruttwell, FRGS, himself who was waiting at the top of the lift shaft. An imposing man: Cruttwell Glacier *in Spitsbergen*, Cruttwell Falls in Venezuela, Mount Cruttwell in the Pamirs . . . marked his travels" (*Scoop* 43, my italics). And Waugh's inadvertently acquired billiard cue haunts the vast miscellany of William's purchases, where it is metamorphosed into the cleft sticks recommended by Lord Copper.

The Spitsbergen Expedition's fundamental contribution to *Scoop* is structurally more significant and much more surprising.

In *Scoop*, not for the first time, Waugh divides himself into two fictional personae. In his first travel book, *Labels* (1930), Waugh played two roles simultaneously—uxorious Geoffrey on honeymoon with his wife (as Waugh had been at the time of the cruise) and a cotraveler and narrator, the hard-bitten *Bachelor Abroad* Waugh had become at the time of writing.[6] In *Scoop*, Waugh's experiences are similarly distributed between two authorial alter egos—John and William Boot. John Boot is a fashionable novelist pointedly reminiscent of Waugh himself in 1934. He is the author of eight books (Waugh's own tally at the time of the Arctic jaunt), the first a life of Arthur Rimbaud, rather than Waugh's *Rossetti* (1928); the last "a studiously modest description of some harrowing months among the Patagonian Indians" (*Scoop* 5), not unlike the studiously modest Brazilian travelogue, *Ninety-two Days*, which Waugh published in 1934.[7] Waugh deliberately sets up his reader at the beginning of *Scoop* by encouraging two misapprehensions: first, that John Boot will be the hero, and, second, that John Boot (like Waugh) is eager to leave England because he is unhappily in love. In the characteristic Waugh manner, this trail is sustained by just four widely separated references. Only at the very end does the reverse emerge. John Boot is far from being "rather lovelorn," as the original *Times Literary Supplement* reviewer carelessly assumed:[8] "I've sent my Boot off to the Antarctic. He said he had to go abroad at once. Apparently some woman is pursuing him" (*Scoop* 213). The biographical reality is pedantically reversed, point by point: Waugh "rather lovelorn," John Boot in flight from unwanted love; Waugh in the Arctic, John Boot in the Antarctic.

It is typical of Waugh that this unobtrusive pattern, set up by a private joke in a narrative detour, should provide a neat microcosm of the whole. The novel is structured on a pattern of reversals. John Boot's harrowing Patagonian travel book, *Waste of Time*, is the antithesis of William Boot's cozy equivalent, the rural biweekly half-column, Lush Places. City sophisticate; rustic recluse—the opposing figures of the two Boots, their contrasting literary modes and lifestyles, mark the two caricature extremes of Waugh's complex personality at the time of this, his climacteric.[9]

Waugh returned from Spitsbergen in time for the publication of *A Handful of Dust* in September 1934. Four further years were to plait together his literary preoccupations and the emotional renaissance of his second marriage, before *Scoop* was published. *Edmund Campion* was written between September 1934 and May 1935. At an unknown point in its composition Waugh took "a *great* fancy to a young lady named Laura" (*LEW* 92).[10] He continued their courtship in letters from Abyssinia, where he spent August–December 1935 as the *Daily Mail*'s war correspondent, awaiting the end of the rainy season and the Italian invasion. In June 1935 the Diocesan Court finally found in favor of his annulment. Ratification from Rome was expected in about three months. Early 1936 was largely taken up with Waugh's burgeoning relationship with Laura, and the composition of *Waugh in Abyssinia* (a title he abhorred). No news arrived from Rome. After six months he made a short pilgrimage to Lough Derg in Ireland. The diary entry on his return is the first since the Spitsbergen Expedition. After two years' silence it is all the more striking for its reticence.

London, Tuesday 7 July 1936

Holyhead midnight; sleeper and sandwich. Euston 5.30 daylight. Drove through empty streets to St James's where I found telegram "Decision favourable. Godfrey."[11] Bath, shaved; lay down but did not sleep. At 8 rang up Bruton Street and was told that Laura had gone out to church. Dressed and went to Farm Street. Laura and Mary there. Knelt behind them and told Laura news in porch. . . . Message to call on Diana [Cooper]; found her with face expressionless in mud mask. (*DEW* 391)

The annulment was formally confirmed a fortnight later. The next day Waugh left for Abyssinia to observe it under fascist rule. In October, within days of his return and the completion of *Waugh in Abyssinia*, his diary records, "On Thursday 15th made a very good start with the first page of a novel describing Diana's early morning" (*DEW* 409; cf. *Scoop* 6). *Scoop*'s first two chapters were finished within a fortnight and deemed by the author "light and excellent."[12]

However, for Waugh, the novel's subsequent gestation was unusually protracted. The couple married in April 1937. Waugh took the unfinished manuscript on the honeymoon. By July he decided it had to be "entirely rewritten."[13] In January 1938 he was complaining, "Work on *Scoop* going slowly, with infinite interruptions and distractions" (*DEW* 430). A year before, in the first flush of cheerfulness, he had observed with detachment that the novel "has good material but shaky structure" (*DEW* 420). It took him another year to put that right.

Scoop was finally published on May 7, 1938. No wonder he was lecturing Connolly on the importance of structure soon after.

Three major elements deriving directly from Waugh's experiences in this period govern the structure of *Scoop*. All three are generically related, being variants on the idea of transposition. They permeate every level of the novel, from recurrent linguistic tropes to the major cross-bindings of plot and character. They are anagram and metathesis, reversal, and mistaken identity.

Anagram and Metathesis

En route by ship to Abyssinia, Waugh was practicing on the typewriter given him by the *Daily Mail*. Like William Boot, he was no adept:

One finger was not enough; he used both hands. The keys rose together like bristles on a porcupine, jammed and were extricated; curious anagrams appeared on the paper before him; vulgar fractions and marks of punctuation mingled with the letters. Still he typed. (*Scoop* 155)

there is no news and if there wrew wr were funny how hard that word is
to get right wr were gotvit were were were were were if there were we
should not be allowed to send it by the censor whom i have tild tou about.
(to Laura, October 1935, *LEW* 99–100)

Unfortunately these metathetic logjams have mostly been editorially
cleared from Waugh's published letters. We have to imagine him reading
his own comic errors day by day. They flourished well beyond the single
paragraph admitted by Mark Amory and the more accurately erratic but
still mildly emasculated versions printed by Artemis Cooper.[14] Especially
in the letters to Lady Diana Cooper, Waugh's habitual amalgam of fri-
volity and political acumen is further compounded by a hail of typos
and underpunctuated private slang into a hectic, semi-incomprehensible
telegraphese: "as I see it three things may happre (a) Brilliant wop victory
with death by gas of bo balfour and the poor News Chronicle chap. Then it
is the soup for Eden and duff is the next prime MINISTER (b) Wops run
away triumphant blacks massacre bo etc. soup for Duce soup for Eurpoe
soup for all except dead bo etc. (c) Wicked partition planned by 3 powers conference Outraged niggers massacre bo etc.great soup for League
and Eden DUFF PM Of course the best thing would be great massacre of
Balfour and Chronicle chap Bo escapes to tell tale Eden soup league soup
Duff sir GARNET great success of bloodcurdler book."[15] This style is particularly characteristic of the *Mr Wu and Mrs Stitch* correspondence, and
appears to be a trick of Lady Diana's own voice, appropriated and outdone
by Waugh in his letters to her. Waugh had reason to be proud of *Scoop*'s
very good start describing Diana's early morning. Mrs. Stitch's headlong
babble in the opening pages of *Scoop* is a recognizable pastiche of Diana
Cooper's flibbertigibbet style.[16] More importantly, it introduces *Scoop*'s
structural principle, in which numerous narrative threads are inserted and
left dangling while others are plaited in—just as Mrs Stitch's conversation
is conducted on several different fronts simultaneously: "You're putting
too much ivy on the turret, Arthur; the owl won't show up unless you
have him on the bare stone, and I'm particularly attached to the owl. *Mu-
nera*, darling, like tumtiddy; always a short a in neuter plurals. It sounds
like an anagram: see if 'Terracotta' fits. I'm *delighted* to see you, John."
(*Scoop* 7).

Mrs Stitch's idiolect is itself analogous to anagram, separate topics being broken up and jumbled together:

> "I absolutely loved *Waste of Time*. We read it aloud at Blakewell. The
> headless abbot is grand."

"Headless abbot?"

"Not in Wasters. On Arthur's ceiling. I put it in the Prime Minister's bedroom." (*Scoop* 7)

Interpretation depends on correct attribution: the headless abbot is on the ceiling, but Wasters is in the prime minister's bedroom. The required technique is that of construing Latin—a sophisticated skill: "'*Floribus Austrum*,' Josephine chanted, '*perditus et liquidis immisi fontibus apros*'; having been lost with flowers in the South and sent into the liquid fountain; *apros* is wild boars, but I couldn't quite make sense of that bit'"(*Scoop* 8). Josephine has made nonsense of Virgil's Eclogue 2:59 because she has matched the wrong words together,[17] just as her mother gets the crossword wrong—she says the clue sounds like an anagram, but (as we later learn) the word it anagrammatizes is not *Terracotta* or even *Hottentot* but *detonated*. In every case the authorial trick is to scramble a lucid text. But, with patience, the waffle can be unscrambled.

REVERSAL

Waugh's hopes of his journalistic assignment in Abyssinia were disappointed in a series of reverses and reversals. His failures as a journalist occasion much facile derision in the biographies. He missed the only scoop to be had, and his own three scoops fell flat. But the experience had rich artistic compensations.

On the boat out to Djibouti Waugh met an entrepreneur named Rickett, a clear partial model for *Scoop*'s Mr Baldwin:

Mr. Rickett spoke openly of a "mission". . . . He spoke more freely about a pack of hounds which he had in the Midlands, and when, as often happened, he received lengthy cables in code, he would pocket them nonchalantly, remarking, "From my huntsman. He says the prospects for cubbin' are excellent."[18]

"I have so much on my hands—naturally—and in winter I am much occupied with sport. I have a little pack of hounds in the Midlands."

"Oh? Which?"

"You might not have heard of us. We march with the Fernie. I suppose it is the best hunting country in England. It is a little hobby of mine." (*Scoop* 56)

Waugh's suspicions were aroused. In midpassage, he wrote a letter (not a telegram) to Penelope Betjeman, a keen hunter, to learn whether she knew anything of Rickett. It was a move of Boot-like naivety, but of more durable literary value than the professionalism of Waugh's journalistic rivals, who scooped the Rickett story in August.[19] At that time Waugh was out of Addis with his friend Patrick Balfour. They had found a scoop of their own in Jijiga, where a resident Frenchman, improbably named Count Maurice de Roquefeuil du Bousquet, and his wife had been imprisoned for spying. Waugh and Balfour were triumphant: "There was no possibility of any other journalist having got it. We happily imagined cables arriving for our colleagues in Addis. 'Badly left Roquefeuil story' and 'Investigate imprisoned countess Jijiga'" (*WiA* 75).[20] Within hours they also stumbled on secret information about the Abyssinians' defense line (*WiA* 76).[21] Neither story was of the least interest to the British press, whose attention was all on Rickett. Triumphantly unaware, Balfour and Waugh left Jijiga for Harar, where they picked up cables demanding, "What do you know Anglo American oil concession?"

> We were not alarmed. I replied, "Apply local agent for commercial intelligence Addis".... Next morning there was another cable, a day old: "Must have fullest details oil concession." I replied: "Absolutely impossible obtain Addis news Harar." Before luncheon there was a third: "Badly left oil concession suggest your return Addis immediately." (*WiA* 77–78)

> "there's some cables for you somewhere."
> William opened them one by one . . .
> BADLY LEFT ALL PAPERS ALL STORIES.
> IMPERATIVE RECEIVE FULL STORY TONIGHT SIX YOUR TIME WHY NO NEWS ARE YOU ILL FLASH REPLY. . . .
> There were a dozen of them in all. . . . The last, which had arrived that morning, read:
> CONFIDENTIAL AND URGENT STOP LORD COPPER HIMSELF GRAVELY DISSATISFIED STOP LORD COPPER PERSONALLY REQUIRES VICTORIES STOP ON RECEIPT OF THIS CABLE VICTORY STOP CONTINUE CABLING VICTORIES UNTIL FURTHER NOTICE STOP LORD COPPERS CONFIDENTIAL SECRETARY.
> "What are they all about?" asked Kätchen.
> "They don't seem very pleased with me in London. They seem to want more news." (*Scoop* 140)

Later Waugh, who was "slappers [on good terms] with the wops" (*MW&MS* 52),[22] obtained advance information about the date of the Italian minister's departure from Addis, which, he knew, signaled the beginning of the Italian invasion. That scoop also got him nowhere.

darling Diana

well I have chucked the Mail it was no good they sent me offensive cables twice a day & i took umbrage & they wanted me to stay in Addis & I took despair. . . . iI got two scoops the first happened the same day as the Rickett concession & I was away so all I got was abuse for not getting that. The second happened on a saturday so the other journalists had 24 hours to catch up the telegraph clerks to sell the news so I thought to be clever and sent it in Latin but no one in the mail office knew that language so I got abuse for that. discouragig. (*MW&MS* 52)

That abortive Latin telegram infiltrates *Scoop* in multiple guises. It is there in the little signpost of Josephine's Virgil. It is everywhere in the journalists' compressed Latinate syntax, encrusted with impacted suffixes and prefixes. In Abyssinia Waugh had employed the agglutinative idiolect with professional relish: "'Request earliest name life story photograph American nurse upblown Adowa.' We replied 'Nurse unupblown'" (*WiA* 111). It becomes a feature of *Scoop*: "ADEN UNWARWISE . . . UNPROCEED LAKUWARD . . . NEWS EXYOU UNRECEIVED . . . CONTRACT UNTERMINATED" (72, 121, 152).[23] Decoding requires classic hermeneutic skills William lacks and he nearly misconstrues his first telegram—"OPPOSITION SPLASHING FRONTWARD SPEEDILIEST STOP ADEN REPORTED PREPARED WARWISE FLASH FACTS BEAST" (*Scoop* 68)—as an order to stop at Aden. Lord Copper's enigmatic imperatives—"STOP ON RECEIPT OF THIS CABLE VICTORY STOP CONTINUE"— are comparable bite-sized waffle scrambles of negation and reversal.

This linguistic code is related to Mrs Stitch's hyperanagrammatical style and is peculiar to *Scoop*. We have clear evidence from Waugh himself that something special is going on here. In his 1957 memorandum to *Scoop*'s would-be scriptwriters, he stipulates that the original dialogue should be retained as far as possible, because "The dialogue of the novel has certain idiosyncrasies which few can imitate successfully. All additional dialogue should be submitted to the original author for translation."[24]

These miscellaneous experiences were already fueling Waugh's fantastical imagination. In the Wu/Stitch correspondence he invented further ironic inversions of his own: "The minister of Commerce has announced that from November 18th Abyssinia will take economic sanctions against Italy." "The heaviest fighting is among the journalists." Metaphor sustains the switchback mode—"I have made friends with a very nice South African nigger who represents a worldwide society for the extermination of the white races. . . . He says the Emperor is on his blacklist as not being a real negro" (*MW& MS* 57).[25] All three of these quotations are from a single letter to Lady Diana Cooper. This pattern is far from haphazard. Waugh is already up to his elbows, playing with the tarnished and dented valuables of his rubbish heap.

The inversions, setbacks, and reversals of the letters turn into a sustained motif in *Waugh in Abyssinia*, where mistaken assumptions are repeatedly reversed in reality. "How wrong we were!" is a recurrent refrain (*WiA* 71, 90). Everyone, including the Abyssinians, thought the main campaign would be fought in the south. The Italians attacked from the north (*WiA* 58). Many colorful fates were predicted for Haile Selassie—suicide, assassination, death in battle, rescue by British airplane. No one guessed that in defeat he would "quietly proceed to the station, board the train and trip down to Djibouti by rail" (*WiA* 47). "How wrong we were!" The motif gathers momentum as Waugh's time in Addis ends. The journalists were finally given permission to visit Dessye, the equivalent to *Scoop*'s Laku. As soon as permission was granted, popular enthusiasm for the journey waned (*WiA* 124). Waugh and a few others decided to go. Two days away from Addis they were turned back—they had permission to visit Dessye but not to leave Addis. On their return they were allowed to leave. When four days' travel finally took them to their goal, "We began to wonder what precisely we had gained by the journey" (*WiA* 138).

For the first time in their protracted Abyssinian sojourn, at Dessye the journalists found a wireless station ready to take messages of unlimited length. All that evening typewriters could be heard around the camp as the journalists spread themselves in color pieces five hundred, eight hundred, a thousand words long. Two days later they were told that none of the messages had been sent; henceforth the limit would be fifty stringently censored words.

An Abyssinian governor who had spent many years in disgrace was received by the local Dedjasmach, reinstated and embraced, withdrew, tripped, and broke his neck—"what must be one of the briefest periods of official favour in recorded history."

The native members of the Ethiopian Red Cross threw a party, dancing around the tent of their American officer, who had that evening purposely removed his quarters from his rowdy Irish colleagues.

Selassie's arrival was expected daily; was finally announced; all day the road was lined with exultant soldiers, disgruntled cameramen, overheated journalists, royal mules in brilliant saddle cloths ready to carry him to his destination. The sun set; cold descended; the crowds departed; the emperor arrived unnoticed in the dark.

All these reversals occur on two successive pages (*WiA* 139–40). Their spirit permeates *Scoop*.

Mistaken identity

Three episodes of mistaken identity were particularly fruitful contributions to *Scoop*'s structure.

In December 1935 Waugh finally left Abyssinia, with intense relief, to spend Christmas in Bethlehem. A funny thing happened to him on his way home. "I did a thing at Bagdad that only happens in nightmares and went to stay in the wrong house. I met a woman in London whose name I didn't hear and she lived, as I thought, in Bagdad, and was a diplomat's wife and she said do come and stay with us. So when I get here [Damascus] I said who is a pretty fair haired woman married to a diplomat in Bagdad, and they said that's easy we can tell you in one she is Tita Clark-Kerr. Well that sounded a likely name, so I sent a telegram saying I was coming to stay" (*MW&MS* 58). "Would I be welcome if I came to you for weekend Evelyn Waugh." The reply was oddly unenthusiastic: "Fairly. Ambassador."[26] Waugh "arrived to find two totally strange people and my real hostess lives in Tehran" (*MW&MS* 58).

Then it happened again. This time it was Waugh's identity that was mistaken.

In 1936 he returned to Abyssinia to observe it under Italian rule for the ending of *Waugh in Abyssinia*. He was given permission to visit the remote northern town of Asmara, in order to describe the great trunk road being built by the Italians. Asmara's original population of 2,000 now accommodated 60,000 Italian navvies and what Waugh tactfully describes as "seven unattached white women" provided by the Italian authorities. The evening Waugh was shown the brothel he estimated there were about eighty men waiting for attention. "Feminine company," Waugh dryly observes, "is a primary need for Italians. . . . It is a romantic rather than a physical need; the latter, in a rough and tumble way, has been catered for" (*WiA* 165). With pardonable optimism, the Italian press officer at Asmara jumped to the wrong conclusion when informed of Waugh's forthcoming visit: "Like many others before him, he was deluded by my Christian name and for two days flitted between airport and railway station, meeting every possible conveyance in a high state of amorous excitement. His friends declared that he had, with great difficulty, procured a bouquet of crimson roses. The trousered and unshaven figure which finally greeted him must have been a hideous blow" (*WiA* 164).

Finally, to earn money, Waugh agreed to assist on a silly film, *Lovelies over London*. He retired to his habitual writing retreat, Mrs Cobb's hotel at Chagford, accompanied by a professional scriptwriter named Kernell: "Yesterday I sent him up to his room to think up some wisecracks and he turned up after 1½ hours & said, 'How would it be if one of the girls said to a policeman "I wish I had stilts, then I'd come up & see ya some time."' . . . I think he may have murdered the real Mr Colonel and come instead of him. I can't believe he was ever really in Hollywood" (*LEW* 112–13, January 1937?). This happy fantasy gave another fillip to the composition of *Scoop*: "I want to get [the film script] all done before the end of next week then I can get going on the novel, for which I am itching and full of ideas. Feeling very cheerful about all this."[27] The idea of mistaken identities provided the double knot binding the three parts of *Scoop* together. William Boot is mistaken for John Boot in part 1. Uncle Theodore Boot masquerades as William Boot in part 3. The Boot is on the other foot.

Thus *Scoop* is built on two major transpositions pivoting on false identities. At the beginning, William inadvertently takes the place of John as the *Beast*'s war correspondent. At the end, Uncle Theodore willingly takes William's place as Lord Copper's guest of honor. Moreover, in a kind of return match, the knighthood intended for William goes to John.[28] Transposition is the novel's camshaft. The wheels of the plot rotate around it; the smallest stylistic cogs are driven by it. In Waugh's characteristically graphic, elucidatory manner, the novel opens with a pointed vignette:

> Algernon Stitch was standing in the hall; his bowler hat was on his head; his right hand, grasping a crimson, royally emblazoned despatch case, emerged from the left sleeve of his overcoat; his other hand burrowed petulantly in the breast pocket. . . . He spoke indistinctly, for he was holding a folded copy of the morning paper between his teeth.
>   "Can't get it on," he seemed to say. (*Scoop* 5–6)

This is an icon of transposition: the minister has his arm down the wrong coat sleeve. Throughout the novel, minor crossovers repeat the leitmotif. In Ishmaelia the lost luggage van finally turns up because "mysteriously it had become attached to the special train; had in fact been transposed" (*Scoop*

107). In the Megalopolitan offices "on a hundred lines reporters talked at cross-purposes" (*Scoop* 179). Mr Salter's first meeting with William is fraught with cross-purposes and Spooneresque metatheses. He has been advised to welcome William with heavy hospitality and light conversation on agricultural matters—swedes, parsnips, and root crops in general:

> There was a pause, during which Mr Salter planned a frank and disarming opening: "How are your roots, Boot?" It came out wrong.
> "How are your boots, root?" he asked.
> William, glumly awaiting some fulminating rebuke, started and said, "I beg your pardon?"
> "I mean brute," said Mr Salter.
> William gave it up. Mr Salter gave it up. They sat staring at one another, fascinated, hopeless. (*Scoop* 27)

Further linguistic crossovers litter the intricate maze. The novel opens on "a biting-cold mid-June morning" (*Scoop* 5). Newsboys in London are selling "the lunchtime edition of the evening papers" (*Scoop* 10). At Boot Magna Hall, the telegram summoning William to London is delivered by "Troutbeck, the aged 'boy'" (*Scoop* 28). Toward the end of the novel, Mr. Salter is met at Boot Magna Halt by a cretinous local, picking the dry paint bubbles on the palings with "a toe-like thumb nail" (*Scoop* 197). Under the moonlight "the warm land lay white as frost" (*Scoop* 189). Dialogue sustains the switchback mode: " 'Come in,' she said, 'I'm just going out'" (*Scoop* 7).

Even the novel's most celebrated phrase is an instance of linguistic inversion, because what looks like agreement is covert dissent: "Capital of Japan? Yokohama, isn't it?" "Up to a point, Lord Copper" (*Scoop* 14).

It is worth noting how carefully Waugh clusters these tropes of transposition and reversal for maximal impact, at the beginning and end of the novel. We are reminded of his scrupulous distribution of Longinus references in *Helena*. Transposition lies behind the laconic directive summoning William to his first journalistic assignment: "*Mrs Stitch. Gentlemen's Lavatory, Sloane Street.*" The sight in the underground toilet is another bold icon of checkerboard opposites: "At the foot of the steps, making, for the photographer, a happy contrast to the white tiles about it, stood a little black motor car" (*Scoop* 39–40). Mockery lurks in further innocent oxymorons, like Lord Copper's "country seat at East Finchley" (*Scoop* 14).[29] Did Lady Diana Cooper register the irony when Waugh's "very good" description of her early morning gave her not *feet*, but a *face* of clay (*Scoop* 7)?[30] Such deadpan inversions mask satiric gibes an insouciant reader might well miss—as when Waugh makes a cat's cradle of two clichés, describing the *Beast*'s journalistic employees as "a multitude of men and women with visible means of support but no fixed occupation" (*Scoop* 36). Thus Waugh derides their extravagant wages and nugatory skills at a blow. A sharper irony invests the Ishmaelite identity cards distributed to William and his colleagues—small orange documents originally printed for the registration of prostitutes, the space for the thumb print replaced by a passport photo, "and the word 'journalist' substituted in neat Ishmaelite characters" (*Scoop* 95). This substitution directly evokes Stanley Baldwin's memorable accusation that the Press exercises "power without responsibility—the prerogative of the harlot throughout the ages."

A comparable but innocuous act of substitution appears to trigger William's original journalistic metamorphosis, when his younger sister, Priscilla, replaces "badger" with "great crested grebe" in his week's copy for Lush Places. His next column's memorable opening, *"Feather-footed through the plashy fen passes the questing vole,"* is in the same mode. "That must be good style," says the *Beast*'s managing editor. "At least it doesn't sound like anything else to me" (*Scoop* 16). It is good style—not because it's lush, but because its yoked incompatibilities of feather and foot, bird and beast, crested grebe and badger, obey the novel's shuttlecock decorum.

Priscilla's mischievous substitution *appears* to trigger William's summons to the *Beast*'s London offices but does not actually do so. This narrative turnaround is characteristic of *Scoop*'s labyrinthine plot of detours, dead ends, U-turns, high drama, and anticlimax, which derive so obviously from Waugh's own disappointing journalistic experiences in Abyssinia. The mode is established in miniature in the novel's first pages, when Mrs Stitch briskly drives off well after eleven in the morning, intending to get to Bethnal Green and back by lunchtime; is foiled by the traffic; abandons her car; and returns by underground. That anticlimactic narrative loop is repeated in the extended bathetic sequence of William's attempts to leave England for Ishmaelia. His one ambition has been to fly. Soaring hopes are ignominiously grounded when he is refused first by the airline (too much luggage), then by the customs (no passport). Acquiring the requisite visas takes another three attempts (two from two rival legations, one Marxist, one Fascist, the Red visa burned by the Fascist consul-general; final triumphant departure with two passports and two visas). In Ishmaelia, the novel's circuitous narrative course is epitomized by literal detours. Taxi rides taken by the journalists invariably take them, irrespective of their intended destinations, to Erik Olafsen's Tea, Bible and Chemist Shop: "When they have a white man they do not understand, they always drive him to me" (*Scoop* 94); later the detour is repeated (103). The main narrative coils around two further meanderingly self-contradictory narratives—the lengthy affair of the Swiss ticket collector (a communist secret agent? No, not a secret agent at all. Yes, a *really* secret agent, working incognito for Mr. Baldwin) and the shaggy-dog story of the journalists' expedition to nonexistent Laku (journalists clamor for permits to visit Laku, are refused leave, and then permitted to leave; leave; are stopped from leaving; leave again). In both, the narrative takes a circuitous route to nowhere strongly reminiscent of Waugh and his colleagues' trip to disappointing Dessye. Multiple other narrative strands, like William's stop-go relationship with Kätchen, and the storm in a teacup of Ishmaelia's short-lived revolution and counter revolution, follow the same anticlimactic pattern. At the end of the novel, poor Mr Salter's painful journey on foot to Boot Magna Hall is a final, rustic equivalent—a good six miles tacking from field to field, scrambling through hedges and ditches, bayed at by dogs, pursued by cattle, the last long mile up the drive the bitterest of all. The entire novel is, in fact, a long trek to nowhere, the essential point being, as Waugh told the novel's prospective scriptwriters, that "Boot should return home without ambition ever to go away again" (Memorandum 29).

This narrative pattern contains its own satiric point. Waugh had no respect for the journalists accompanying him to Abyssinia, nor for the political parties squabbling over it. *Scoop* is primarily *A Novel about Journalists*, as its subtitle proclaims. Its political situation is not important—as Waugh also made clear to the novel's prospective scriptwriters: "No great pains need to be taken to make a plausible plot for the central section. The essentials are that a potentially serious situation is being treated frivolously, sensationally and dishonestly by the assembled Press" (Memorandum 29). In opposition to the established Jackson regime, Ishmaelia has two political parties, the Marxists and the Fascists. In the real world, Waugh had no liking for either.[31] In *Scoop* they are diametrically identical, indistinguishably opposed. William asks Mr Salter:

> "Can you tell me who is fighting who in Ishmaelia?"
> "I think it's the Patriots and the Traitors."
> "Yes, but which is which?"
> "Oh, I don't know *that. That's* Policy, you see. . . ."
> "I gather it's between the Reds and the Blacks."
> "Yes, but it's not quite as easy as that. You see they are all Negroes. And the Fascists won't be called Black because of their racial pride, so they are called White after the White Russians. And the Bolshevists *want* to be called Black because of *their* racial pride. So when you say Black you mean Red, and when you *mean* Red you say White." (*Scoop* 43)

Mr Salter is understandably confused here. He should have ended, "and when you *mean* Black [not Red] you say White." The Ishmaelite Fascists are White Shirts. By the same inverted logic the Bolshevists are led by Dr. Benito, the racially black but politically Red antitype of the racially white but politically black Benito Mussolini. In Waugh's habitual manner, this checkerboard motif is sustained in minor cameos, such as the Ishmaelite foreign minister glimpsed on a gilt chair at Jacksonburg railway station, "like a daguerreotype, stiffly posed, a Victorian worthy in negative, black face, white whiskers, black hands" (*Scoop* 106). Similarly, when the Bolshevists take control of the Jacksons' Presidential Residence, "a red flag hung black against the night sky" (*Scoop* 175).

Mr. Salter's mistake is an instructive one. In spite of their apparent differences, there is nothing to choose between the two parties. Political propaganda renders black white, and vice versa. The Marxist consul-general of Ishmaelia claims all whites are really black: "As that great Negro Karl Marx has so nobly written" (*Scoop* 50). At his rival embassy, the Fascist consul-general maintains all blacks are really white: "As you will see for yourself, we are pure Aryans" (*Scoop* 51). Both sides think of themselves as Patriots and the opposition as Traitors.

Hence Pip and Pop the Bedtime Pets, and their later, alliterating echo in the Popotakis Ping-Pong Parlour at Jacksonburg.[32] Ping-Pong's instant reversibility—its high-speed ricochet to and fro getting nowhere—epitomizes the novel's elaborately inconclusive narrative structure and the op-art flicker of its identically opposed political parties. The novel's interchangeable press magnates, Lords Copper and Zinc, of the *Beast* and the *Brute,* respectively, are merely further players in the same tournament. The *Beast,* Lord Copper claims, "stands for strong mutually antagonistic governments everywhere" (*Scoop* 14). Patriot or Traitor; journalist or whore? There is no difference between the mendaciously aggressive, infantile worlds of press and politics, the Pip and Pop of *Scoop*'s phantasmagoria.

Of course *Scoop* is not a serious satire. And yet, from secret meetings with Muslim elders in Harar, Waugh knew how much Selassie's subjects suffered from exorbitant taxation. His impatience with what he called the "humane humbug of [Ras] Tafari's regime" (*WiA* 136) and the West's naïve support informs his tart résumé of Ishmaelite history, particularly the merger of its national defense and fiscal authorities into two armed companies, "the Ishmaelite Mule Tax-gathering Force and the Rifle Excisemen, with a small Artillery Death Duties Corps for use against the heirs of powerful noblemen; it was their job to raise the funds whose enlightened expenditure did so much to enhance President Jackson's prestige among the rare foreign visitors to the capital" (*Scoop* 76). General Gollancz Jackson heads the Mule Tax-gathering Force, in honor of Victor Gollancz, the creator of the Left Book Club.[33] Waugh's antipathy to the sentimental supporters of Abyssinia as the League of Nations's youngest and most colorful member is expressed in the names of Ishmaelia's ruling dynasty: "A Mr Rathbone Jackson held his grandfather's office in succession to his father Pankhurst, while the chief posts of the state were held by Messrs Garnett Jackson, Mander Jackson, Huxley Jackson, his uncle and brothers, and by Mrs Athol (*née* Jackson), his aunt" (*Scoop* 75).

Miss Sylvia Pankhurst was the leading organizer of the Abyssinia Association from 1936.[34] Its council included two active MPs, Miss Eleanor Rathbone (Independent member for the English Universities), a vociferous supporter of sanctions against Italy, and the strongly pro-League Liberal Geoffrey Mander. According to the historian Daniel Waley, the Duchess of Atholl spoke in Parliament in favor of the Hoare-Laval Pact "in terms that persuaded many to oppose it."[35] The others were private vendettas— Waugh gave Aldous Huxley an acid review at the time of *Scoop*'s composition. David Garnett wrote a negative review of *Waugh in Abyssinia*.[36]

High-profile literary vilification holds a masochistic appeal for its victims. The press has always had a strong affection for *Scoop*, just as the bright young things loved *Vile Bodies*. In both cases, the satirized originals and their fictional personae were exultantly identified.[37] Yet the details of attribution offer little more than mild curiosity value. Waugh's overwhelming animus was against the journalistic profession in its entirety. Hence his literalization of Stanley Baldwin's celebrated attack on Lord Beaverbrook and Lord Rothermere, two of Lord Copper's three originals, in 1931.[38] Their newspapers, Baldwin said, "are not newspapers in the ordinary acceptance of the term. They are engines of propaganda for the constantly changing policies, desires, personal wishes, personal likes and personal dislikes of two men. What are their methods? Their methods are direct falsehood, misrepresentation, half-truths. . . . What the proprietorship of these papers is aiming at is power, but power without responsibility—the prerogative of the harlot throughout the ages." Waugh's own sense of profound moral alienation from journalism emerges with increasing intensity in his letters from Addis Ababa. There he was, he tells Lady Diana, with "74 journalists mostly American all lying like hell & my job to sit here contradicting the lies they write" (*MW&MS* 52). And to Katharine Asquith, "The journalists are lousy competitive hysterical lying. It makes me unhappy to be one of them" (*LEW* 98). When he was finally recalled, he was delighted, telling Lady Diana, "I suppose it is priggish to despise ones job but there it is. I felt ashamed all the time" (*MW&MS* 57). A sense of shame is recurrent in these letters.[39]

The journalists' lies recur just as often: "The Mail now takes all its war news from a chap at Jibouti; he doesnt speak French, has never set foot in Abyssinia or met any Abyssinians except consular officials who refused him admission. He sits in his hotel describing an entirely imaginary campaign—18,000 abyssinians and 500,000 sheep killed by poison gas . . . ton weight bombs raining down and destroying seven mosques in a place he found on the map which in point of fact consists of one brackish well and a dozen huts and so on" (*MW&MS* 56). On his departure from Djibouti a month later Waugh found confirmation of this story: "There were a number of journalists there reporting the war at leisure from their imaginations. One of them waged a pretty little war in his hotel bedroom with flags and a large scale map" (*WiA* 143)—a clear model for *Scoop*'s Sir Jocelyn Hitchcock, reporting the Ishmaelia crisis incommunicado from his annex in the hotel grounds. The allegation also occurs earlier in the novel in a sharp reference to real events: "Mr Salter smiled. . . . 'You'll be surprised to find how far the war correspondents keep from the fighting. Why, Hitchcock reported the whole Abyssinia campaign from Asmara and gave us some of the most colourful eye-witness stuff we ever printed'" (*Scoop* 32).[40] Asmara was well out of the way of the real fighting, in the far north of Abyssinia.

Waugh in Abyssinia coolly catalogs Waugh's perception of his colleagues' professional mendacity.[41] Haile Selassie's ambitious modern buildings, everywhere left unfinished and in ruins, were snapped by press photographers hoping later to pass them off as the "ravages of Italian bombardment" (*WiA* 47). The day of the Maskal ceremony, marking the end of the rainy season so long awaited by Mussolini's troops and the impatient press, dawned bright and sunny. Most of the journalists dispatched their stories before the ceremony began. Guests filled the open-air stands; cameramen set up their tripods. A cold wind rose; single raindrops turned to downpour, thunder, and hail. The more honest journalists who took their typewriters with them found the paper turning "to pulp under the keys" (*WiA* 98–99).[42] A week later they were invited to hear Selassie summon his people to arms: "Over his shoulder I watched an American journalist typing out a description of the women under their mushroom-like umbrellas. There were no women and no umbrellas" (*WiA* 102). When the invasion finally occurred, the world's predominantly pro-Abyssinian press was encouraged to publicize Italian atrocities, especially the use of gas and the bombing of first-aid stations and hospitals, which were supposed to be marked by a red cross visible from the air. But in Abyssinia a red cross was the normal sign for a brothel, and a traditional charm on saddle cloths. Newspaper photos of mules bearing the mark were disingenuously designated "ambulance transports."[43] Naturally the Abyssinians played the press along. The Abyssinians themselves, with high drama, reported the opening of Italian hostilities with the bombing at Adowa of a nonexistent hospital filled with phantom women, children, and an American nurse whose existence Waugh exploded in his terse denial, "Nurse unupblown."[44] Major events, like the general mobilization, the bombing of Adowa, the mass emigrations choking the railway station, were predicted and preemptively described so often that when they finally came to pass, their news value was lost. The press had, in fact, a fairy-tale capacity for making nonevents occur and real events not occur—another paradox to riddle the fantastical structure of *Scoop*.[45]

When Corker first initiates William into the mysteries of his craft, he tells many stories of this kind: "the classic scoops and hoaxes . . . the confessions wrung from hysterical suspects . . . the innuendo and intricate misrepresentations, the luscious, detailed inventions that composed contemporary history . . . how Wenlock Jakes . . . scooped the world with an eye-witness story of the sinking of the *Lusitania* four hours before she was hit; how Hitchcock . . . straddling over his desk in London, had chronicled day by day the horrors of the Messina earthquake" (*Scoop* 66). Such are the self-fulfilling prophecies of the press. When Wenlock Jakes was sent to cover a revolution in the Balkans, he overslept in the train, got out at the wrong station, and went straight to a hotel to cable an eyewitness account of the imaginary conflict ("a dead child, like a broken doll, spread-eagled in the deserted roadway below his window—*you* know"). Within days press convergence on the peaceful city triggered a real revolution and Jakes won the Nobel Prize in peace for his "harrowing descriptions of the carnage" he had caused (another ironic inversion): "There's the power of the press for you" (*Scoop* 67). The press are, however, the impotent slaves of their own inventions. In the long nonstory of the Swiss ticket collector, Shumble turns him into a Red spy with a false beard—the first scoop of the Ishmaelite crisis. Jakes gets Benito to issue a denial and the story dies at birth. When William finds out that there is a genuine Russian agent but that he is not the Swiss ticket collector, the scoop is unusable though true, as Corker explains: "No one's going to print your story after the way it's been denied. Russian agents are off the menu, old boy. It's a bad break for Shumble, I grant you. . . . The false beard was a very pretty touch. His story was better than yours all round, and we killed it" (*Scoop* 101–2). As in Addis Ababa, real news loses its value because it has been preempted, reported before it occurs. Lies and inventions acquire the status of reality, while reality loses its status altogether. When Hitchcock scoops the world with his firsthand account of the Fascist camp at Laku, all the other journalists have to go there, even though it does not exist. Since it is splashed across the front page of the *Daily Brute*, it does exist. Indeed, the *Brute* alone has summoned it into existence.

Language is sacrificed to professional mendacity: things are, because they are called so—a philosophy playfully evoked by a light refrain. An indignant correspondent complains about Lush Places's approval of baiting great crested grebes in the "so-called twentieth century" (*Scoop* 20).[46] Journalism is a skilled exercise in the misattribution of terms. The so-called is so only because it is called so. Take expenses. As Mr Salter explains to William, "Supposing you want to send flowers to your girl. You just go to a shop, send a great spray of orchids, and put them down as 'Information'" (*Scoop* 33). What's in a name? Terms like *Patriot* and *Traitor* are meaningless, because each side attributes the same term to the opposite side. That is why policy is so simple, and Lord Copper's requirements are failsafe: "A few sharp victories, some conspicuous acts of personal bravery on the Patriot side, and a colourful entry into the capital. That is the *Beast* Policy for the war" (*Scoop* 42). Whoever wins is the Patriot, and by definition he will be brave. Thus the press inhabits a cloud-cuckoo-land where language is robbed of meaning and fantasy turns into transitory reality—where even Laku appears to exist for a little while and where no one is surprised when Sir Jocelyn Hitchcock claims £300 on expenses—for camels. In Shanghai.

The cub reporter who meets William on his triumphant return to London asks anxiously, "You do think it's a good way of training oneself—inventing imaginary news?" "None better," William replies. The cub is a student at the "Aircastle School of Journalism" (*Scoop* 188)—a heavy hint more subtly prefigured at the novel's beginning, where Mrs Stitch's levée is attended by a small throng of retainers, including "an elegant young man at the top of a step ladder painting ruined castles on the ceiling" (*Scoop* 7). In fact, the journalists have only the capacity to build castles in the air, not to make dreams come true. *That* is the prerogative of the novelist.

Scoop was written during Waugh's emotional rebirth, his happy courtship and marriage to Laura—"virgin, Catholic, quiet & astute" (*LEW* 92), and nearly half his age. In the diaries and letters the intense joy of recaptured innocence is distinctly audible.[47] *Scoop* catches the same glow. It is a fairy tale with William transformed, like Cinderella, from incompetent green-horn to the cynosure of Fleet Street, the mercurial Mr Baldwin as fairy godmother, and indiscriminate happy endings for everyone.

It should not surprise us, then, that *Scoop*'s two major literary sources come from children's literature.

Its tripartite structure is based on the classic fable of the town mouse and the country mouse, specifically as told by Beatrix Potter: "Johnny Town-Mouse was born in a cupboard. Timmy Willie was born in a garden. Timmy Willie was a little country mouse who went to town by mistake in a hamper."[48] William Boot, "a retiring, bucolic, innocent young man" (Memorandum 26–27), is Timmy Willie. Book 1 revolves around his apprehensive journey up to the city, away from his secure country nest. At this point John Boot is, self-evidently, his sophisticated urban cousin, Johnny Town-Mouse. In book 3 John's role passes to Mr. Salter, reluctantly forced out of frenetic, familiar London into the bucolic terrors of Boot Magna. William, in obedience to the classic fable, and Waugh's strictures to *Scoop*'s scriptwriters, returns home without ambition ever to go away again. Thus the novel's characteristic narrative line leads William down a long, meandering detour through London, Ishmaelia, the excitements of calf love for Kätchen and his scoop, back to London and the quiet bathos of his own chosen happy ending, at Boot Magna again.

Waugh teases his reader with indistinct echoes of his second narrative source for most of the novel. It is tantalizingly half-heard in the premonitory coupling of the two rival papers, the *Brute* and the *Beast*. It surfaces for a flash in Mr. Salter's confused overture, "How are your boots, root? . . . I mean brute." It recurs in William's schoolboy nickname, "Beastly" (*Scoop* 95). It finally emerges from the shadows on William's triumphant return to London, where newspaper placards and Lord Copper's invitation hail him as BOOT of THE BEAST (*Scoop* 185, 193). It is, of course, Beauty and the Beast.[49]

In the novel's recurrent mode, we are encouraged to decode these tantalizing suggestions incorrectly—first, by assuming that the Beastly references simply draw attention to the beastly behavior of the journalists themselves. Their names—*Shumble, Pigge, Whelper*—suggest it. The *Beast*'s telegraph code, *UNNATURAL*, confirms it. Or so you would have thought. Then the reader is decoyed into another false detour by the appearance of Kätchen. She is a self-evident Beauty, reminiscent of Garbo—no, "Not Garbo . . . Bergner" (*Scoop* 115)[50]—but not at her best when William first sees her spattered with mud, tatty umbrella dripping at her feet. As soon as William gives her some of his expense money, she is transformed—fluffy new haircut, new dress, red sandals, red toenails. But this too is a false trail. In the classic fairy tale it is the Beast, not Beauty, who is transformed. Kätchen, as does Beauty, helps to initiate the metamorphosis of "Beastly" William with trivial scandal picked up from her hairdresser. In his turn, Mr. Baldwin transforms her gossip into the authoritative headlines that scoop the world and makes a star of William.

For all their apparent omnipotence, neither the journalists, nor even Lord Copper, nor Mrs. Stitch least of all, has the capacity to make miracles happen or to create order out of *Scoop*'s ever-intensifying chaos. On the contrary, editors and subeditors have the daily "humdrum task of reducing to blank nonsense the sheaves of misinformation" placed before them (*Scoop* 179). It is only the polyglot Mr. Baldwin who can construe the novel's complex syntax and impose order on the chaos at last. He epitomizes cosmopolitanism, intelligence, and gourmet good taste—everything lacking in the shambolic world of Shumble, Corker, and Pigge. In crepe-de-chine shirtsleeves he plays a dazzling game of Ping-Pong at Popotakis's Parlour. In his luxurious little pied-à-terre he provides William with a private wireless transmitter, a delicious meal, and a lucid explanation of the political situation in Jacksonburg. Then he writes William's story for him.

Mr. Baldwin drops from his airplane with balletic grace, an explicit answer to William's prayer "Was there not, even in the remorseless dooms of antiquity, a god from the machine?" (*Scoop* 166). In *A Handful of Dust* Mrs. Rattery is a flawed goddess also descending from the skies with comparable comic literalism, but failing to halt Tony Last's tragedy. The happier world of *Scoop* is provided with two potent, benevolent deities—Mr. Baldwin and Erik Olafsen.

Olafsen, like William, is a figure of naïve simplicity and truth. Like William, he is no party to the lies of the other journalists. He knows that the Swiss ticket collector is nothing more than a Swiss ticket collector. He dismisses with puzzled politeness Hitchcock's palpable whoppers about talking parrots and gorillas on the road to Laku. He has no illusions about Benito's invented outbreak of bubonic plague, a ruse to get him out of town for the revolution. His humble strength is glimpsed early on, significantly mending his hymn books with patient hands: "One by one the tattered books were *set in order*, restored and fortified" (*Scoop* 132, my italics). Waugh describes him as "a blinded and shackled Samson with his bandages and Bibles . . . scarcely able to shift a pebble from the vast mountain which oppressed humanity" (*Scoop* 104). But his time also comes. Just as Mr Baldwin is lamenting the lack of local might to dislodge the Bolshevist takeover, Olafsen roars into Popotakis's Ping-Pong Parlour on his motorbike—another literal, if drunken deus ex machina:

> He rode slowly between the ping-pong tables, then put his feet to the floor and released the handle-bars. *The machine shot from under him* . . . while the rider, swaying ponderously from side to side like a performing bear, surveyed the room in a puzzled but friendly spirit.
>
> It was the Swede, but a Swede *transfigured*, barely recognisable as the mild apostle of the coffee-pot and the sticking plaster. . . .
>
> "Might," said Mr Baldwin reverently. (*Scoop* 173, my italics)

Finally awakened and stirred to action, Olafsen, as does Samson in the temple of Dagon, brings down the unholy Marxist rule, and the Jacksons return to power in Jacksonburg.

There is a logical, incremental sequence in the novel's stylistic markers, from anagram and metathesis to reversal, from reversal to transposition, from transposition to transformation and transfiguration. Olafsen's transfiguration is one of many filling the novel's final pages in Ishmaelia. Transformative awakenings, like those of the Beast or Sleeping Beauty, are the stuff of fairy tale. In Ishmaelia they have a natural source in the long-awaited ending of the rainy season and the coming of summer: "Next morning William awoke in a new world. As he stood on his veranda calling for his boy, he slowly became aware of the *transformation* which had taken place overnight. The rains were over. The boards were warm under his feet; below the steps the dank weeds of Frau Dressler's garden had suddenly burst into crimson flower" (*Scoop* 143–44, my italics). Waugh evokes this transfigured world in transcendent terms reminiscent of his most impassioned letters to Laura: "It was a morning of ethereal splendour—such a morning as Noah knew . . . such a morning as only the angels saw on the first day" (*Scoop* 147). Stranded on the road to nonexistent Laku, the "earth-bound journalists" are blind to the newly wakened world: "Look at the flowers," says Pigge. "Like a bloody cemetery," Corker replies (*Scoop* 147). Transformation is reserved for the good of the novel—not the lying journalists and politicians like Sir Jocelyn, Benito or his superior accomplice, whom the milk goat, rejoicing in the new season, butts gloriously into the kitchen garbage.[51]

Ever-increasing order gradually takes over as the rainbow fills the sky. At the beginning of the novel, William was a magnet for miscellaneous rubbish—cleft sticks, collapsible canoe, astrolabe, portable humidor, camp operating table, Christmas hamper complete with Santa Claus costume and tripod mistletoe stand; synthetic ivory elephants stored for Corker at Frau Dressler's; stones he charitably buys from Kätchen on expenses. Kätchen and William have a happy game unpacking and assembling the canoe and paddling through an imaginary sea of shavings. This is fantasy. But as the novel draws to a close, the miscellany of rubbish finds a practical function. William feeds the Christmas dinner to Kätchen's starving prospector husband. Kätchen and her husband escape in the collapsible canoe. Even Lord Copper's cleft sticks turn up again on William's return to England, where he is met by a telegraph boy carrying his name "stuck, by a felicitous stroke of fancy, into a cleft stick" (*Scoop* 185).

Thus the novel's resolution replays Waugh's own aesthetic practice. Dented valuables are retrieved from the smoldering rubbish tip, polished, and arranged. Every disorderly element finds its proper place, and Kätchen's "stones" turn into valuable samples of gold ore.

Lord Copper's banquet draws to a close in a pleasant haze of vinous optimism. With his toast to "the Future," Lord Copper, Uncle Theodore, Mr Salter, Mrs Stitch, John Boot, Corker, Pigge, Kätchen, and her husband are given the happy endings of their dreams. William is left in the nocturnal calm of Boot Magna, composing his column for Lush Places: *"The waggons lumber in the lane under their golden glory of harvested sheaves . . . maternal rodents pilot their furry brood"* (*Scoop* 222).

Waugh, however, was a realist and a truth teller. The novel's last words strike a chillier note. "Outside the owls hunted maternal rodents and their furry brood" (*Scoop* 222). World war was on its way. The fairy tale was over.

APPENDIX: WAUGH AND THE ITALIAN INVASION OF ABYSSINIA

David Garnett was not the only one to give *Waugh in Abyssinia* a hostile review. From the safe retrospect of 1946 Rose Macaulay dismissed it as "a Fascist tract."[52] Waugh's openly pro-Italian stance at the time of the invasion has won him much popular disfavor and infects criticism of the antipolitical *Scoop* to this day.[53] Yet it is clear from Daniel Waley's history of public opinion on the Abyssinian crisis that Waugh's position was shared by many politically acute thinkers of the time.

Waley divides British opinion into two camps. The vast majority were the idealists, believers in the power of the League of Nations and vociferous defenders of the rights of Abyssinia, its youngest and most vulnerable member. Opposing them were the minority, "the cautious realists, believers in the essential immutability of human nature, in the inescapability of selfishness and power."[54] It should not surprise us that Waugh belonged to this skeptical group. To the British politician of 1935, Italy was more important than Abyssinia, as a potential ally against Germany's growing military strength. Italy had already curbed German expansionism in July 1934, when Mussolini sent three Italian divisions to the frontier to discourage German annexation of Austria after the assassination of Engelbert Dolfuss. In April 1935 England and France joined Italy in the Stresa front against Germany. Among the politicians and cautious realists, as opposed to the sentimental idealists, approval of pragmatic British fraternization with Fascist Italy was combined with growing skepticism over the efficacy of the League of Nations, whose inadequacies first emerged in 1931 after its failure to respond effectively to the Japanese attack on Manchuria. The Conservative attitude to the League of Nations was one of contemptuous distrust: "In any place where what are generally called the upper and middle classes foregather, anyone who asked the assembled company whether they felt personally more secure for the existence of the League of Nations would have aroused laughter."[55] However, it was not an attitude that could be publicly acknowledged.

As a Catholic Conservative, Waugh belonged to this strong dissident minority. His views coincide startlingly with those of his diametric opposite, the Fabian agnostic George Bernard Shaw. No less outspoken than Waugh, Shaw declared roundly that "Ethiopia is not a nation" (therefore unworthy of league membership) and derided "our love of exalted moral attitudes," as vaunted by the pro-League, pro-Abyssinian idealists.[56] Shaw voiced Waugh's sympathies precisely when he wrote to the *Times* on October 22, 1935: "As between the Danakil warrior and the Italian engineer I . . . am on the side of the engineer." In *Waugh in Abyssinia*, Waugh's historical introduction to the political situation in 1935 is titled "The Intelligent Woman's Guide to the Ethiopian Question"—a manifest echo of Shaw's 1928 essay "The Intelligent Woman's Guide to Socialism and Capitalism." Waugh's objectivity is widely acclaimed. His skepticism about the ideals justifying the nineteenth-century rush to colonize Africa is uncompromising. His distaste for British hypocrisy in its parade of benign colonial intentions corroborates Shaw's dislike of Britain's exalted moral attitudes. Waugh was not a knee-jerk colonialist. The final chapter of *Waugh in Abyssinia* could not be written until he was able to see with his own eyes the great Italian trunk road being built from Asmara to Addis Ababa. Like Shaw, he was on the side of the Italian engineers.

Waugh in Abyssinia was written and published in 1936, when England's position on the successful Italian invasion was still a matter of intense debate. Waley observes that by December 1935, when the Italian invasion was three months old, those unsympathetic to Abyssinia's cause could be divided into "pessimistic isolationist imperialists" (a label inappropriate to Waugh's robust rationalism) and the politicians. Waley identifies a wide rift between Waugh's bugbear, the popular majority of pro-League idealists and supporters of Abyssinia, "who cogitated and proclaimed ideas," and the decision-making minority, "those who held responsibility and exercised power."[57] Waugh would have fallen naturally into the latter group. Lady Diana's husband, Duff Cooper, became secretary of state for war in December 1935. The leading politicians' perception of the crisis emerges from Harold Nicolson's diary entry summarizing a speech made by the prime minister, Stanley Baldwin, at a small dinner on June 11, 1936: "We knew that our great danger was not Italy, but Germany. We knew that if we crushed Italy we should not only destroy a possible ally, but weaken ourselves tremendously during the next two critical years, which are so dangerous. How could I [Baldwin] say that publicly? Yet we in the room knew that to be true."[58] In the conflicting cross-currents of the time, Waugh held a rational and consistent line that was, as he said of *Waugh in Abyssinia*, "quite honourable" (*MW&MS* 61). It is both condescending and ill informed of Martin Stannard to dismiss Waugh's views as those of "a politically naïve aesthete."[59]

And yet Waugh's final position was that of the uncommitted observer. When he returned to Abyssinia in July 1936 to gather material for *Waugh in Abyssinia*'s last chapter, he wrote to Katharine Asquith, "I am sick of Abyssinia and my book about it. It was fun being pro-Italian when it was an unpopular and (I thought) losing cause. I have little sympathy with these exultant fascists now" (*LEW* 109). *Scoop* betrays Waugh's total disaffection from any political party, whether Left or Right. Apart from William, the novel's heroes are the pragmatic, apolitical order makers and individualists—Olafsen and Mr Baldwin. And even Mr. Baldwin's familiar name is shaded with irony.

NOTES

1. Frederick J. Stopp's *Evelyn Waugh: Portrait of an Artist* (London: Chapman & Hall, 1958) remains the best critical study of Waugh's work—partly because it was written with assistance from Waugh himself. Stopp offers a good understanding of the overall structure of the novels and suggests the point of some of their details.

2. Evelyn Waugh, "Present Discontents," *Tablet*, December 3, 1938; rep., *The Essays, Articles and Reviews of Evelyn Waugh*, ed. Donat Gallagher (London: Methuen, 1983), 238. Hereafter cited as *EAR*.

3. Evelyn Waugh, *The Diaries of Evelyn Waugh*, ed. Michael Davie (London: Weidenfeld & Nicolson, 1976), 640-41. Hereafter cited as *DEW*.

4. The adjustments Waugh refers to occur in *Helena*, chapters 1 (pages 15-16), 3 (62-63), and 4 (69) in the first edition (London: Chapman & Hall, 1950). Waugh's manuscripts, as analyzed by Robert Murray Davis in his groundbreaking *Evelyn Waugh, Writer* (Norman, OK: Pilgrim Books, 1981), demonstrate this technique repeatedly. For his account of *Scoop*'s manuscript alterations, see 87–106.

5. Evelyn Waugh, *Scoop* (1938; rep., Harmondsworth, UK: Penguin, 1943), 16. Hereafter cited as *Scoop*.

6. *Labels, A Mediterranean Journal* was titled *A Bachelor Abroad* in the American edition. Waugh's first marriage broke down during its composition.

7. Rimbaud died in Abyssinia. On Waugh's first visit to report the coronation of Haile Selassie for the *Times*, he fantasized about finding a half-caste son of Rimbaud's there. See Evelyn Waugh, *Remote People* (1931), in *Waugh Abroad: Collected Travel Writing* (New York: Everyman's Library, 2003), 261.

8. See Martin Stannard, ed., *Evelyn Waugh: The Critical Heritage* (London: Routledge & Kegan Paul, 1984), 197.

9. Cf. letter to Laura, August 5, 1936: "Sometimes I think it would be lovely to lead the sort of life with you that I have led alone for the last ten years—no possessions, no home. At other times I picture a settled patriarchal life with a large household." See Evelyn Waugh, *The Letters of Evelyn Waugh*, ed. Mark Amory (London: Weidenfeld & Nicolson, 1980), 110. Hereafter cited as *LEW*.

10. January? 1935. The precise dating of the fancy's inception is unknown. Waugh first notes meeting "white mouse named Laura" at the Herberts' family home in Portofino in September 1933 (*LEW* 80), when Laura was seventeen and Waugh, still in pursuit of Teresa Jungman, was thirty. He stayed at the Herberts' English home in April 1934. The consensus is that the friendship probably began in September 1934.

11. William Godfrey, then domestic prelate of His Holiness, and rector of the English College in Rome. Archbishop of Westminster (1956–63).

12. Martin Stannard, *Evelyn Waugh: The Early Years 1903–1939* (London: Dent, 1986), 440.

13. Ibid., 464.

14. Mark Amory says he reproduces verbatim only the first paragraph of Waugh's first typewritten letter to Laura. See *LEW* 96 n. 1. Artemis Cooper is unsystematically more accommodating: "Not all the idiosyncrasies and inconsistencies . . . have been ironed out." See Cooper, ed., *Mr Wu and Mrs Stitch: The Letters of Evelyn Waugh and Diana Cooper* (London: Hodder & Stoughton, 1991), 9. Hereafter cited as *MW&MS*.

15. August 1935. A glossary, with thanks to Artemis Cooper—*bo*: Waugh (whose nickname was "Boaz"); *balfour*: Patrick Balfour, Waugh's friend and special correspondent for the *Evening Standard*; *News Chronicle chap*: Stuart Emeny; *duff*: Diana's husband, Duff Cooper, then financial secretary to the Treasury and model for Algernon Stitch; *Sir GARNET*: everything as it should be (military slang of 1880s); *bloodcurdler book*: *Waugh in Abyssinia*. See *MW&MS* 51. (a) came to pass with the successful Italian invasion in December 1935; there were gas attacks but no journalistic casualties. (c) was partly

fulfilled by the abortive Hoare-Laval Pact of December 1935, when Duff was also Sir Garnetted minister of state for war. The League of Nations and Anthony Eden (minister without portfolio for League of Nations affairs) found themselves in the soup in June 1936 when they had to abandon sanctions against Italy. "Soup for Eurpoe" came with the Second World War in 1939.

16. E.g., "Dearest Bo. I've read Handfulers aloud to Barbie . . . the success has been dynamic. The book has, and is now being fought for by the men. As for myself I can not tell you, because I am not educated, and inarticulate and uncoordinated in thought how beautiful I think it. . . . I read the whole of the 2nd ½ with a lump in my throat, produced by the chapter, and the verse, if you follow me." See *MW&MS* 45–46. The subsequent quotation, on reading "Wasters" aloud, seems to echo this letter quite deliberately.

17. "*floribus* (1) *Austrum* (2) / *perditus* (3) *et* (4) *liquidis* (5) *immisi* (6) *fontibus* (7) *apros* (8)" = "I, ruined man (3), have let in (6) the South wind (2) to my flowers (1), and (4) wild boars (8) to my crystal (5) springs (7)." For an alternative reading of this Latin quotation as an image of the fallen world, see Douglas Lane Patey, *The Life of Evelyn Waugh: A Critical Biography* (Oxford: Blackwell, 1998), 162.

18. Evelyn Waugh, *Waugh in Abyssinia* (1936; rep., Harmondsworth, UK: Penguin, 1984), 44–45. Hereafter cited as *WiA*.

19. As a representative of a group of American financiers, Rickett negotiated a vast concession of mineral rights from the emperor, in the terrain to be covered by the Italian advance. It was an ingenious act of self-defense on Haile Selassie's part. But it did not succeed. Early reports mistakenly assumed that, since Rickett was English, he represented an Anglo-American company. French and Italian suspicions were aroused: was England's publicly censorious attitude to Italy merely a cover for promoting its own commercial interests? The State Department at Washington blocked the concession's ratification, to keep out of the conflict. Waugh's political bias is evident in *Scoop*'s dénouement, where a comparable situation is resolved by Mr. Baldwin, who foils the rival Communist and Fascist attempts to annex Ishmaelia by reinstating the Jackson regime, under whose rule he owns extensive tracts of Ishmaelia's unmined goldfields.

20. "Badly left" = you have been badly left behind on this story.

21. Waugh's other scoop occurred earlier: his spy informed him of Italian troop movements, whose verification, a month later, triggered the order for general mobilization (*WiA* 69).

22. Waugh was on good terms with the Italians in Addis because he represented the *Daily Mail*, one of only two British papers supporting Mussolini.

23. According to Patrick Balfour, Waugh was the author of "Nurse unupblown." See Christopher Sykes, *Evelyn Waugh: A Biography* (London: Collins, 1975), 156.

24. See Evelyn Waugh, "Memorandum for Messrs. Endfield & Fisz," April 12, 1957, introduced by Donat Gallagher, in "Notes on the Film Adaptations of 'Brideshead Revisited' and 'Scoop,'" *Areté* 14 (2004), 28. Hereafter cited as Memorandum.

25. Even Waugh's most trivial jottings naturally fall into unity of metaphor: "loafers crumbling crusts of bread" (*DEW* 403).

26. See Sykes, *Evelyn Waugh*, 153, 157. This event, recounted in detail, is unaccountably omitted from the biographies by Stannard, Patey, and Selina Hastings, *Evelyn Waugh: A Biography* (London: Sinclair-Stevenson, 1994). In fact, "after the first very grave shock it was O.K. and they laughed a lot and I had quite a funny week-end" (*MW&MS* 58).

27. Stannard, *Early Years*, 445. Stannard prints the preceding letter (with variant readings) as unpublished.

28. Stopp has a good understanding of the novel's tripartite structure and the crisscrossed substitutions of John, William, and Uncle Theodore Boot, and Mr Salter, within this structure. See Stopp, *Evelyn Waugh*, 83–89.

29. East Finchley, in North London, began to be developed in the 1890s, initially providing what Wikipedia ironically calls "some grand 'country' estates of wealthy Londoners." Nevertheless it is merely a London suburb.

30. The ironic implication of Mrs Stitch's feet of clay was reaffirmed when the first section of *Scoop* was published in the *Bystander* (in the United Kingdom) and *Town and Country* (in the United States) in November 1937 under the equally ambivalent title "Mrs Stitch Fails for the First Time."

31. In answer to a questionnaire of 1937 demanding "Are you for or against Franco and Fascism?" Waugh replied that "As an Englishman I am not in the position of choosing between two evils. I am not a Fascist nor shall I become one unless it were the only alternative to Marxism. It is mischievous to suggest that such a choice is imminent" (*EAR* 187).

32. Cf. "two indistinguishable Japanese, who beamed at the world through horn-rimmed spectacles and played interminable, highly dexterous games of ping-pong in Mme Idot's bar" (*WiA* 82). The rival establishments run by Mme Idot and Mme Moriatis follow the same pattern of indistinguishable opposition. Both Frenchwomen had cad husbands who beat them and served unspeakable refreshments. Both establishments boasted a cinema and bar: 'after an hour in either place, one longed for the other' (*WiA* 54).

33. Cf. Evelyn Waugh, *Robbery under Law: The Mexican Object-Lesson* (London: Chapman & Hall, 1939), 16: the English, "bored with the privilege of a free press, have lately imposed on themselves a voluntary censorship; they have banded themselves into Book Clubs so that they may be perfectly confident that whatever they read will be written with the intention of confirming their existing opinions."

34. Daniel Waley, *British Public Opinion and the Abyssinian War, 1935–36* (London: Temple Smith, 1975), 116.

35. Ibid., 54, 77, 65. "Geoffrey Mander MP made the unrealistic proposal that Britain should offer to treat the war as an attack on Britain itself, if other members of the League agreed to take the same step." Ibid., 72. Patey, less probably, identifies Pankhurst Jackson with the suffragette Emmeline Pankhurst, who died in 1928, and Mander Jackson with Lionel Mander, a socialist author and radio commentator. See Patey, *Life of Waugh*, 162, 383 n. 38. For more on Waugh and the Italian invasion of Abyssinia, see the appendix.

36. See Evelyn Waugh, "More Barren Leaves" (review of Huxley's *Ends and Means*, December 23, 1937), in *EAR* 213–14; Garnett, review of *WiA* (*New Statesman*, November 7, 1936), in *Critical Heritage*, 188ff.

37. For further details, see W. F. Deedes, *At War with Waugh: The Real Story of Scoop* (London: Macmillan, 2003), and Michael Salwen, *Evelyn Waugh in Ethiopia: The Story behind Scoop* (Lampeter, UK: Edwin Mellen, 2001), particularly chapter 8, "Journalistic Practices," 159–90. Hitherto unnoticed is the ironic link between Wilfred Courtenay Barker of the *Chicago Tribune*, the only correspondent to die (of malaria) on this assignment, and John Courteney Boot, who never got to Ishmaelia at all. Waugh refers casually to the unnamed Barker's death (*MW&MS* 52).

38. Lord Copper's derivation from Lord Beaverbrook and Lord Rothermere of the *Daily Mail* is well known. Sykes points out that Copper's "megalomania bordering on insanity" is more reminiscent of the mad last years of Lord Northcliffe, Rothermere's predecessor

on the *Daily Mail*. See Sykes, *Evelyn Waugh*, 177. In his 1931 review of Northcliffe's biography, Waugh singled out details he later clearly recreated in Copper. Most significant are Northcliffe's dizzyingly inappropriate promotions of his staff ("the amusing story of the sudden mock-elevation of Mr Glover from the post of hall porter to that of advertising manager"—an obvious source for William's apotheosis) and Northcliffe's "policy of exorbitant payment to journalists . . . [encouraging] an atmosphere of uncertainty in his staff; there were continual drastic changes, sudden, generous rewards; sudden, ungenerous reprisals" (*EAR* 99). This is replayed in the uncertainty of Copper's employees, willfully transposed from one desk to another: Mr. Salter shot from the quiet nook of Clean Fun into the hurly-burly of Foreign News, before coming to rest in the haven of Home Knitting.

Baldwin's speech was delivered on March 17, 1930, opposing the Beaverbrook-Rothermere candidate in the St. George's Westminster by-election. Duff Cooper, the candidate backed by Baldwin, won by a large majority. Rudyard Kipling, Baldwin's cousin, is often credited with the authorship of Baldwin's memorable peroration.

39. To Penelope Betjeman he wrote, "I am a very bad journalist, well only a shit could be good at this particular job." In December 1935 he left Abyssinia for Jerusalem, where he told Katharine Asquith he was spending "four days penance for the shame of the last four months in intense discomfort at Franciscan Monastery" (*LEW* 102). The result was that Waugh's factually accurate dispatches were pointedly dull, unlike the highly colored lies of his colleagues—to the extent that Lady Diana wrote demanding "more pep in my messages more fantastic stories fewer place names etc" (*MW&MS* 55), and Waugh himself admitted to Laura, "Goodness how stale and meagre my cables are" (*LEW* 100).

40. Fortunately Sir Jocelyn Hitchcock's obvious original, Sir Percival Phillips of the *Daily Telegraph*, died in 1937, before *Scoop* was published.

41. Waugh's revulsion was shared by several colleagues. See Salwen, "The Culture of Lying," *Evelyn Waugh in Ethiopia*, 174–78, and O'Dowd Gallagher of the *Express*, as cited by Philip Knightley, *The First Casualty: From the Crimea to Vietnam: The War Correspondent as Hero, Propagandist, and Myth Maker* (New York: Harcourt Brace Jovanovich, 1975), 176–77. The telegrams received by O'Dowd are strongly reminiscent of William's: "PHILLIPS IN TELEGRAPH SAYS ABYSSINIAN SPEARSMEN MASSING ON TIGRE FRONT STOP WHAT YOU FOLLOW UP EXYOU . . . DANKIL [*sic*] TRIBESMEN ANNIHILATED ITALIAN SCOUTING PARTY ACCORDING TO PHILLIPS IN TELEGRAPH STOP AWAIT ACTION REPORT EXYOU . . . BEG YOU EMULATE PHILLIPS STOP YOUR LACK CABLES MOST DISCONCERTING STOP NOT ONLY YOUR JOB BUT MINE AT STAKE." Both of these stories from Phillips were false.

42. Cf. *MW&MS* 54: "Today there are great celebrations for the cessation of the rains. It is hailing."

43. For misuse of the Red Cross symbol by the press, see Waugh's "Appendix VIII to the Official Note addressed by the Italian Government to the League of Nations," in *EAR* 185–86.

44. The Abyssinian announcement of the bombing of Adowa is the climactic ending of *Waugh in Abyssinia*'s fourth chapter, "Waiting for the War." The reader takes the atrocity seriously. The next chapter is titled "Anticlimax" and the false bombshell is defused over several pages—another striking instance of the pattern of reversal and anticlimax that was later transferred to *Scoop*.

45. When the press were summoned to the palace to hear Selassie's announcement of general mobilization, "I remember saying to the Reuter's correspondent, 'Well, now

that they *have* at last mobilized, I suppose—and—(naming two abnormally untruthful colleagues who had anticipated the morning's order by ten days) will have to start announcing the bombardment of Adowa'" (*WiA* 102). For the preempted stories listed here, see *WiA* 102, 103–04, 110–113.

46. The blatantly inappropriate use of "so-called" at this early stage alerts the reader to two more anodyne usages in *Scoop* (51, 80). The term significantly recalls Wynant Davis Hubbard's *Fiasco in Ethiopia: The Story of a So-Called War by a Reporter on the Ground* (London: Harper & Bros., 1936). Hubbard, a relative journalistic neophyte, was as shocked as Waugh by his colleagues' mendacity. See *Fiasco in Ethiopia*, 195–96.

47. "Leaf-catching with Laura" (*DEW*, October 24, 1936, 410); "my darling love child," "darling child," "lovely child," "darling child . . . my blessed child" (*LEW* 95, 98, 107, 110). "This light-hearted tale was the fruit of a time of general anxiety and distress but, for its author, one of peculiar personal happiness." See Evelyn Waugh, preface, in *Scoop* (1938; rep., London: Chapman & Hall, 1964).

48. Beatrix Potter, *The Tale of Johnny Town-Mouse* (London: Warne, 1918), 1.

49. Davis points out that the names *Brute* and *Beast* "occurred to [Waugh] very late in the process of composition." See *Evelyn Waugh, Writer*, 99. But the significant substitution of these names for the original *Voice* and *Excess* are then inserted into the text from early on, in Waugh's habitual manner.

50. Elisabeth Bergner, star of *Catherine the Great* (1934) and *Escape Me Never* (1935). Garbo or Bergner? Ping-Pong, Pip and Pop alternatives.

51. For nature's rebellion against Sir Jocelyn's lies, see *Scoop* 128. For the goat's transfiguration and the fall of the welterweight champion of the Adventist University of Alabama, see *Scoop* 153. Stopp recognizes the importance of the milk goat. See Stopp, *Evelyn Waugh*, 88.

52. Stannard, ed., *Critical Heritage*, 193.

53. "When the spotlight moves to Ishmaelite/Abyssinian affairs, the standard drops. . . . His treatment of the Ishmaelite revolution engineered by [*sic*] the Jackson family with the comic left-wing names—Huxley Jackson, General Gollancz Jackson, Earl Russell Jackson . . . is comparatively poor stuff." See Hastings, *Evelyn Waugh*, 372–73.

54. Waley, *British Public Opinion*, 13.

55. R. B. McCallum, *Public Opinion and the Last Peace* (Oxford: Oxford University Press, 1944), 138.

56. George Bernard Shaw, letters to *Time and Tide*, October 12 and 16, 1935 (and see Donat Gallagher, introduction, in *EAR* 157). Cf. Waugh: "When Abyssinia applied for membership of the League, England opposed her admission, France and Italy supported it. Both parties realised that she did not constitute a homogeneous or orderly nation of the sort that could be admitted on equal terms to the councils of the world" (letter to the *Times*, May 19, 1936; rep., *EAR* 187).

57. Waley, *British Public Opinion*, 136–37.

58. Ibid., 142.

59. Stannard, *Early Years*, 435.

Violence, Duplicity, and Frequent Malversation: *Robbery under Law* and Evelyn Waugh's Political Critique

Baron Alder

> I see nothing quite conclusive in the art of temporal government,
> But violence, duplicity and frequent malversation.[1]

IN 1938, EVELYN WAUGH TRAVELED TO MEXICO TO SEE FOR HIMSELF THE EFFECTS of General Cardenas's radical and far-reaching economic reforms. The observations he made during his two months in Mexico are recorded in *Robbery under Law*, which was published in Great Britain in 1939 but not reprinted until 1999. *Robbery under Law* is one of Waugh's least-known books, and the fact that it remained out of print for sixty years reflects possibly Waugh's own reservations[2] but certainly the general critical indifference toward the book. This reaction is unfortunate because *Robbery under Law* presents a coherent statement of political and social principles that are not given overt expression elsewhere in Waugh's works. Waugh wrote *Robbery under Law* at the end of a decade that, to a large extent, is defined in terms of its ideologically inflamed consciousness. In Waugh's view, however, the conversations that his contemporaries were having about episodes such as the Spanish civil war reflected only the immaturity of the modern, essentially political outlook. Waugh's critique was not simply concerned with what he regarded as the facile theoretical discourse of class, nation, and race. As *Robbery under Law* indicates, Waugh considered the pursuit of political solutions to human problems an inherently misguided project that neglected the spiritual and cultural requirements of a civilized society.

There are numerous reasons for the general obscurity in which *Robbery under Law* has lain since publication. Most notably, there is a tendency to dismiss the book as a transparently tendentious apologia prepared on behalf of British and American capital. *Robbery under Law* was commissioned by Clive Pearson, the son of Lord Cowdray, the founder of the Mexican Eagle Oil Company, as part of a campaign against Cardenas's nationalization of the mostly American- and British-owned oil industry. At the same time, Waugh's treatment of the Mexican government's persecution of the Roman Catholic Church is inadequate, and it appears selective and disingenuous in parts.[3] Probably *Robbery under Law* has also suffered from unavoidable comparison with Graham Greene's *The Power and the Glory* and *The Lawless Roads*: certainly, as Christopher Sykes has pointed out, the anthropologist Sir Robert Marett considered Greene's contribution to the literature of the Mexican Revolution more valuable than Waugh's.[4] At the time of its publication, a book that proposed—even lightheartedly—the establishment of a College of Arms "to polish the pedigrees and titles of the colonial families" as a means of salvaging Mexican social life is likely to have had its contemporary significance drawn into question.[5] Even with the passage of time, Waugh's general call for a European renaissance in Mexico is very difficult for the postcolonial reader to credit. As a commentary on international affairs, certain of Waugh's predictions about North American geopolitics—for example, that Mexico would be absorbed into the United States—appear groundless.

While Waugh himself was not *Robbery under Law*'s harshest critic—Donat Gallagher suggests that aspects of the book's religious polemic are "of interest only as an example of how bad [Waugh's] work could sometimes become"[6]—it is well known that in 1946, Waugh chose not to include any part of the book in the collection of extracts from his travel writing published as *When the Going Was Good*. Rather, Waugh recommended that *Robbery under Law* be left in oblivion because "it dealt little with travel and much with political questions."[7] Waugh's own attitude to *Robbery under Law* does not, however, devalue his critique of modern politics and the significance of the book in any discussion of these.

On the one hand, Waugh liked to pretend that he had no interest in politics. He once explained, for example, that he had never voted in a parliamentary election because he "did not aspire to advise [his] sovereign in her choice of servants."[8] This outward attitude has sustained the assessments of Martin Stannard, who considered Waugh a "politically naive aesthete," and Selina Hastings, who stated that Waugh "was never seriously interested in politics and his political understanding was and remained simplistic and immature."[9] On the other hand, the important political issues of the day are always clearly present and often prominent in his novels: the General Strike in *Brideshead Revisited* (1945), the Nazi-Soviet Pact in *Men at Arms* (1952), and the welfare state in *Love among the Ruins* (1953). As Donat Gallagher has pointed out, February 1935 to June 1945 was Waugh's "political decade," and the articles and reviews produced by Waugh in that period were marked by the politics of the time.[10]

Waugh objected to the overt politicization of literature in the 1930s and, in *Work Suspended* (1942), satirized the literary Left of the period as a coterie of self-referential partisans, sanctimonious, absurd, and hypo-critical. He tackled one of the most notable political issues of the day in a very forthright manner when he gave an elaborate defense of Mussolini's invasion of Abyssinia. He also expressed a preference for the insurgents over the loyalists in the Spanish civil war and described himself in *Robbery under Law* as a partisan of Franco. As a result, he often emerges, in the words of an editorial in the *Socialist Review* in 1979, as a "vile reaction-ary monster"[11] or, in the assessment of Christopher Hitchens and others, a crypto fascist.[12] David Cannadine has found significance in the rediscovery of Waugh in Margaret Thatcher's England by "a small group of misogynist, High-Church Tories whose obscurantist resentment and parochial belliger-ence found ample echoes in the less attractive aspects of Waugh's work," as well as in the success of the television version of *Brideshead Revisited* in Ronald Reagan's United States.[13]

The fact is that Waugh's fiction and nonfiction reflect an acutely politi-cal temperament. Above all, as *Robbery under Law* demonstrates, Waugh was clearly attuned to the importance of politics in his age and the division between Left and Right in the modern political mind. *Robbery under Law* contains what is usually described as Waugh's "Conservative Manifesto," an articulate explanation of why he was a Conservative when he went to Mexico. Douglas Lane Patey has identified the tacit influence of "Boling-broke, Burke, Coleridge and Disraeli,"[14] but Waugh was not an ideologue in any real sense of the word. Indeed, Waugh was scathing about ideologues, and throughout life he declaimed against the distinction between compet-ing political ideologies—"the idiotic dichotomy between Left and Right" (*RuL* 254)—which he considered as "meaningless and as mischievous" as the "circus colours of the Byzantine Empire." In *Robbery under Law* Waugh imagined a conversation between two moderns anxious to size up a third party: "'How does so-and-so stand, Left or Right?' 'Well it's hard to say exactly.'" The third party cannot be placed on the political spectrum, its value undermined by categorical dualism, so he is denied any relevance according to the moderns' criteria: "Ah, sitting on the fence. No contem-porary significance" (*RuL* 265).

According to Patey, the key to understanding Waugh's politics, at least in the 1930s, is "his rejection of the conventional oppositions of Right and

Left, Fascist and Communist, which he viewed simply as alternative totali-tarianisms equally opposed to what he called 'individualism.'"[15] In George Orwell's words, Waugh found "nothing to choose between Communism and Fascism."[16] However, Waugh's political critique did more than question the language of modern political discourse; it also profoundly questioned the principles and objectives of modern political philosophy. *Robbery under Law* certainly reconsiders the ideology of Mexican political history in the language of modern politics: Waugh's intention was to demonstrate the extent to which modern political ideology actually confounded the real issues. Of the international reaction to the Mexican government's program of nationalization, he wrote:

> The Mexicans had a Left Book Club vocabulary. It so happened that the Mexican regime showed features which elsewhere would be damning: the government was autocratic; the autocrat was a General; there was only one political party; educational appointments were political and the teaching purely state-propagandist; history books were being edited on the lines of national self-assertion. . . ; but to the politically minded vocal minority, one thing was of paramount importance: when the Mexicans saluted their bosses they raised the arm with clenched fist, not with extended fingers. So they were all right. (*RuL* 80)

In this sense, *Robbery under Law* referred to an argument Waugh had raised in *Scoop* (1938) and would raise again in *Work Suspended*: the fruit-ful discussion of politics had been debased by canalized phrases with no real meaning. Yet it was not Waugh's principal objective to show the mis-chief in modern political discourse when he opened *Robbery under Law* with the unambiguous statement that it was going to be "a political book" (*RuL* 1). He was instead interested in something more fundamental. By 1939, Mexico had known "Napoleonic-masonic monarchy, liberal-repre-sentative democracy, German-enlightened-constitutional-monarchy, inter-national-individualist-capitalism, socialism, dictatorship of the proletariat, and [seemed likely to] develop a species of Hitlerism" (*RuL* 277–78). After all these varied experiences, Mexico offered an "object lesson" in the effect of attempts at progress through secular political means.

Waugh was writing at a time when political issues had assumed an overwhelming significance: the modern consciousness was a political con-sciousness. For Virginia Woolf, for example, it was impossible in the 1930s "not to be interested in politics; not to find public causes of much more pressing interest than philosophy. In 1930 young men . . . were forced to be aware of what was happening in Russia; in Germany; in Italy; in Spain.

They could not go on discussing aesthetic emotions and personal relations."[17] For Waugh, however, the decade's preoccupation with political
solutions was misconceived in a fundamental sense. Probably the most
significant point of Waugh's critique disclosed in the "Conservative Manifesto" is his view that forms of government were transient and did not,
from one variant to the next, have any real influence over the iniquities
inherent in the human condition. Waugh believed that humans' chances of
happiness were "more or less constant through the centuries, and generally
speaking, [were] not much affected by the political and economic conditions in which he live[d]." Accordingly, "there [was] no form of government
ordained from God as being better than any other" (*RuL* 16). In Waugh's
view, while good government was important, there was more to a successful society than redistributing wealth, maintaining territorial integrity, or
asserting national achievement. A society wishing to become a civilization
required philosophical, artistic, and, above all, spiritual vitality, the very
things that, Woolf declared, young men in the 1930s could not afford to be
concerned with. Waugh considered that incessant political agitation and the
crises that politics engendered were distractions from the full-time task of
defending the material and spiritual achievements of Western civilization
against the assaults of modern barbarians.

As did T. S. Eliot, Waugh found that proposals for secular renewal lacked
"respect for the needs of the individual soul."[18] Also like Eliot, Waugh believed that the only way to control political enthusiasm was to encourage "religious control and balance."[19] According to Eliot, the "only hopeful course
for a society that would thrive and continue its creative activity in the arts
of civilization [was] to become Christian";[20] according to Waugh in *Robbery under Law*, Mexico could revitalize its culture only by rediscovering
its Catholic origins. Most importantly, though, Waugh did not think vigor
could be achieved simply by reestablishing the hierarchy and reopening the
churches. These moves would have been another political solution, no more
effective than the installation as emperor in the 1860s of Archduke Maxi-
milian, who, according to Waugh, posed as a Catholic prince while breaking
the church's laws and doubting its teaching. Waugh was instead suggesting
that Mexican salvation required a program for renewal more fundamental
than politics: the restoration of "the people to a state of faith without which
no political programme had any value." The kind of government that would
be adopted was really a secondary issue: "a good people [would] evolve its
own political organization" (*RuL* 256). In *Robbery under Law,* Waugh was
effectively answering the question posed rhetorically by Eliot: is "our form
of government to be more important than our Christianity?"[21]

A number of considerations sustained Waugh's mistrust of political programs. As did a number of religiously guided writers, he thought that political ideas, unlike religious truths, were ephemeral and incapable of imparting any usefully enduring dogma. In *Black Mischief* (1932), he made the point that modern political reforms were essentially faddish and insubstantial:

> "You know, [said Basil Seal to the emperor Seth] we've got a much easier job now than we should have had fifty years ago. If we'd had to modernize a country then it would have meant constitutional monarchy, bi-cameral legislature, proportional representation, women's suffrage, independent judicature, freedom of the Press, referendums. . . ."
> "What's all that?" asked the Emperor.
> "Just a few ideas that have ceased to be modern." [22]

In *Robbery under Law*, Waugh elaborated on this point when he complained about the demise of the rule of law in modern government. In earlier times, according to Waugh, law had been the product of highly evolved traditions, and revealed wisdom and morality. Divorced from its divine foundations, application of the law was subject to capricious social experiment. Furthermore, it was "merely a formulation of the whims of the party in power . . . and lightly abandoned if it prove[d] unpopular." In modern politics, Waugh considered that "rulers [rose] to power largely on their promises to make new laws or repeal old ones" (*RuL* 85).

Waugh also disdained politicians and bureaucrats of any ideological hue and thought that the modern political machine promoted illusory or counterproductive freedoms while actually disenfranchising the individual, discouraging individual creativity, and cultivating mediocrity. Adam Fenwick-Symes falls victim to the state in *Vile Bodies* (1930) when an officious customs officer destroys his manuscript: "'Now just you wait while I look up these here *books*'—how he said it!—'in my list. Particularly against books the Home Secretary is. If we can't stamp out literature in the country, we can at least stop its being brought in from outside. That's what he said the other day in Parliament, and I says "Hear, hear."'"[23] Although his tone is less frivolous, Waugh conveys this feeling of individual impotence in the face of the state in *Robbery under Law* when he describes the plight of a friend whose property had been confiscated by the government. According to Waugh, his friend had been operating a successful and profitable plantation, employing local Indians and maintaining very good relations with them. At some point, a government official presented the owner with a forged petition indicating that his plantation was to be divided and given to a neighboring village. Waugh visited the confiscated estate with its former owner to discover that a tolerably prosperous venture had started to revert to waste and that the Indians who had been employed on the plantation now produced only a bare subsistence. Others had left their holdings and had drifted into town. In Waugh's view, wanton neglect results from maliciously misguided bureaucratic intervention and the intrusion of the state into the realm of productive labor.

Waugh belonged to a generation who experienced the state's assumption of responsibilities that went beyond the traditional role of maintaining the king's peace. In A. J. P. Taylor's words, "Until August 1914 a sensible, law-abiding Englishman could pass through his life and hardly notice the state."[24] The First World War changed all that, and Englishmen became, for the first time, active citizens whose lives—from working conditions to where and when they could travel, the potency of their beer, and what they could read—were shaped by what Waugh derided in *Brideshead Revisited* as a profusion of "humane legislation."[25] Of course Waugh agreed that government was necessary and believed that "men could not live together without rules." He believed that the rules should be "kept to the bare minimum of safety" (*RuL* 16)—safety, one presumes, for the development of individual talent and creativity. The state had, however, assumed the position in society that the church had once held. In *Robbery under Law*, he observes that in the sixteenth century talent was stultified by an obsession with theology, but "today we are plague-stricken by politics" (3). Given the state's inordinate influence over the individual in the twentieth century, the separation of church and state appeared to Waugh to be a specious benefit. According to Waugh, Western Europeans felt superior to Latin American republics for a number of reasons; in Latin America, for instance, education was a monopoly of the church. Waugh asked, "Which is sounder, the catechism, or the race-mythology taught in half the schools of Europe today?" (*RuL* 15).

Waugh proposed that civilization in Mexico had been destroyed by the country's obsession with politics. The Enlightenment's conception of society was humanistic and materialistic in that it valorized sociological and economic considerations over spiritual and emotional life. The modern age reflected these skewed priorities and believed in political solutions to human problems. Waugh considered that politics, "everywhere destructive, [had] dried up [Mexico], frozen it, cracked it and powdered it to dust" (*RuL* 3). Political strife had, in Waugh's view, severed Mexico from its traditions, especially its spiritual and ethical foundations. Secular politics, with its emphasis on "the power and weakness of great possessions,"[26] was, by its very nature, self-serving: if the highest goal humanity could conceive was the enjoyment of consumable goods, it was very easy to start "to accumulate the goods exclusively for oneself" (*RuL* 278). In *Scott-King's Modern Europe* (1947), Dr. Arturo Fe has entered politics as a business venture: "I am not a party man. You think because I wear the badge and give the salute I am of the New Neutralia. . . . I have six children, two of them girls of marriageable age. What can I do but seek one's fortune."[27] Waugh thought Mexico had declined because people lacked a sense of civic duty; instead, "rival politicians [were] appealing to the interests of rival groups." In Waugh's view, altruism, or morality, did "not flourish without religion."[28]

NOTES

1. T. S. Eliot, *Murder in the Cathedral* (1935; rep., London: Faber & Faber, 1938), 14.

2. See Christopher Sykes, *Evelyn Waugh* (1975; rep., Harmondsworth, UK: Penguin, 1977), 254.

3. Donat Gallagher, "The Mind of Evelyn Waugh: A Study of the Aspects of the Mind of Evelyn Waugh through his Non-Fiction" (PhD diss, James Cook University), 512ff.

4. Sykes, *Evelyn Waugh,* 259.

5. Evelyn Waugh, *Robbery under Law* (1939; rep., Pleasantville, NY: Akadine Press, 1999), 29. Hereafter cited as *RuL*.

6. Gallagher, "Evelyn Waugh," 512.

7. Evelyn Waugh, *When the Going Was Good* (Boston: Little, Brown, 1946), 9.

8. Evelyn Waugh, "Aspirations of a Mugwump," in *The Essays, Articles and Reviews of Evelyn Waugh*, ed. Donat Gallagher (London: Methuen, 1983), 537.

9. See Douglas Lane Patey, *The Life of Evelyn Waugh: A Critical Biography* (Oxford: Blackwell, 1998), 376 n. 1; Martin Stannard, *Evelyn Waugh: The Early Years 1903–1939* (London: Dent, 1986), 435; and Selina Hastings, *Evelyn Waugh: A Biography* (London: Sinclair-Stevenson, 1994), 100.

10. Donat Gallagher, ed., *The Essays, Articles and Reviews of Evelyn Waugh* (London: Methuen, 1983), 153ff.

11. C. Sparks, "Waugh and War," *Socialist Review*, March 1979, 22.

12. See Christopher Hitchens, "The Permanent Adolescent," *Atlantic Monthly,* May 2003, 107–16; see also Conor Cruise O'Brien, *Maria Cross: Imaginative Patterns in a Group of Catholic Writers* (1953; rep., London: Burns & Oates, 1963).

13. David Cannadine, "Stand Up and Sneer," *New York Times*, January 7, 1990, sec. 7, 11.

14. Patey, *Evelyn Waugh,* 167.

15. Ibid., 145.

16. See Humphrey Carpenter, *The Brideshead Generation: Evelyn Waugh and His Friends* (London: Weidenfeld & Nicolson, 1989), 390–91.

17. Virginia Woolf, "The Leaning Tower" (1940), in *Collected Essays,* vol. 2 (London: Hogarth, 1966), 172.

18. T. S. Eliot, "The Reformation of Society" (1939), in *Selected Prose*, ed. John Hayward (Harmondsworth, UK: Penguin, 1953), 210.

19. Ibid.

20. Ibid.

21. T. S. Eliot, "Church and State" (1939), in *Selected Prose*, 211.

22. Evelyn Waugh, *Black Mischief* (1932; rep., Harmondsworth, UK: Penguin, 1965), 128.

23. Evelyn Waugh, *Vile Bodies* (1930; rep., London: Compact Books, 1993), 25.

24. A. J. P. Taylor, *English History: 1914–1945* (1965; rep., Harmondsworth, UK: Penguin, 1981), 57.

25. Evelyn Waugh, *Brideshead Revisited* (1945; rep., Harmondsworth, UK: Penguin, 1962), 15.

26. Evelyn Waugh, *Saint Edmund Campion: Priest and Martyr* (1935; rep., Manchester, NH: Sophia Institute, 1996), 7–8.

27. Evelyn Waugh, *Work Suspended and Scott-King's Modern Europe* (Harmondsworth, UK: Penguin, 1951), 231.

28. Ibid., 278.

Homosexuality in *Brideshead Revisited:* "Something quite remote from anything the [builder] intended"

Peter G. Christensen

INTRODUCTION

OVER THE YEARS MANY GAY MEN HAVE FOUND *BRIDESHEAD REVISITED* (1945) A rewarding and moving book, while a number of influential critics have played down or otherwise disparaged the same-sex relationship between Sebastian and Charles, as if it were Waugh's intent either to show homosexual relations as immature or perverted or else to devalorize the love between two men as only a first step on the road to grace. Same-sex love does not survive or triumph in the novel, and Sebastian never overcomes his alcoholism, so it may seem as if the book is just another entry in the sad-fate-for-gays sweepstakes. If so, gay men would at best find reading the novel a masochistic pleasure or at worst another dramatization of their own persecution and marginalization.

Critics want to hold Waugh to a rigid view of Catholicism to which they seldom dream of submitting his contemporary Graham Greene. As a gay male reader, I believe that in *Brideshead* male same-sex love is treated by the Roman Catholic Waugh with dignity very different from Vatican orthodoxy, which conceives of all gay relationships as fundamentally disordered. The appearance of the professed Catholic John Boswell's groundbreaking *Christianity, Social Tolerance, and Homosexuality* (1980) and *Same-Sex Unions in Premodern Europe* (1994) led many gay Catholics to wonder whether there actually was a time when they were not denigrated and persecuted by the Roman Catholic hierarchy. *Brideshead Revisited* deserves reevaluation in the light of Boswell's challenge to the establishment.[1]

I try to account for the continuing appeal of *Brideshead Revisited* to gay readers, stressing that the novel treats homosexuality sympathetically instead of condemning it. A chief tension in the novel is the struggle between two Catholicisms, a stifling version and a more generous and *catholic* spirit. By the end of the novel, catholic spirit triumphs. I begin with the critical reception of the novel, continue with comments by Waugh relating to homosexuality, move to a reading of the novel that foregrounds gay elements of the plot and fills in ellipses in Charles's narrative, and conclude by contextualizing the novel in terms of gay spirituality and living gayness as a value.

CRITICAL RECEPTION

Unfortunately, many critics have failed to take the relationship of Sebastian and Charles and the role of homosexuality in the novel seriously. This trend is evident in criticism from 1958 to 1998. Frederick J. Stopp sets the pattern of seeing Sebastian not as a partner in a serious relationship with Charles but rather as a metaphysical aid to Charles, the hero: "Sebastian only partially wishing his actions, and not at all their end, has served the purpose for which he was summoned into the life of Charles Ryder."[2] Even worse, Sebastian "degenerates into alcoholism and homosexuality" in Marston LaFrance's reading.[3] Kurt Schlüter describes Charles's relationship with Sebastian as "Freundschaft" as compared to "Liebe" with Julia, yet he finds Sebastian incapable of sustaining a real friendship.[4] Harvey Curtis Webster ingenuously opines that "Ryder's long journey of faith starts when he meets and falls in love (not homosexually) with Sebastian."[5] Gene D. Phillips follows LaFrance and laments that Sebastian gradually "sinks into both dipsomania and homosexuality."[6] Calvin W. Lane writes off the picnic scene: "Although a homosexual idyll may be suggested by this passage, of greater significance is Sebastian's wish to escape to an idealized timeless world."[7] Jeffrey Heath claims that Sebastian is "pernicious when loved as an end in himself but valuable as an avenue to the divine."[8] For Ian Littlewood, Waugh approves of Cara's warning about the relationship between Charles and Sebastian, and Sebastian's view of life is so unrealistic as to "foster a state of mind that is infected."[9] In a peculiar turn of phrase, Jacqueline McDonnell states that "the child Cordelia loves [Sebastian], and so, after a fashion, does Charles."[10] Robert R. Garnett declares that Charles's "love for Sebastian had been naughty but schoolboyish."[11]

The tide begins to turn in the 1990s, albeit with reservations. For Robert Murray Davis, the relationship of Charles with Sebastian returns to "nursery innocence."[12] In Katharyn W. Crabbe's words, the relationship is simply a "friendship,"[13] but in Annette Wirth's view, it "transcends sexuality."[14] Evelyn Toynton writes that Charles Ryder's "(asexual) love for Sebastian at Oxford has provided all the major revelations of his youth."[15] I am not saying that every single critic of this often analyzed novel denies a homosexual relationship to Charles and Sebastian, but critics have marginalized its importance, often by denouncing it, deeroticizing it, or infantilizing it.

The articles exchanged by David Bittner and John W. Osborne in the *Evelyn Waugh Newsletter* between 1987 and 1990 finally called more attention to same-sex attraction. Bittner claimed it had been imposed on the text, but Osborne felt it was clearly implied.[16] Writing in 1994 in *Ariel*, David Leon Higdon declared that *pace* Bittner, "it is impossible to regard Sebastian as other than gay; that Charles is so homoerotic he must at least be considered cheerful, and that Bittner's [response to Osborne's 1989 essay]—and others like it—is a representative skirmish in a much larger and more important sexual war being fought as entrenched heterosexuality strives to maintain its hegemony over important twentieth-century works."[17] Higdon maintained that Osborne as well as Bittner took a patronizing view of homosexuality and that a refusal to face homophobic assumptions led to misreadings of the text by many critics.[18] Higdon stated that the relationship between Sebastian and Charles was "homosexual, though perhaps not sexually active,"[19] a position with which I agree. However, he also claimed that for Waugh, "Charles's and Sebastian's mutual love is enticingly seductive, but thematically appears the most corrupted and the most distant from Waugh's God."[20] I do not share this assessment of "corrupted" love: it does not seem corrupt at all.

Since Higdon's article, the theme of homosexuality in *Brideshead Revisited* can be faced more squarely. To do so requires rejecting Charles as a reliable narrator. Some critics have not found Charles an appealing character. Robert Murray Davis wrote that Charles as "narrator is sometimes uncharitable and often unpleasant" and that he "refuses to criticize his own past,"[21] while Jean-Louis Chevalier called Charles "a *fides* [*sic*] *Achates* and Peeping Tom by turns."[22] In addition, Charles leaves sizable gaps in describing his feelings for Sebastian, forcing one to wonder whether a more complete narrative would reveal Charles in a bad light.

Frederick L. Beaty argued in *The Ironic World of Evelyn Waugh* that Sebastian is a figure who helps Charles and turns out to be a type of Good Samaritan.[23] This claim counters many earlier critics, who saw Sebastian as a danger to Charles. Ironically, Beaty's generous reading of Sebastian's character was not developed out of a gay perspective, while Higdon's gay reading maintained the accepted view that Sebastian was low in Waugh's esteem. When he compared *Brideshead Revisited* with E. M. Forster's *Maurice*, D. H. Lawrence's *Lady Chatterley's Lover*, and David Storey's *Radcliffe*, Roberto A. Valdeón-García found Waugh's novel less radical and important than Forster's, since Valdeón-García did not analyze religious themes with respect to homosexuality.[24] His reading overvalorizes Forster's concern with freeing middle-class gay men from British prudery so that they can sleep with noneffete, rougher men.

Finally, in a 1999 comparison of *Brideshead Revisited* and Yukio Mishima's *Confessions of a Mask*, John Howard Wilson portrayed Charles as both unreliable and unpleasant. Wilson suggested that Charles was sadistic and treated his wife and Sebastian cruelly. In Wilson's view, Charles's behavior made sense if he were a repressed gay man not doing well at converting to heterosexuality and glad that Celia had been unfaithful. As in the interpretation of Beaty, Sebastian is more sinned against than sinning. In Wilson's evaluation, Charles is latently homosexual throughout the novel.[25] This is not the position I take, for I believe that Charles's homosexual relationship with Sebastian was the only one in his life. Indeed, a major conflict in the novel arises from the fact that Sebastian is gay and Charles is not. Thus I depart from the long line of critics who desexualize the relationship and the minority who find Charles gay or latently so. Sebastian is an exceptionally appealing person, and Charles's love for him is a unique experience.

In "Romantic Friendship, Homosexuality, and Evelyn Waugh's *Brideshead Revisited*," Tison Pugh in 2001 cited Bittner and Higdon on homosexuality in the novel. In response to their opposed positions, he wrote that "the polarized consideration of hetero- and homosexuality in *Brideshead Revisited* is too reductive a formula to fit the subtleties and shades of meaning in the text."[26] Although this statement was fair, it minimized the number of years before critics even considered the issue and began to apprehend its subtleties. Pugh claimed that Charles and Sebastian have a "romantic friendship" of the kind "common in the segregated societies of the nineteenth and early twentieth centuries in such institutions as all-male and all-female colleges and boarding houses."[27] Many critics would agree with this evaluation, though it was restated in gay-friendly terms. Pugh chided readers for wanting to know about Charles and Sebastian's activities and identities and for interpreting their norm-resistant "queer desire" as "gay" to suit current gay-male-liberation identity politics. He recognized that through his novel Waugh admirably breaks down straight and gay as binary categories.[28] Thus, Waugh's refusal to name same-sex desire and to "out" characters as "homosexuals" once looked like a problem of clarity in the novel, but it can now be recognized as a major virtue. Many queer critics, who stress mismatches in sex, gender, and desire, insist that same-sex attraction falls prey to reductionism when it is labeled, while gay critics are emotionally invested in identity politics for men professing same-sex attraction.[29]

Although I agree with Pugh's desire to avoid reductive classifications, I do not similarly conclude that "both the same-sex and the heterosexual relationship prove meaningless to Charles as he finds himself without a sexual partner but with God."[30] Also, Pugh does not perceive that much of the intensity of the novel results from the young men's markedly different positions: Sebastian is oriented toward men, whereas Charles is not, except in the case of Sebastian. Arguing that we should avoid binaries and the terms *gay* and *straight*, Pugh lumps the protagonists together. In my view, more attention has to be paid to their lives as a whole: their behavior shows that this binary (gay/straight) actually exists, though we may wish to avoid categories.

To understand Charles's understated narration, we should also reevaluate Charles's sexuality in relation to "homosexual panic" as explained by Eve Kosofsky Sedgwick.[31] "Homosexual panic" results from the pressure on all men, whatever their sexual orientation, to avoid expressing feelings and making gestures that might be interpreted as homosexual. Society arbitrarily divides men's acceptable behavior from unacceptable behavior, and these lines can shift at any time, leaving a man suddenly labeled homosexual. To escape from this conundrum, one has to be completely open about being gay or leave the society altogether. Sebastian opts out of this world of "homosexual panic," removes himself from a policed society, and goes to Morocco to live more freely. In London, in contrast, Charles dislikes the "pansy bar,"[32] a classic site for homosexual panic. Pugh sees a narrative style that avoids simplistic labels, but Charles's narration is also panicky, given his inadequate attempt to help Sebastian fend off breakdown and alcoholism.

WAUGH'S COMMENTS

In "Fan-Fare," Waugh's April 8, 1946 article in *Life*, readers will not be able to find any declared intention regarding the relationship of Sebastian and Charles. Waugh speaks in traditional terms of having "little control" over characters: "I start them off with certain preconceived notions of what they will do and say in certain circumstances but I constantly find them moving another way."[33] More pointedly, at the beginning of *The Ordeal of Gilbert*

Pinfold (1957), the narrator recognizes that he cannot control the reception of his books: "Mr. Pinfold gave nothing away. Not that he was secretive or grudging by nature; he had nothing to give these students. He regarded his books as objects which he had made, things quite external to himself to be used and judged by others."[34] In the preface to the revised edition of *Brideshead Revisited*, Waugh expressed certain intentions, such as desire to show the operation of divine grace, and bypassed other intentions, such as the depiction of homosexuality.[35] We will consider *Brideshead Revisited* as "external" to the Pinfold-like author.

Authors may not be the most accurate or truthful interpreters of their own work. Jeffrey Heath, after giving an excellent overview of critics' very diverse positions on the novel's themes,[36] shows that Waugh's memorandum on filming *Brideshead* "does not square with a careful reading of the novel." Heath implies that we should interpret the text on the basis of what it says, not of what Waugh said about it. In the memorandum, Waugh briefly mentions Charles's "romantic affection" for Sebastian,[37] and if one is looking for authorial intent, one cannot expect anything more specific, since Waugh was aware of Hollywood censorship, as when he notes that Anthony Blanche's character will have to face "considerable modifications."[38]

Waugh's reviews of novels by other writers provide relevant information. In the *Sunday Times* of June 10, 1936, under the title "A Story with a Moral," Waugh reviewed Compton Mackenzie's *Thin Ice*, a novel about a homosexual politician. In Waugh's words, the story is "the deterioration of a human character," and the politician's profile in English society is totally different from Sebastian's. Waugh claims that "there is a radical difference between heterosexual and homosexual relationships" and that "'normality' is certainly an almost meaningless expression," since the "absolute norm is an abstraction from which all men vary in greater or less degree."[39] Waugh seems more interested in praising realistic characterization than in making statements about homosexuality.

Homosexuality is frankly discussed by Waugh in the chapter on his Oxford years in his autobiography, *A Little Learning* (1964). He notes that the Hypocrites' Club had members known for "flamboyance of dress and manner which was in some cases patently homosexual."[40] He recalls the "strikingly handsome 'hearty' for whom Harold [Acton] conceived a romantic attraction" (*ALL* 198). He also mentions Brian Howard, "an incorrigible homosexual, subject to a succession of delusions . . . who died by suicide at the time when he at last became rich" (*ALL* 205). As for his own life, Waugh writes that he "loved [Richard Pares] dearly, but an excess of wine nauseated him and this made an insurmountable barrier between us" (*ALL* 191–92). Waugh conceals the name of Pares's "successor as the friend of my heart," the undergraduate whom he calls "Hamish Lennox" (*ALL* 192). As Martin Stannard notes in his biography of Waugh, the real name of Waugh's beloved was Alastair Graham.[41] These reflections on Oxford are mixed with memories of drinking, which Waugh compares and contrasts with those of Sebastian and Charles in *Brideshead Revisited* (*ALL* 191). In another link with *Brideshead*, Waugh mentions that Hamish's mother "made friends with me as a link with her wayward son and constantly appealed to me to mediate between them; always without effect" (*ALL* 193).

Brideshead Revisited: A Reading

Brideshead Revisited should join other first-person novels told by narrators who do not reveal everything about male same-sex attraction, such as Gide's *L'Immoraliste* and Marguerite Yourcenar's *Le Coup de grâce*. Waugh creates a complicated retrospective narration with the past filtered through new knowledge granted to Charles. Charles avoids specific details about his relationship with Sebastian because they never discussed its essence. If it had been verbally explored, the fragile nature of love between a gay man and a straight man would have been exposed and undermined. However, neither wished to risk calling a spade a spade, and their strategy worked for a while but, not surprisingly, failed in a crisis.

Charles deflects the issue of openness with Sebastian by discussing maturity in generalized terms. Charles believes that prolonged adolescent indulgence promotes maturity in its proper time. We wonder how Charles experienced events as they were actually happening, for he recalls his time with Sebastian through a thick, romantic glaze: "Looking back, now, after twenty years, there is little I would have left undone or done otherwise. I could match my cousin Jasper's game-cock maturity with a sturdier fowl. I could tell him that all the wickedness of that time was like the spirit they mix with the pure grape of the Douro, heady stuff full of dark ingredients; it at once enriched and retarded the whole process of adolescence as the spirit checks the fermentation of the wine, renders it undrinkable, so that it must lie in the dark, year in, year out, until it is brought up at last fit for the table" (*BR* 45). This description is so metaphoric and aesthetic that it makes one wonder what deeds are being remembered. Charles is more concerned with creating an effect than telling what actually happened. Each reader is compelled to put together a coherent narrative based on suggestion. When we accept what Charles tells us, we face the stalemate that has afflicted *Brideshead*'s reception: some find it inhuman, cold, or snobbish, while others find it mature, good-hearted, and consoling.[42] Once we learn to read around Charles, particularly Charles's interpretation of Sebastian, we can create more dialogue between the two factions.

Even recent gay critics have failed to see through Charles's metaphors and recognize the opening scenario. Sebastian is a young gay man who falls in love with Charles, who, Sebastian knows, is straight. Their lives and emotional inclinations reveal the situation, so the end of the affair is inevitable, although Charles does not want to admit it. When called before Lady Marchmain, Charles thinks, "It was impossible for me to explain to her what I only half understood myself" (*BR* 136). As Sebastian drinks more and more, Charles thinks: "He did not fail in his love, but he lost his joy of it, for I was no longer part of his solitude. As my intimacy with his family grew I became part of the world which he sought to escape; I became one of the bonds which held him" (*BR* 127–28). Charles does not make the connection between Sebastian's love and his solitude. He phrases the sentence so that he does not have to tell us to whom this love is directed. Actually Sebastian does not fail in his love for Charles, but Charles escapes from Sebastian's "solitude," his feeling of isolation as a young gay man. Charles's intimacy with the family indicates ability to move successfully in the straight world.

Charles is blind to the fact that Sebastian is gay and he is not, but their difference is expressed symbolically:

> Julia used to say, "Poor Sebastian. It's something chemical in him."
> That was the cant phrase of the time, derived from heaven knows what misconception of popular science. "There's something chemical between them" was used to explain the overmastering hate or love of any two people. It was the old concept of determinism in a new form. I did not believe that there was anything chemical in my friend. (*BR* 129)

Charles never explains Julia's reference to "it." She could be referring to Sebastian's drinking or to alcoholism as a disease. Charles fails to realize that there once was something "chemical" between Sebastian and him, but he also fails to see that there is something chemical in Sebastian, namely, that he is gay by nature, whereas Charles is not.

When Charles decides to go to art school in Paris after his second year at Oxford, there is no indication that he has consulted Sebastian (*BR* 146). Charles was in love with Sebastian, the only time in his life that he has had a same-sex attraction. Having undergone the "hard bachelordom of English adolescence" (*BR* 44), Charles is attracted to Julia even when he is most interested in Sebastian. She is "especially female," and he catches her "thin bat's squeak of sexuality" in late summer 1923 (*BR* 76). Fifteen years later, he thinks that Sebastian "was with me daily in Julia; or rather it was Julia I had known in him, in those distant Arcadian days" (*BR* 303).

Sebastian does not articulate his feelings for Charles, as his letter, ending "Love or what you will," indicates (*BR* 73). When they first get to know each other, Sebastian hopes he "was mysterious about everything" (*BR* 39), and he writes in a style of "remote fantasy" (*BR* 43). Sebastian demonstrates the old saw that homosexuality is acceptable when veiled with aristocratic eccentricity. When he hurts his foot, he hobbles in a "pantomime of difficulty" (*BR* 80). Other characters share this desire to conceal their real selves: Anthony Blanche has a "self-taught stammer" (*BR* 32), Mr. Ryder affects a "shuffling mandarin-tread" (*BR* 63), Lord Marchmain exudes "normality" that is "studied" (*BR* 97), Bridey's face is a "rock-crystal mask" (*BR* 131), and Mr. Samgrass engages not only in "bluffing but cheating" (*BR* 151). Following the stereotype of British men, these characters do not reveal emotions to others, and they create an aura that conceals sexuality.

The novel obliquely presents Sebastian's beginning to understand his own sexuality through his relationship with Charles. Sebastian finds out that he is same-sex oriented, but Charles is not. As Sebastian becomes more aware of their difference, he feels more desperate. When Sebastian reads in the *News of the World* about "another naughty scout-master," he seems to be prodding Charles for some comment on what appears to be a sexual encounter, but he gets none. Charles is certainly understating the case when he begins "to realize how little I really knew of Sebastian, and to understand why he had always sought to keep me apart from the rest of his life" (*BR* 94). Charles assumes that his own relationship with Sebastian is stable, unlike Sebastian's relationship with his family.

Rather than examining their friendship, Charles refers to the "anarchy" that he shared with Sebastian (*BR* 44, 107), but this term hardly explains their experiences. Fear of wrecking their relationship prevents them from discussing their sexuality. Instead, they live intensely in the present, as there will be no future together. If Charles were to face this fact, he would have to admit that he was stringing Sebastian along, whether he wanted to or not.

Martin Stannard describes the close relationships of gay and straight men at Oxford:

It is too easy in an age of Gay Liberation to misinterpret the male domain
that Oxford represented in the `twenties. "Homosexual" friendships were
the norm because women were rarely admitted to the life of the University. . . . An unembarrassed delight existed in the exclusiveness of male
company and, inevitably, intimate friendships developed. Among Waugh's
Oxford acquaintances there were, of course, men who were and remained
homosexual in the full sense that the word now implies—including [Brian]
Howard and [Robert] Byron. And Waugh undoubtedly moved further towards this more fantastic world of extroverts and "prancers" in his last
year. But there is every reason to suppose that his relationship with Pares
was idyllically platonic.[43]

Harold Acton suggested that the love between Waugh and Pares was platonic, and Stannard also underplays its sexual nature. Waugh described
Pares as "my first homosexual love" in a letter to Nancy Mitford of December 18, 1954.[44] Stannard's portrayal of Oxford squares with Charles's
description of the "rabble of womankind" during Eights Week (*BR* 21).
Charles, at age nineteen and "completely ignorant of women" (*BR* 100), is
not fundamentally gay, but Sebastian is. Gay and straight men mixed at the
university and formed temporary but deep emotional liaisons.

Charles is ready for love because, living with his sarcastic and cruel father, he has been deprived of affection. Like Lord Marchmain, Mr. Ryder is
a bad role model for his son. A widower, he has been damaged by the death
of his wife and provides another example of dysfunctional heterosexuality. Charles gladly leaves his father to attend Sebastian, who has hurt his
foot. Mr. Ryder, who could not care less about his son's sexual orientation,
describes Sebastian as that "very good-looking friend of yours" (*BR* 146),
perhaps to see whether he can provoke anger with vague innuendo. The
most bittersweet moment of the young men's relationship occurs when
Charles goes to the injured Sebastian.

Sebastian begins to depend on his straight friend, who has to extricate
himself from their relationship. Charles writes, "It is thus I like to remember Sebastian, as he was that summer, when we wandered alone together
through that enchanted palace" (*BR* 79–80). The palace was enchanted, not
just because they were able "to cut the muscat grapes and choose orchids
for our buttonholes" (*BR* 80), but also because they were in love. Charles
is psychologically inclined to fall in love with Sebastian because he needs
to escape from his father. Before Sebastian hurt his foot, he sent a letter to
Charles, indicating that he would soon travel to his father in Venice. His
escape from Mr. Ryder and Bayswater blocked, Charles confesses, "For
days after that I thought I hated Sebastian" (*BR* 73).

Charles develops a conception of youth that shields him from having failed Sebastian. Everything can be recaptured or redeemed, he claims, except "the languor of Youth—how unique and quintessential it is! How quickly, how irrevocably, lost! The zest, the generous affections, the illusions, the despair, all the traditional attributes of Youth—all save this— come and go with us through life; again and again in riper years we experience, under a new stimulus, what we thought had been finally left behind, the authentic impulse to action, the renewal of power and its concentration on a new object; again and again a new truth is revealed to us in whose light all our previous knowledge must be rearranged" (*BR* 79). Once he has fallen in love with Julia, Charles believes that Sebastian has pointed the way to her. His meditation is very self-centered, and he does not have to think about the consequences of his actions on the way to maturity.

Not surprisingly, Sebastian starts to suffer emotionally when he realizes that he will lose Charles. He is bound to do so because of their different sexual orientations, but this incompatibility has not been discussed by critics, who have focused on Sebastian's anger when Charles is drawn into Lady Marchmain's orbit. Sebastian knows that there are laws against male homosexuality in the United Kingdom, that men are arrested for soliciting, and that once past the freedom of Oxford, it will be hard to find a boyfriend except through the bar culture. He will be leaving the university that blended eccentricity and homosexuality. Even at Oxford, the site of the gay Hellenic revival of Pater and Wilde, Sebastian remains a sincere Catholic and never uses philosophical arguments to defend his feelings.[45] He does not have the intellect or the bravery of Quentin Crisp. If Sebastian is indeed in love with his childhood, as Cara claims, he has good reason to be, since he realizes that life will be hard for a gay man in Great Britain. Cara reminds Charles that she saved Lord Marchmain from alcoholism (*BR* 103), but Charles is too immature and selfish to realize that he should pay more attention to her pointed warning about Sebastian: "He will be a drunkard if someone does not come to stop him" (*BR* 103).

Insisting that Sebastian wants to be left alone, Charles ignores Sebastian's anxiety over the end of their relationship. Charles "had no mind then for anything except Sebastian, and I saw him already as being threatened, though I did not yet know how black was the threat" (*BR* 127). Unfortunately, Charles's single-mindedness does not permit frank discussion of their relationship. Again, Charles retreats into metaphor and describes Sebastian as a Polynesian hiding from the "big ship [that] dropped anchor beyond the coral reef" and a hunted deer (*BR* 127), disturbed solitaries rather than someone seeking love.

Although critics usually view Lady Marchmain as oblivious to homosexuality, she knows that Sebastian is in love with Charles: she tells him
that "Sebastian loves you" (*BR* 136) and that "Sebastian is fonder of you
than of any of us" (*BR* 137). She wants Charles to prevent Sebastian from
becoming alcoholic. She tries to discover Charles's sexuality through long
conversations and his response to her brothers, killed in the Great War.
Never really sure, Lady Marchmain decides to accept him for her son,
hoping that Charles can prevent Sebastian from becoming a pathetic case
like Lord Marchmain, who is vacuous and selfish. She does not ask Charles
about the nature of their relationship, but it would be difficult for even a
close friend to do so. Meanwhile, she asks Mr. Samgrass to spy on them,
suspecting that Samgrass's sexual orientation should help, especially when
he takes Sebastian on a grand tour of the less inhibited Levant. Samgrass
may be presumed gay because he describes Proust's seedy Baron de Char-
lus as "incomparable" (124), a ticket of intimacy between gay men. To
assume that Samgrass is straight is to assume that people are heterosexual
unless they can be proved otherwise.

Although he represents himself as protecting Charles from Sebastian
and the rest of the Flytes, Anthony Blanche is actually looking out for his
old school friend by evaluating the artistically gifted Charles. When he
invites Charles to dinner, Anthony tries to find out how trustworthy he is.
Anthony makes up many outlandish tales about the Flytes to see whether
Charles will carry these stories back to Sebastian. In one example, Anthony depicts Lady Marchmain as a vampire who has sucked Sir Adrian
Porson dry (*BR* 56). Anthony makes a halfhearted come-on to Charles,
asking him to join the circle around Cocteau, who, thanks to Anthony, is
all "agog" about Charles (*BR* 52). To make his proposition less obvious, he
magnifies his relationship with Stefanie de Vincennes into a grand amour
(*BR* 52–53), although later Sebastian deflates their intimacy.

Sebastian has obvious intellectual failings, so Charles appeals to Anthony.
Charm is a word Anthony uses half a dozen times to describe the Flytes,
reinforcing Sebastian's statement that his family has dangerous "charm" (*BR*
37). Anthony suspects that Charles is a social climber who takes cues from
the charming Flytes: Charles despises the taste of Rex Mottram, though Rex
pays for dinner in Paris (*BR* 175). During the General Strike in 1926, Anthony claims that Charles "threw over" Sebastian (*BR* 203), a shrewd evaluation. In the Blue Grotto Club, Anthony calls Charles's pictures "charming,"
not once but three times (*BR* 271–73). Since he has been with Celia and
Julia, Charles has declined as an artist. Anthony takes him to the "pansy
bar" (*BR* 273), where they meet a boy engaged in blatant "gold-digging" (*BR*

271). Charles recognizes that he too has been a gold digger, prostituting his talents in his career as a painter. Charles is not even latently homosexual, so he has no sympathy for Anthony Blanche and his friends; nor is he given to sociological reflection about gay bars as gold mines.

Charles avoids reflections that are too troubling. When Sebastian accuses him of taking his family's side at Easter 1924, Charles claims that he "said more than I can bear to remember" (*BR* 134), and the reader has to assemble a story from this self-serving black hole of memory. Charles admits that with Lady Marchmain, "Everything was left unsaid" (*BR* 128), but he still feels that he understands her and that she wants to "suborn" him (*BR* 138). She is generous to say that only Charles can save Sebastian (*BR* 137), and when she mentions Sebastian's being "ashamed" of something, she may be referring to his homosexuality.

Lady Marchmain is usually blamed for Sebastian's increasing problem with alcohol, but Charles also contributes. When Lady Marchmain confronts Charles about funding Sebastian's drinking during the hunt in December 1924, she realizes that Charles has failed Sebastian. Although Charles initially refused to lend any money (*BR* 157) and then gave Sebastian only a pound note (*BR* 159), he blames Lady Marchmain for Sebastian's disgrace. Creating an aggrandized and noble role for himself in this debacle, he spites her, his hostess, though there was little chance of his loan's saving Sebastian from a family argument. He does admit weeks later that he let Sebastian "go without comfort" (*BR* 142), but he seems to be admitting guilt for only one incident while never expressing a clear view of the end of the whole relationship. Once Sebastian's love has given Charles what he needs, escape from his father and his prim, dull world, he abandons Sebastian to his fate. Sebastian goes abroad, but Charles does nothing to keep in touch.

When he goes to Morocco, Charles dismisses Sebastian's love for the repellent Kurt. Charles prefers a policy of "don't ask and don't tell," so that he does not have to try to understand the nature of Kurt and Sebastian's relationship, whether it is mutually strengthening or alcoholic codependency. If the latter, Charles may have contributed to codependent behavior in Sebastian. The monk does not realize that Sebastian and Kurt are more than friends, so Charles calls him a "poor booby" (*BR* 214). Charles tells the obtuse Bridey that Kurt and Sebastian are two waifs fallen together. Too shallow to see love in others, Charles nevertheless protects Sebastian's allowance, sensing that Bridey would not want to support a homosexual relationship. After Lady Marchmain's death, the only member of the family who understands and loves Sebastian is Cordelia.

Charles, for want of anything better to do, marries Celia when she asks him. He has only vague interest in his two children. Consequently, Charles falls head over heels in love with Julia when he meets her again by chance on the ocean liner. Julia has left Rex, who was morally and spiritually not all there, but Rex, in his vacuity, shows the stupidity of dogmatic, catechizing Catholicism. As he has sex with Julia, Charles is excited by the thought of possessing a woman, of making her emotionally "his," as Celia, apparently, was not. He states not only that he "took formal possession of her as her lover" but also that "the act of possession was a symbol, a rite of ancient origin and solemn meaning" (*BR* 261). With each woman, Charles falls into a dreary heterosexual pattern nurtured by the society around him. There is no comparable symbol and rite for a man who "possesses another man": men are not supposed to be possessed. Given their health problems, including Kurt's "secondary syphilis" (*BR* 213), Sebastian and Kurt probably do not possess each other and are far better off. They are more open about needing each other than Charles was with Sebastian. Need is not possession.

To Charles, Sebastian was the forerunner (like John the Baptist) who introduced him to Catholicism. Nevertheless, in his years with Julia, Charles seems to make no intellectual or emotional advances and resists Christianity until Lord Marchmain's death. Julia, a woman, does not lead him to religious faith. Instead, the old man's deathbed conversion, orchestrated by Father Mackay, man to man, leads Charles to God. The celibate man, the priest, achieves more than Julia's love and speech about sin.

When Sebastian tries to save Kurt, the man he loves, he blends homosexuality and Christian spirit, and he is rewarded by being accepted by the monks' community. The monks may have more gay men than any other community Sebastian has known since Oxford, though there are also European gay men in Morocco, fleeing potential jail sentences or blackmail. Sebastian ends his life in a community of men, a major consolation for a gay man, although mainstream criticism has considered being with men at best a consolation prize for Sebastian. Charles does not like the men around him in the army, and that is not surprising, because he is fixed on his loss of Julia, and he cannot benefit from the affection of men at arms in wartime.

In Cordelia's intelligent assessment, Sebastian's life is pathetic because he lacks will in its most profound sense, but Charles's is even more pathetic. Distancing himself from a community of well-meaning men at a time of crisis, he can only relive his heterosexual despair at being "homeless, childless, middle-aged, loveless" (*BR* 350). As Cordelia observed, just before the war, six years of Sebastian taught Kurt more than a year of Hitler. Homosexuality exposes the horror of Nazi ideology: Kurt has been given a pink triangle and reduced to slave labor in a concentration camp, but if he had been straight, he might have tolerated the Third Reich. Sebastian was happy in North Africa, away from homophobic England, but he hunted for Kurt after they had gone to visit Greece. Sebastian lacks dignity and the power of will, and Cordelia expresses the key that haunts the novel: no one is ever holy without suffering (*BR* 307).

When Lord Marchmain dies, Julia realizes that she has to leave Charles because being with him is incompatible with her relationship with God. As her last speech makes clear, the separation is prompted not by the Roman Catholic prohibition of divorce and remarriage but by her finding the proper place for God. As do Cordelia, Charles, and Sebastian, Julia ends up single, and her resolution to part from Charles underlines the novel's neglected message of how little we are to value heterosexual pairings and the fetishism of procreative marriage, at the heart of Catholic persecution of gay people. Beryl, who judges Julia by feelings, not dogma, will also be happy in a marriage to Bridey that will not bring any children into the world, though she does have three children by her first marriage.

Fortunately, military service gives Charles a chance to fight on God's side even though he could not care less about the men around him. He does not read the homoerotic poets of the First World War, Wilfred Owen and Siegfried Sassoon, and live in communion with brave lads like Lady Marchmain's three brothers. Despite its squalid state, Brideshead transcends deterioration, as we understand from the beaten-copper lamp "burning anew among the old stones" (*BR* 351), when Charles revisits the chapel in the Second World War. As a base for British soldiers in their efforts against the Nazis, Brideshead takes part in the war against godless fascism and persecution, including the killing of gay men. The lamp reminds Charles of the Christian triumph over the Muslims and the creation of a Frankish kingdom, including Acre and Jerusalem, during the First Crusade. However, Charles is casting an unduly romantic light on Crusader knights, probably as a result of falling out of love with the army, since there is nothing glamorous about everyday duties as a serviceman in the war.

Unable to overcome his own snobbery toward common men like Hooper, Charles has not been liberated as Sebastian has. Downward social mobility enables Sebastian to die among men who serve God. Sebastian, as do the monks, renounces wealth. He is far less materialistic than Charles, who gets caught up in country-house living. Before fighting the Nazis, Charles does not do anything more important than Sebastian does, one of the chief ironies of the book. Charles throws away his talent for painting. Failing to heed Anthony Blanche, he has no Diaghilev to command "Astonish me!"

Unlike Cocteau, a bête noir of Waugh's mentioned twice in the novel, Charles had no Raymond Radiguet to be his muse. Cocteau's years with Radiguet correspond almost exactly with Charles's period with Sebastian. Arguably, Waugh respects Sebastian much more than he does Charles, and generous Catholicism wins over mean-spirited Catholicism, most apparent in the novel when marriage is a consideration.

First, Bridey marries Beryl, who is too old to have any more children. Simply having children is not the justification of marriage.[46] Second, Cara never marries Lord Marchmain, but she behaves like a good wife. She perceives that he is bonded to her not by love, but by hatred and fear of his legal wife. Facing his death, Cara acts with dignity even if she does not know much about religion. Her relationship with Lord Marchmain is no less sinful after Lady Marchmain dies. Third, Rex has forgotten his first wife, so discussing an annulment seems silly. His wife is less important than his mistress, Brenda Champion, who is not an impediment to marriage. Fourth, Cordelia, the most admirable character in the novel, never marries but rather leads a life of service. She sees what remains viable and decent in Sebastian's partially wrecked life. Finally, Lady Marchmain, a well-meaning person, gains nothing by remaining legally bound to a man who hates her. Her marriage is a formality and an empty shell.

When Julia gives her monologue by the fountain and expresses her guilt over "*Living in sin*, with sin, by sin, for sin, every hour, every day, year in, year out" (*BR* 287), she is hysterical, as she succumbs to self-loathing that Catholic teaching instills in people in committed relationships not approved by the hierarchy. This misguided morality is a prime example of mean-spirited Catholicism, which competes with the more generous version in *Brideshead*. Gay people perhaps even more than straight people have suffered from the special opprobrium accorded to "living in sin." According to this perverse idea, a mutually enriching relationship over a long period is a much greater sin than a string of degrading one-night stands. Legions of gay Christians endure this stigma, and Julia applies it to her adulterous relationship with Charles, though it would be absurd to go back to their marriages.

Lord Marchmain's rambling review of generations of Flytes is not profound, and Waugh considered deleting it. When Lord Marchmain says that "Julia's son will be called by the name his fathers bore before the fat days," he means that the barony will continue through a child of Julia's, though the family will lose their more impressive titles (*BR* 332). Images of farm life, such as "swelling fruit and surfeited bees," suggest fertility and procreation, in which gay men have little emotional investment. Continuation of a family is perhaps more important than titles of nobility, since inheritance cannot make a person perform a noble deed.

Sebastian does not attend his father's funeral, but the gospels show that the community doing the work of God is more important than the family and that the dead should bury the dead. As does Christ (with his elusive sexuality), Sebastian lives as a member of a small group of men, even though he has a family. As the gospels do, *Brideshead Revisited* questions the value of the traditional family. Thus the novel appeals to gay men: its Catholicism is not the Vatican's well-publicized hatred of gay people.

CONTEXTUALIZATION

Waugh's mix of Catholicism and homosexuality probably makes the novel more topical now than at any other period since its appearance, considering that homosexuality is tearing Christian churches apart. Gay men generally have strong opinions about the Roman Catholic Church. Ellis Hanson stresses the fascination of gay men with Catholicism. In *Decadence and Catholicism* (1997), he claims that *Brideshead Revisited* belongs to the genre of the gay Catholic decadent novel. The novel has a leading character, Sebastian, who, at university age, went to the Levant, and as a gay alcoholic expatriate lived in the Maghreb. Oscar Wilde, André Gide, and Paul and Jane Bowles made Fez and Marrakech famous as escapes for gay men. Hanson sees Waugh in transition from the "mystical and witty" in fin-de-siècle decadent Catholic writing[47] to the "doctrinal and dour" in modernist Catholic writing:

> By the 1920s the notion of Anglo and Roman Catholicism as a magnet for homosexuals had passed from a running joke to a simple fact. Radclyffe Hall, herself a lesbian and a convert to Rome, is positively solemn in her 1928 novel *The Well of Loneliness*. This book, the first great lesbian novel, is rich in Christian imagery, culminating in what appears to be a rhetorical question: "And what of that curious craving for religion which so often went hand in hand with inversion?" In the following decade, in Evelyn Waugh's novel *Brideshead Revisited*, Charles Ryder is warned to stay away from Anglo-Catholics, since they are invariably sodomites.[48]

Hanson notes that "it is interesting to examine Waugh's conversion to Rome in light of his own anxious fascination with homosexuality." For Hanson, Waugh's "novel may be seen as a modernist classic of decadent Catholicism, with its homoerotic saga of a decaying aristocratic family given to Catholic guilt, fashionable poses, and sexual self-indulgence."[49] Although Catholicism has not been "fashionable" since the Stonewall Inn riot in New York City in 1969 drew attention to gay rights in the United States, Hanson states that nonheterosexual people remain entranced by the church.[50] Waugh joins a list of homosexual or bisexual converts such as Wilde, Walter Pater, Paul Verlaine, Lord Alfred Douglas, Lionel Johnson, John Grey, Montague Summers, Frederick Rolfe, John Francis Bloxam, Michael Fields, and Renée Vivien. Hanson is partially misleading, for he makes the novel seem more campy and decadent than it is, and the Flytes are by no means given to sexual self-indulgence.

In *The Silence of Sodom* (2002), Mark D. Jordan agrees that many queer people are still attracted to Roman Catholicism; however, he is much less optimistic about it than Hanson is. Jordan finds the attraction partially grotesque, and he tries to explain why so many gay men subscribe to a religion that destroys them. Why are they in bondage to the enemy? To answer his question, Jordan analyzes queer culture within the Catholic Church, such as popular culture surrounding priesthood.[51] We do not see such popular culture in Waugh's novel. The priest is a good man who helps to save Lord Marchmain's soul.

In *Gay and Lesbian Theologies* (2002), the queer theologian Elizabeth Stuart suggests that Christianity can be queer-positive, not by promoting fashionable but meaningless gay pride, but by recovering theology that has always been queer, or challenging to heterosexual norms.[52] Stuart's approach enables one to live gayness as a value. Gay critics of *Brideshead Revisited* have failed to imagine that male homosexuality can be lived as a value (as distinct from an identity). By recognizing their tenderness, beauty, virtue, and uniqueness, men learn to treat all men decently, with greater concern than straight men show. A gay man may be capable of loving another man, his partner, but if he remains indifferent to what happens to other men, he is living gayness only as an attraction, not as a value. Charles fails in the army, but by living gayness as a value, Sebastian succeeds with the monks.

In *Strangers and Friends: A New Exploration of Homosexuality in the Bible* (1995), Michael Vasey claims that homosexuality emphasizes friendship over sex, and that gay people are thus within the Christian tradition.[53] Unfortunately, discussions of *Brideshead Revisited* since 1990 have tended to advance the repressive notion that homosexuality is primarily about sexual desire and sexual acts. Kurt's request for cigarettes and Sebastian's sense that it is his job to fetch them mark a gay friendship that does not fit into the constrictive pattern of heterosexual friend-or-lover dichotomies. The "are-they-or-aren't-they?" approach to same-sex relations in *Brides-*

head Revisited blinds us to deeper relationships that cannot be described in simple terms, such as sexual acts.

The religious symbolism of Sebastian's name is important in his relationship with Kurt. To help fellow Christians, the future Saint Sebastian joined the military under cover at the time of Diocletian's persecution. The emperor ordered soldiers to kill him with arrows, but he survived the attack. Martyred at a later date, Sebastian became the patron saint of soldiers. In this way he was a forerunner for the soldier Charles.[54] Yukio Mishima was attracted to the beautiful body pierced with arrows, but Waugh perhaps preferred the man who loved other men and lived with them in a caring community. Eroticism and friendship are similarly blended in gay men's lives. Kurt, a wretched and hapless military man, is still a human being to love.

In *Sex and the Church: Gender, Homosexuality, and the Transformation of Christian Ethics* (1997), Kathy Rudy states that "Christianity does not need the categories of male and female. Christianity does not reproduce itself through biology but through conversion. What matters is not whether two Christians can bear children but whether they can embrace outsiders."[55] This message is made clear at the end of *Brideshead Revisited* when Lord Marchmain is reconverted, and his return to the fold is much more important than the fact that his sons will be childless.

As Stuart reminds us, Catholic celibates have shown that "heterosexuality, marriage and family life are not identical with Christian discipleship. . . . The decline of and increasing invisibility of the religious life in western Christianity constitutes a huge crisis for the Church in general and for its discourse on sexuality in particular. It is both a product of and has contributed towards the collapse of Christian discipleship into heterosexual marriage. In public discourse on sexuality the western Churches currently give every impression of wanting to produce heterosexual desire rather than desire for God."[56] Cordelia mentions the monks in North Africa (*BR* 308–10), who suggest that heterosexual marriage must be dislodged from its central status in Christianity. Julia ultimately resists the transformation of Catholicism into heterosexuality: she takes up a single life of war service. There are no immediate prospects of a grandchild for the deceased Lord Marchmain, but good works and contribution to the war effort count more than the perpetuation of family.

CONCLUSION

One can better appreciate *Brideshead Revisited* through an understanding of issues in gay men's lives, such as the blending of love and friendship, the bonding of gay and straight men, and the need to live homosexuality as a value rather than an identity. The novel pits two versions of Roman Catholicism against each other, the generous and the dogmatic, and the generous version prevails. In *Brideshead*, celibate religious prevent Roman Catholicism from degenerating into a fertility cult, and conversion, not procreation, ensures survival of the Christian Church.

As Mark D. Jordan points out, gay Roman Catholics are faring worse now than in 1945, thanks to various documents, particularly the *Declaration regarding Certain Questions of Homosexual Ethics* (1975) and the *Letter to All Catholic Bishops* (1986). In the first, the reigning pope was Paul VI; in the second, John Paul II.[57] Jordan shows that these documents are poorly argued and disrupt Thomas Aquinas's conception of natural law. In the *Declaration*, "acts of homosexuality are disordered by their very nature."[58] According to the *Letter*, only the Roman Catholic hierarchy can determine the truth on matters of homosexuality. Such knowledge is considered beyond the ken of anyone else. Thoughtful readers of Waugh's novel will disagree. Decades after publication, *Brideshead Revisited* challenges these prejudices, even if it is "something quite remote from anything the [builder] intended" (*BR* 351).[59]

NOTES

1. See John Boswell, *Christianity, Social Tolerance, and Homosexuality: Gay People in Western Europe from the Beginning of the Christian Era to the Fourteenth Century* (Chicago: University of Chicago Press, 1980), and *Same-Sex Unions in Premodern Europe* (New York: Villiard Books, 1994).

2. Frederick J. Stopp, *Evelyn Waugh: Portrait of an Artist* (London: Chapman & Hall, 1958), 118.

3. Marston LaFrance, "Content and Structure of Evelyn Waugh's *Brideshead Revisited*," in *Evelyn Waugh*, ed. Robert Murray Davis (St. Louis: Herder, 1972), 59.

4. Kurt Schlüter, *Kuriose Welt im modernen englischen Roma, Dargestellt an ausgewählten Werken von Evelyn Waugh und Angus Wilson* (Berlin: E. Schmidt, 1969), 86–87.

5. Harvey Curtis Webster, *After the Trauma: Representative British Novelists since 1920* (Lexington: University of Kentucky Press, 1970), 85.

6. Gene D. Phillips, *Evelyn Waugh's Officers, Gentlemen, and Rogues: The Fact behind His Fiction* (Chicago: Nelson-Hall, 1975), 64.

7. Calvin W. Lane, *Evelyn Waugh* (New York: Twayne, 1981), 92.

8. Jeffrey Heath, *The Picturesque Prison: Evelyn Waugh and His Writing* (Montreal: McGill-Queen's University Press, 1982), 178.

9. Ian Littlewood, *The Writings of Evelyn Waugh* (Oxford: Blackwell, 1983), 133.

10. Jacqueline McDonnell, *Evelyn Waugh* (Basingstoke, UK: Macmillan, 1988), 95.

11. Robert R. Garnett, *From Grimes to Brideshead: The Early Novels of Evelyn Waugh* (Lewisburg, PA: Bucknell University Press, 1990), 150.

12. Robert Murray Davis, Brideshead Revisited: *The Past Redeemed* (Boston: Twayne, 1990), 74.

13. Katharyn W. Crabbe, *Evelyn Waugh* (New York: Continuum, 1988), 95–96.

14. Annette Wirth, *The Loss of Traditional Values and Continuance of Faith in Evelyn Waugh's Novels*: A Handful of Dust, Brideshead Revisited, *and* Sword of Honour (New York: Peter Lang, 1990), 56.

15. Evelyn Toynton, "Revisiting *Brideshead*," *American Scholar* 67, no. 4 (1998): 135.

16. See David Bittner, "The Thread with the Built-in Twitch, or The Case for Lady Marchmain," *Evelyn Waugh Newsletter* 21, no. 2 (Autumn 1987): 1–2; John W. Osborne, "Sebastian Flyte as a Homosexual," *Evelyn Waugh Newsletter* 23, no. 3 (Winter 1989): 7–8; and Bittner, "Sebastian and Charles—More than Friends?" *Evelyn Waugh Newsletter and Studies* 24, no. 2 (Autumn 1990): 1–3.

17. David Leon Higdon, "Gay Sebastian and Cheerful Charles: Homoeroticism in Waugh's *Brideshead Revisited*," *Ariel* 25, no. 4 (October 1994): 77–78.

18. Ibid., 78.

19. Ibid., 83.

20. Ibid., 87.

21. Robert Murray Davis, "Imagined Spaces in *Brideshead Revisited*," in *Evelyn Waugh: New Directions*, ed. Alain Blayac (New York: St. Martin's Press, 1992), 22.

22. Jean-Louis Chevalier, "Arcadian Minutiae: Notes on *Brideshead Revisited*," in *Evelyn Waugh: New Directions*, 45.

23. Frederick L. Beaty, *The Ironic World of Evelyn Waugh: A Study of Eight Novels* (DeKalb: Northern Illinois University Press, 1992).

24. Roberto A. Valdeón-Garcia, "El tratamiento de la tematica homosexual en cuatro novelistas ingleses: Lawrence, Forster, Waugh y Storey (1914–1963)," *Cuadernos de Investigación Philologica* 23–24 (1997–98): 139–62.

25. John Howard Wilson, "Mishima's *Confessions of a Mask*: Brideshead Revisited?" *Journal of Evolutionary Psychology* 20, nos. 1–2 (March 1999): 22–32.

26. Tison Pugh, "Romantic Friendship, Homosexuality, and Evelyn Waugh's *Brideshead Revisited*," *English Language Notes* 38, no. 4 (2001): 64–65.

27. Ibid., 65.

28. Ibid., 71.

29. Annamarie Jagose, "Queer Theory," *Australian Humanities Review* 4 (December 1996– February 1997): 1. Web site: http://www.lib.latrobe.edu.au/AHR/archive/Issue-Dec-1996/ jagose.html.

30. Pugh, "Romantic Friendship," 70.

31. Eve Kosofsky Sedgwick, "The Beast in the Closet: James and the Writing of Homo- sexual Panic," in *Epistemology of the Closet* (Berkeley: University of California Press, 1990), 185.

32. Evelyn Waugh, *Brideshead Revisited: The Sacred and Profane Memories of Captain Charles Ryder* (Boston: Little, Brown, 1945), 269–73. Hereafter cited as *BR*.

33. Evelyn Waugh, "Fan-Fare," in *Evelyn Waugh: The Critical Heritage*, ed. Martin Stannard (London: Routledge & Kegan Paul, 1984), 251.

34. Evelyn Waugh, *The Ordeal of Gilbert Pinfold* (Boston: Little Brown, 1957), 4.

35. Evelyn Waugh, "Preface to the 1960 Revised Edition of *Brideshead Revisited*," in *Critical Heritage*, 271–72.

36. Jeffrey Heath, "*Brideshead:* The Critics and the Memorandum," *English Studies* 56, no. 3 (June 1975): 222–30.

37. Ibid., 227.

38. Ibid., 228.

39. Evelyn Waugh, *The Essays, Articles and Reviews of Evelyn Waugh*, ed. Donat Gallagher (Boston: Little, Brown, 1983), 511.

40. Evelyn Waugh, *A Little Learning: The First Volume of an Autobiography* (Boston: Little Brown, 1964), 179. Hereafter cited as *ALL*.

41. Martin Stannard, *Evelyn Waugh: The Early Years 1903–1939* (London: Dent, 1986), 90–95.

42. Stannard, *Critical Heritage*, 233–87, and Joseph Hynes, "Two Affairs Revisited," *Twentieth Century Literature* 33, no. 2 (Summer 1987): 252.

43. Stannard, *Early Years*, 82–83. See also Jeffrey Weeks and Kevin Porter, eds., *Between the Acts: Lives of Homosexual Men, 1885–1967* (New York: New York University Press, 1998), especially "An Academic Life" (70–90), which coincidentally includes a report about a scoutmaster of the 1920s dismissed for "interfering" with scouts, and David Hugh, *On Queer Street: A Social History of British Homosexuality, 1895–1995* (London: HarperCollins, 1997), especially on Oxford in the 1920s, where homosexuality is described as "certainly more than simply *comme il faut*" (80). Humphrey Carpenter in *The Brideshead Generation* (London: Weidenfeld & Nicolson, 1989) describes Waugh's love of men at Oxford: "This homosexual episode or phase, whatever it was and whomever it involved, passed swiftly and was not to be repeated" (125).

44. Charlotte Mosley, ed., *The Letters of Nancy Mitford and Evelyn Waugh* (London: Hodder & Stoughton, 1996), 357.

45. See Andrew Elfenbein, *Romantic Genius: The Prehistory of a Homosexual Role* (New York: Columbia University Press, 1999), and Linda Dowling, *Hellenism and Homosexuality in Victorian Oxford* (Ithaca, NY: Cornell University Press, 1994).

46. Donat Gallagher explains that "matrimonial consent in canon law must therefore embrace four elements, viz. voluntary union; an intention that the union will last for life; an exclusive relationship between one man and one woman; and an exchange of the right to procreative (not merely sexual) acts" (70). He adds that a marriage is "invalid if the right to beget children [*ius ad prolem*] is *excluded* by one or both parties, either temporarily or permanently. But a marriage is not considered invalid if one or both parties intend merely to *violate* that right [to beget children], e. g. by using birth control" (75). See Gallagher, "Evelyn Waugh and Vatican Divorce," in *Evelyn Waugh: New Directions*, 62–84.

47. Ellis Hanson, *Decadence and Catholicism* (Cambridge, MA: Harvard University Press, 1997), 366.

48. Ibid., 25.

49. Ibid., 368.

50. Ibid., 25.

51. Mark D. Jordan, *The Silence of Sodom: Homosexuality in Modern Catholicism* (Chicago: University of Chicago Press, 2002).

52. Elizabeth Stuart, *Gay and Lesbian Theologies: Repetitions with Critical Difference* (Aldershot, UK: Ashgate, 2002).

53. Michael Vasey, *Strangers and Friends: A New Exploration of Homosexuality and the Bible* (London: Hodder & Stoughton, 1995).

54. Joachim Heusinger von Waldegg shows how in painting and literature the image of St. Sebastian has been used to create the compound figure of the artist-martyr. He gives examples from writers such as Rainer Maria Rilke in *Neue Gedichte*, Thomas Mann in

"Death in Venice," Georg Trakl in "Sebastian in Traum," and Gabrielle d'Annunzio in *The Martyrdom of St. Sebastian*, set to music by Claude Debussy. See Von Waldegg, *Der Kunstler als Martyrer: Sankt Sebastian in der Kunst des 20. Jahrhunderts* (Worms: Wernersche Verlagsgesellschaft, 1989), 19. Charles Hutton-Brown suggests analogies between Sebastian and St. Aloysius, after whom the teddy bear is named. See Hutton-Brown, "Sebastian as Saint: The Hagiographical Sources of Sebastian Flyte," *Evelyn Waugh Newsletter* 11, no. 3 (1977): 1–7.

55. Qtd. in Stuart, *Gay and Lesbian Theologies*, 95.

56. Ibid., 109.

57. Mark D. Jordan, *Silence of Sodom*, 24.

58. Ibid., 28.

59. The relevance of *Brideshead Revisited* to gay men's place in Roman Catholicism continues to increase. The situation for gay men in the Catholic Church becomes graver, as Vatican policy spreads the myth that gay men are more likely than heterosexual men to be child molesters. The Vatican has also tried to drive gay men out of seminaries. Since the 1970s, serious discussion of sexual ethics in the church has been discouraged. Mark D. Jordan reports that in 1972 the Catholic Theological Society of America set up a committee that reported on recent trends in sexual ethics and theology. Such committees are unwelcome today. The committee published Anthony Kosnick's *Human Sexuality: New Directions in American Catholic Thought, A Study* (New York: Paulist Press, 1977), which was condemned by various Catholic bishops and agencies. Kosnick and his colleagues suggested seven criteria for sexual acts: self-liberating, other enriching, honest, faithful, socially responsible, life-serving, and joyous. See Jordan, *The Ethics of Sex* (Oxford: Blackwell, 2002), 147. These criteria are more meaningful than those the Vatican endorses.

The World's Anachronism:
The Timelessness of the Secular
in Evelyn Waugh's *Helena*

Marcel DeCoste

THE SUCCESSFUL PUBLICATION OF *BRIDESHEAD REVISITED* (1945) IN GREAT BRITAIN and its selection as Book of the Month in the United States made Evelyn Waugh a transatlantic best seller and celebrity. Yet *Brideshead*'s publication represented a turning point for Waugh in another sense as well. While he had first shown himself a willing Catholic apologist with the 1935 publication of *Edmund Campion*, *Brideshead* marked a watershed in his career by being, as Martin Stannard observes, Waugh's "first overtly apologetic novel."[1] Unfortunately, Waugh's first Catholic novel marries apologetics to an ostensible requiem for the aristocracy represented by the Flyte family, and *Brideshead* has engendered a tradition of criticism that identifies Waugh's faith with reactionary nostalgia for a feudal past. Marred, in Henry Reed's view, by "an overpowering snobbishness,"[2] dismissed by Edmund Wilson as "extravagantly absurd" in its piety and "shameless" in its toadying admiration for the English aristocracy,[3] *Brideshead*'s rendering of Waugh's Catholicism was to be even more forcefully condemned by Conor Cruise O'Brien for presenting the Catholic faith as "an almost idolatrous reverence for birth and wealth" and a bitter pining for a lost "golden age" of the peerage's proper ascendancy.[4] Indeed, responses to Waugh's first Catholic novel have done much to create the image of Waugh as archconservative chronicler of Christendom's historic decline and fall, which remains a critical commonplace to this day. Thus later readers such as Malcolm Bradbury, or more recently David Rothstein, have seen in the novel a distillation of Waugh's consistent nostalgia, proof, for Bradbury, that in Waugh's eyes "values exist in the past,"[5] and for Rothstein, that Waugh's art seeks the "fictional reconstitution of an aristocratic Catholic heritage in England."[6] Coupled with self-portraits that paint Waugh as the nemesis of "plastics, Picasso, sunbathing and jazz—everything in fact that had happened in his own life time,"[7] *Brideshead* has been central to the depiction of Waugh's sense of history as encompassing only degeneration and loss.

Considerably less attention, however, has been devoted to Waugh's second Christian fiction, *Helena* (1950). While Waugh himself predicted it would be his masterwork[8] and according to Jeffrey Heath declared it, as late as 1960, his finest novel,[9] it has been dismissed by such readers as Christopher Sykes as Waugh's signal failure.[10] As any search of the MLA International Bibliography will reveal, it has certainly failed to generate much scholarly comment. As Stannard notes, Waugh's fictional hagiography "is rarely included in the canon of [his] major works."[11] Indeed, its status in the Waugh oeuvre is such that of the fourteen major novels, including the unfinished *Work Suspended* (1942), listed by the Web site *Doubting Hall*, *Helena* is the only one granted neither a graphic nor a précis, and it can be a very difficult text to purchase,[12] as I came to possess a Canadian first edition discovered by the American *AbeBooks*. That this novel has fallen into obscurity is unfortunate, for *Helena* seriously challenges the simple equation of Waugh's faith with elitist nostalgia that has enjoyed such currency and *durée* in Waugh scholarship. More specifically, I argue that this novel's flagrant and obtrusive anachronisms foreground a historical sensibility at odds with this equation. Waugh presents a view of history in terms not of cultural decline and forfeiture, but rather of parallels and repetitions, of a profound changelessness relieved only by brief glimpses in time of that which transcends the drearily monotonous temporal realm. Rather than a history divided into a glorious "then" and a diminished "now," Waugh's second Catholic novel presents history as indicating, in the words of Waugh's 1939 credo in *Robbery under Law*, "that man is, by nature, an exile and will never be self-sufficient or complete on this earth [and] that his chances of happiness and virtue, here, remain more or less constant through the centuries."[13]

That Waugh himself was, at least on one occasion, uneasy with the reading of his faith prompted by *Brideshead* is revealed by his 1947 response to Conor Cruise O'Brien's angry review. Waugh adduces *Brideshead*'s caustic portraits of the millionaire Rex Mottram and Lady Celia Ryder and asks, with some justice, "Why did my reverence for money and rank not sanctify those two?"[14] To a great extent, *Helena* itself can be read as a corrective response to *Brideshead*'s reception, a pointed rebuttal of the charges laid by O'Brien and others, and an insistence on the radical inclusiveness and equality posited by his own Christian faith, a position also articulated in such contemporary essays as "Come Inside" and "The American Epoch in the Catholic Church."[15] In *Helena*, we find a narrative that, despite its focus on the empress dowager of Rome, conspicuously rejects any equation of grace with rank[16] and instead suggests the irrelevance of temporal hierarchies to the soul's worth and fate. Thus, Helena's early readiness for the Christian message is signaled in her questioning of her husband, Constantius's, love for the walls that keep barbarians at bay and Roman civilization pure and secure. While Constantius, gazing on the Swabian Wall, carves the world up into a hierarchical binary set—"inside, peace, decency, the law . . . outside, wild beasts and savages"—Helena challenges such thinking and, refusing the legitimacy of barriers and ranks, champions a universalist definition of "civilization": "Instead of the barbarian breaking-in, might The City one day break out?"[17]

This leveling of distinction is essential to her later experience of Christianity itself, as we are told of the seemingly momentous event of her baptism in terms that stress its commonness: "Privately and humbly, like thousands of others, she stepped down into the font and emerged a new woman" (*Helena* 140). That this act is to be understood as standing apart from matters of caste and politics, even from the historical record, is only emphasized by Waugh's cursory mention of it. What a reader might take to be the dramatic center of Helena's narrative is never described but, in a virtual aside, merely reported in a single paragraph that underlines how this crucial act is at odds with the history of the great or governing: "None knows when or where. No record was made. Nothing was built or founded. There was no public holiday" (*Helena* 140). Moreover, when, at long last, Helena reaches Rome itself, she finds her home there not within the murderous, intrigue-ridden ruling class, but in a church presented as embracing all classes and kinds: "The barrow-man grilling his garlic sausage in the gutter, the fuller behind his reeking public pots, the lawyer or the lawyer's clerk might each and all be one with the Empress Dowager in the Mystical Body" (*Helena* 146).

Helena's treatment of that Mystical Body entails more than an occasional defense against charges that Waugh's church is a closed club. What it involves is a meditation on history that highlights its status as a narrative not of decline and fall, but of abhorrent recurrence. So treated, history in this novel fails to underwrite any notion of, or nostalgia for, some temporal golden age that makes our present seem uniquely fallen. Rather, history, in its totality, seems to emerge as the very badge of our fallen nature, typified not by grand heights and catastrophic cultural loss, but by, in William Myers's words, "an endless recycling of the same old problems."[18] The primary means through which the novel communicates this apparent timelessness of historical time is its conspicuous and insistent use of anachronism in rendering the third- and fourth-century world that is its setting. Interestingly, Waugh's preface to the novel is at some pains to call the reader's attention to such "wilful, obvious anachronisms which are introduced as a literary device," though he declines to mention what purpose this device is meant to serve (*Helena* x). Their effect in the text, though, is to make us Helena's contemporaries, to conflate her world and ours, and to deflate historical distance. While such a gesture might have a proselytizing motive— demonstrating that the problem of belief and its Christian answer are still central to our own increasingly secular time—it also works to present all times as equally secular, hence equally problematic.

This is true despite those moments in the novel when the narrator seems to insist on his, and our, distance from Helena and her age. For the novel does, at times, advertise its status as a twentieth-century retrospective and our own significant historical remove from the events it chronicles. Thus, early on, our narrator comes forth in the role of a modern cultural historian, introducing his heroine with the observation that "there would be decades in the coming seventeen centuries, when she would have been thought beautiful" (*Helena* 2). Likewise, in the novel's conclusion, our storyteller identifies himself as a creature of "our" age by stressing that "above all the babble of her age and ours, [Helena] makes one blunt assertion" (*Helena* 265). Yet this concluding admission of his own historical situation is telling, in that it is part of an assertion of likeness, if not identity, between the fourth and twentieth centuries, and of the benign timelessness of Helena's assertion, namely, that Christ did, in fact, live and die in historical time. Such confessions, on the part of the narrator, of his own historical distance from his subject do not serve to establish the fundamental dissimilarity of historical epochs. Rather, when combined with the novel's anachronistic rendering of the past, they serve to foreground parallels between these supposedly discrete ages and to underscore the fundamental sameness of different times. By stressing how distant is Helena's time, on one hand, and insisting on a depiction that makes it mirror our own, on the other, the text makes more forceful its implied claim of changelessness through historical time.

The anachronisms that help give this claim its force are of three main types. The first and most obvious results from Waugh's transplantation to the age of Helena of a gratingly class-bound British idiom.[19] We first meet Princess Helena eager for what she dubs "tonight's beano," her father's feast in honor of Constantius: she voices her approval of its extravagance by exclaiming "What a blow out!" (*Helena* 3, 18). Nor is such anachronistic slang—so at odds, as R. J. MacSween has observed, with readerly expectations of the historical novel as a genre[20]—limited to or expressive only of Helena's youth. Helena in her maturity will likewise speak both bluntly and in the argot of another age, dismissing, for example, the mystery cults in Ratisbon with "It's all bosh, isn't it?" (*Helena* 54). In the midst of her quest for the true cross, Helena's language remains anything but exalted or Latinate, as she rejects various speculations concerning the composition and fate of the Cross with such curt rejoinders as "Rot" and "Bosh" (*Helena* 231–32). While Helena's vocabulary is particularly marked by such anachronisms, they are not hers alone. Her tutor Marcias, for example, informs her that Christianity is "all the rage in Antioch" (*Helena* 8), and other characters too speak of "eyesore[s]," "sucker[s]," and "togs" (*Helena* 105, 188, 245), so that the whole of this ancient world is tied to Waugh's own through flamboyant linguistic contiguity.

The second type of anachronism takes the form of characters serving as transhistorical figures, able, in the midst of Helena's era, to foresee, articulate, and in a sense embody all future times. Despite being situated in Helena's own time, they partake of the twentieth-century narrator's knowledge of all subsequent time and, by describing it to a fourth-century audience, collapse the distance between historical periods. There are two of these characters in the novel. First is the African "witch" used by Constantine's wife, Fausta, to predict betrayals and thus to convince the emperor to eliminate whomever Fausta dislikes. While initially presented as a fraud, this character becomes, in chapter 8, a genuine conduit of both past and future history, as she is seized by a "music . . . drumming from beyond the pyramids, wailing in the *bistro* where the jazz disc spun" (*Helena* 187). In this music's grip she conveys Constantine's growing, precarious power, but she also shouts "Heil" and tells of the "plenty big chief" who is "lost to the world on Helena's isle" in reference to future emperors such as Hitler and Napoleon (*Helena* 188). Her tale of power and nemesis is thus transhistorically descriptive and true, revealing the destiny of what Helena herself calls "Power without Grace" (*Helena* 198), whatever the century that power dominates. The second such figure is the Wandering Jew, who, appearing in a dream of Helena's while she searches the Holy Land for the true cross, not only speaks in 1940s Hollywoodese—"I'm in incense, see" (*Helena* 246)[21]—but also discloses to her the future course of Christendom's traffic in relics true and false: "She saw the sanctuaries of Christendom become a fairground, stalls hung with beads and medals, substances yet unknown pressed into sacred emblems; heard a chatter of haggling in tongues yet unspoken" (*Helena* 250). Again, the effect is to collapse historical distance, to make Helena's age capable of reflecting our own, and to treat history as something traversed by the same repeated acts and characters. That Helena's son, Constantine, has already—with his Labarum—begun the business of proclaiming and praising false relics only heightens this sense of identity through time (*Helena* 201–03).

The last and perhaps most significant type of anachronism lies in the text's persistent treatment of the political, social, and aesthetic "changes" of Helena's day as parallel to those of Waugh's own. Thus, for example, Helena's confidante, Calpurnia, offers her worldly counsel on conjugal matters that might well be heard in Waugh's century: "My dear, nowadays people marry again and again" (*Helena* 84). Later, when Constantine arrives, in the midst of warfare over the contested imperial succession, to take Helena from Dalmatia to safer territory, he is alarmed by her suggestion that no one would bother with her and replies in a manner worthy of Orwell himself: "You don't understand modern politics, mamma. There are no private lives nowadays" (*Helena* 111). Later still, Constantine himself is held captive to aesthetic "innovations" that aptly mirror and mock the antirepresentationalism regnant in Waugh's own lifetime. Having waited twelve years for completion of his triumphal arch, the emperor calls architect and sculptor before him to explain the delay and why the statues "are lifeless and expressionless as dummies" (*Helena* 171), only to be condescendingly schooled in the orthodoxies of modernism, according to which simple mimesis "would not be the least significant" (*Helena* 173). The sculptor Carpicius ultimately admits that he is unable to execute realistic figures, as Waugh—who would sign letters "Death to Picasso!" (*LEW* 218)—once more attacks trendy avant gardism. More importantly, these various parallels make the past with which the novel deals—a past that, as it charts the rise of the institution of Waugh's own church, we might expect him to romanticize—no lofty, lost age of splendor, but the twentieth century's own mirror image. Parallels argue for the fundamental consistency or sameness of historical time and undermine notions of history as progress or degeneration. As Stannard rightly notes, "Helena's world, then, *is* Waugh's. It is the world as it always has been and always will be."[22]

So what sort of world is this? If the nature of cultural and political history is such that Waugh's own era can substantially reproduce the fourth century, what sort of past has been so conserved? On the evidence of *Helena*, the past is not very desirable. Far from representing some classical, or even ecclesiastical, golden age, the twentieth century's doppelganger in the late empire is a time and place of gratuitous violence—Constantine himself celebrates his rise to emperor "by slaughtering an entire army of unarmed Franks in the theatre" (*Helena* 117)—incessant warfare, bloody insurrection, cynical political and conjugal treachery, and vainglorious hypocrisy. Superficially, changes abound; certainly emperors and wives are replaced at a dizzying rate. But the course of historical events, even in the midst of that most epochal event—the elevation of Christianity to the status of state religion—is presented as both monotonous and monstrous; history in *Helena* is simply one war, one assassination, one purge after another. As does Waugh's own time, marked by the inglorious warfare and endemic treachery that are the meat of his other major historical fiction, *Sword of Honour* (1965), Helena's era too reveals human affairs to be mired, both locally and globally, in the bloodiest of ruts: "The oblivious Caesars fought on. They marched across frontiers, made treaties and broke them, decreed marriages and divorces and legitimizations, murdered their prisoners, betrayed their allies, deserted their dead and dying armies, boasted and despaired, fell on their swords or sued for mercy. All the tiny mechanisms of Power regularly revolved like a watch still ticking on the wrist of a dead man" (*Helena* 139). We get a portrait of worldly affairs as vicious, bloody, futile, and, as the device of the anachronism highlights throughout, repetitive. While the closing image of this passage suggests that the empire, the reign of the "oblivious" Caesars, is already over, superseded by the church's ascendancy, still the history of the *saeculum* mechanically runs its deadly circular course, as indeed the ties between Helena's then and Waugh's now indicate. Hence Helena's wise admonition to her son, "Keep out of history" (*Helena* 112).

Yet if changeless history is, in this novel, something we are best out of, it is nonetheless the case that Helena's whole story hinges upon the redemptive character of history, or at least of certain historical facts. Helena's quest for the true cross is, after all, a search for historical evidence, the absence of which she derides in gnosticism and the various mystery cults she encounters. That the cross and Christ are facts of history is central to Helena's understanding of Christianity. Helena's tale reveals the dreary and hopeless sameness of secular history, and it expressly states that meaningful change occurs not in this arena, but only in adopting the Christian faith. As she tells her son, "There is only one way in which things can be made new" (*Helena* 196), and this is through the baptismal font, through the commitment of oneself to an eternal truth and a suprahistorical reality. As Waugh and his empiricist heroine are both aware, in Christianity, access to such eternal truth hinges upon a specific historical event. It hinges on the intersection of the eternal and the temporal in the Incarnation, an event in history that offers to redeem us from the lapsarian history that this novel discloses. Thus, as the narrator informs us, the significance of the cross derives from its "stat[ing] a fact" (*Helena* 265), something its very status as a historical artifact permits it to do. As Waugh would elaborate in his 1952 essay "St. Helena Empress," it was just this factual basis that permitted Christianity to survive as Christianity, as our one means of redemption: "Everything about the new religion was capable of interpretation, could be refined and diminished; everything except the unreasonable assertion that God became man and died on the Cross; not a myth or allegory; true God, truly incarnate, tortured to death at a particular moment in time, at a particular geographical place, as a matter of plain historical fact" (*ALO* 183). Faith does intertwine with history in Waugh's view, not as the sole possession of one age or one class to the exclusion of all others, but as that which, grounded in historical reality, transcends the gruesome sameness of secular time. For Waugh, as for Eliot, "only through time time is conquered,"[23] and change happens for the individual believer *in* historical time, though not *for* historical time, whose watch keeps tragically ticking.

This essay began by claiming that the marginalization of Waugh's second Catholic novel is to be lamented, not only because it offers a Waugh interestingly at variance with portraits, not excluding his own, depicting *him* as an anachronism, a Jacobite lost in the twentieth century and mourning the irreparable passing of a worthier culture, a truer civilization. *Helena* does complicate such a picture of this writer and his faith and, for this alone, merits greater attention than it has received. I would argue that the value of *Helena* lies not in its being in unique counterpoint, in the Waugh canon, to the worldview discernible in *Brideshead*, or even in *Decline and Fall* (1928) or *The Ordeal of Gilbert Pinfold* (1957). Rather, consideration of this text offers the occasion for new readings of both earlier and later works. Through the lens of *Helena*, the much-noted circularity of Waugh's early narratives—*Decline and Fall*, with its wheel at Luna Park, or *Vile Bodies* (1930), with its car races and endless circuit of parties[24]—might reveal the present's standing vis-à-vis the past as rather different from Michael Gorra's "lament for the end of the old English agricultural and aristocratic order."[25] Likewise, *Helena* might help us appreciate just how Guy Crouchback's initial eagerness to wage war against "the Modern Age in arms"[26] and to recapture the glory of his crusading antecedent, Roger of Waybrooke, by the end of the trilogy begins to appear both deluded and culpable, an instance of the "will to war, [the] death wish" that defines modernity.[27]

To be sure, Waugh waged his own war against the modern age: its art, its politics, its secularism, its etiquette (or lack thereof). What is more, he would often, in the midst of this campaign, not only decry the present, but also wax nostalgic for the past, thus lending support to treatments of him as a writer beguiled by "a Giant Race before the Flood."[28] This is, after all, the novelist who would puzzle over the destination sought by H. G. Wells's Time Traveller: "The future, dreariest of prospects! . . . To hover gently back through centuries (not more than thirty of them) would be the most exquisite pleasure of which I can conceive."[29] *Helena* suggests that Waugh's quarrel with his own day was also a reaction against the belief in modern superiority to the past, which he saw as a retreat from unprecedented failings. As his anachronistic tale of the empress dowager shows, Waugh held "that man's capacity for suffering keeps pretty regular pace with the discoveries that ameliorate it,"[30] and this very conviction concerning man's fallen nature is a significant spiritual compass pointing toward the faith he had embraced. Modernity's own overarching philosophy of innovation and amelioration, its "vile & frivolous panglossisme" (*LEW* 296), could only draw his suspicion and ire. Such conservatism, rooted in his sense that there was only one way things could be made new and made right, in his belief that history repeatedly demonstrates our need for this blunt fact, may very well be seen to underpin more of Waugh's oeuvre than conventional identifications of him as elegiac satirist have permitted us to see.

NOTES

1. Martin Stannard, *Evelyn Waugh: The Later Years 1939–1966* (New York: W. W. Norton, 1992), 128.

2. Henry Reed, review of *Brideshead Revisited*, in *Evelyn Waugh: The Critical Heritage*, ed. Martin Stannard (London: Routledge & Kegan Paul, 1984), 239.

3. Edmund Wilson, review of *Brideshead Revisited*, in *Critical Heritage*, 246.

4. Conor Cruise O'Brien, review of *Brideshead Revisited*, in *Critical Heritage*, 258.

5. Malcolm Bradbury, *Evelyn Waugh* (Edinburgh: Oliver & Boyd, 1964), 50.

6. David Rothstein, "*Brideshead Revisited* and the Modern Historicization of Memory," *Studies in the Novel* 25, no. 3 (1993): 318.

7. Evelyn Waugh, *The Ordeal of Gilbert Pinfold, and Other Stories* (London: Chapman & Hall, 1973), 126. One might also number among such "portraits" Waugh's famous credo in "Aspirations of a Mugwump," which defends his avowed intention not to avail himself of the franchise, first, by observing that Britain is a monarchy; second, by lamenting a century's worth of dignity granted the mechanism of popular election; and third, by confessing, "I do not aspire to advise my Sovereign in her choice of servants." See Evelyn Waugh, *A Little Order: A Selection from His Journalism*, ed. Donat Gallagher (London: Eyre Methuen, 1977), 139–40. While a more reactionary persona is hard to find, even in Waugh's writings, he strikes comparable notes in a 1959 piece for the *Daily Mail*, collected

as "I See Nothing but Boredom . . . Everywhere" in *A Little Order* (45–48), and throughout his caustic satire on the postwar welfare state in 1953's *Love among the Ruins*. See Waugh, *Pinfold, and Other Stories*, 179–223.

8. Evelyn Waugh, *The Letters of Evelyn Waugh*, ed. Mark Amory (London: Weidenfeld & Nicolson, 1980), 312. Hereafter cited as *LEW*.

9. Jeffrey Heath, "Concluding *Helena*," *Evelyn Waugh Newsletter* 10, no. 2 (1976): 4.

10. Christopher Sykes, *Evelyn Waugh: A Biography* (Boston: Little, Brown, 1975), 320. While Sykes concedes that the novel displays all of Waugh's writerly merits—"his wit, his broad humour, his irony [and] some of the best pieces of evocative writing that he achieved at any time" (318)—he nonetheless sees it as muddled and undermined by its own apologetics: "The book becomes discordant, without clear intention, and ends lamely, almost in a pietist spirit" (320). A more recent biographer, Selina Hastings, further argues that such was the judgment of the majority of Waugh's contemporary admirers, who found *Helena* "an embarrassing aberration, a distasteful mix of slangy girls' school adventure with an emotional sanctimoniousness." See Hastings, *Evelyn Waugh: A Biography* (1994; rep., London: Vintage, 2002), 538. Both thus chastise the novel for its mixing of perspectives and discourses that, in their view, should not go together. They criticize *Helena* for that very reliance upon anachronism which I argue is central to Waugh's purpose.

11. Stannard, *Later Years*, 274.

12. Loyola Press of Chicago issued an affordable paperback edition in its Loyola Classics series in 2005. The reviewer Patrick Query has questioned this edition's apparent goal of recuperating the novel from obscurity only by treating it "as a spiritual guidebook" and Catholic apology. See "The Idea of Europe," *Evelyn Waugh Newsletter and Studies* 36, no. 2: http://www.lhup.edu/jwilson3/Newsletter_36.2.htm. Nonetheless, it has the merit of offering this underread text to a new age and a new audience, however small or pious.

13. Evelyn Waugh, *Robbery under Law* (London: Chapman & Hall, 1939), 16.

14. Evelyn Waugh, letter to the editor of the *Bell*, in *Critical Heritage*, 271.

15. Evelyn Waugh, *A Little Order: A Selection from His Journalism*, ed. Donat Gallagher (Boston: Little, Brown, 1977), 147–49, 167–79. Hereafter cited as *ALO*.

16. Not all readers, it should be noted, have agreed with this assessment; indeed, some have taken *Helena* as proffering the title character's sanctity precisely as deriving from her social position. Most notoriously, Fr. Gerald Meath implied, in a 1951 *Tablet* review of Dorothy Sayers's *The Emperor Constantine*, that Waugh presented his heroine as "a woman who was made a Saint . . . by her aristocratic inheritance." Waugh's response to what he dubbed "this odious imputation" (qtd. in Stannard, *Later Years*, 297) is itself highly revealing. Enraged, Waugh responded with an angry letter and threats of legal action. Father Meath relented, and no action was taken. Martin Stannard uncharitably suggests that Waugh's intemperate and litigious reaction is best explained in terms of fear that such remarks might undermine the radio adaptation of his favorite novel being prepared at this time by Christopher Sykes. See Stannard, *Later Years*, 299. Just two years later Waugh would passionately instruct Nancy Mitford that "it is not true that any Catholic thinks the poor go to a servants' hall in heaven. Read Bossuet's great sermon on the Eminent Dignity of the Poor. Also Gospels. Dives & Lazarus" (*LEW* 411). Similarly, in a 1949 essay for the *Month*, Waugh heaps praise upon the faithful poor of America, who have "covered their land with schools, colleges and universities," and insists that "honour must never be neglected to those thousands of coloured Catholics who so accurately traced their Master's road amid insult and injury" (*ALO* 175, 173). All of this suggests that

Waugh, during the period of *Helena*'s composition and first reception, at any rate, was both sensitive to claims that his Catholicism granted dignity only to the nobility and eager, in good faith, to refute such claims.

17. Evelyn Waugh, *Helena* (Toronto: Chapman & Hall, 1950), 47–48. Hereafter cited as *Helena*.

18. William Myers, *Evelyn Waugh and the Problem of Evil* (London: Faber & Faber, 1991), 91.

19. Selina Hastings, in particular, finds this "idiomatic informality of the dialogue" difficult to square with "the reverential tone" elsewhere adopted by the narrator in his treatment of his "great Christian theme." See *Evelyn Waugh*, 539–40. Indeed, Hastings identifies this anachronistic idiom as a central part of the novel's overriding difficulty, namely, that the novel, for all its diligent research, evokes Waugh's century much more forcefully than Helena's. Hastings is baffled by and hostile to Waugh's use of anachronism. Whether or not we take this technique to be aesthetically satisfying, we should acknowledge its deliberateness and attempt, as Hastings does not, to understand its intent.

20. R. J. MacSween, "*Helena*: Waugh's Failure," *Antigonish Review* 14, no. 1 (1988): 29–30.

21. Perhaps relying too much on my own North American outlook, and on the proximity to the composition of *Helena* of Waugh's own 1947 adventures in Los Angeles (and at Forest Lawn Memorial Park), I hear in this voice the Cagneyesque argot of 1930s and 1940s Hollywood. By contrast, and perhaps more accurately, Christopher Sykes describes this character as speaking "in the accents of a London East End go-getting Yid, the kind that Jewish comedians for years portrayed on the music-hall stage." See Sykes, *Evelyn Waugh*, 319.

22. Stannard, *Later Years*, 281.

23. T. S. Eliot, *Four Quartets* (1944; rep., London: Faber & Faber, 1986), 15.

24. The circular structure of these early novels has been widely remarked. James Carens, for instance, reads Paul Pennyfeather's tale as a parodic conversion narrative, a story of rebirth in which our hero is neither transformed nor redeemed. See Carens, *The Satiric Art of Evelyn Waugh* (Seattle: University of Washington Press, 1966), 11. Similar observations appear in Bradbury, *Evelyn Waugh*, 35; Frederick J. Stopp, *Evelyn Waugh: Portrait of an Artist* (London: Chapman & Hall, 1958), 69; and George McCartney, *Confused Roaring: Evelyn Waugh and the Modernist Tradition* (Bloomington: Indiana University Press, 1987), 11. Likewise, Brooke Allen argues for the fundamentally static character of *Vile Bodies*, a world that endures "remarkably unchanged," despite all its frenetic activity and even the advent of war. See Allen, "*Vile Bodies*: A Futurist Fantasy," *Twentieth Century Literature* 40, no. 3 (1994): 325. As both Stopp and Stanley Kaplan note, a similarly "circular movement expressive of changelessness and—ultimately—of futility" also characterizes Waugh's third novel, 1932's *Black Mischief*. See Stopp, *Evelyn Waugh*, 82; cf. Kaplan, "Circularity and Futility in *Black Mischief*," *Evelyn Waugh Newsletter* 15, no. 3 (1981): 3.

25. Michael Gorra, *The English Novel at Mid-Century: From the Leaning Tower* (London: Macmillan, 1990), 186–87.

26. Evelyn Waugh, *Men at Arms* (1952; rep., Harmondsworth, UK: Penguin, 1970), 12.

27. Evelyn Waugh, *Unconditional Surrender* (1961; rep., Harmondsworth, UK: Penguin, 1975), 232.

28. Bradbury, *Evelyn Waugh*, 89.

29. Evelyn Waugh, *A Little Learning: An Autobiography* (London: Chapman & Hall, 1964), 1.

30. Evelyn Waugh, "To an Unknown Old Man" (1932), MS, Harry Ransom Center, University of Texas at Austin.

Guy Crouchback's Disillusion:
Crete, Beevor, and the Soviet Alliance
in *Sword of Honour*

Donat Gallagher

> To the living we owe respect; to the dead we owe the truth.
> —*Voltaire*

THE TYRANNOUS VOICE OF FASHION NOWADAYS DECREES THAT THE CRUX OF Evelyn Waugh's trilogy *Sword of Honour* (1965) shall be the evacuation of Crete in 1941. Antony Beevor has taught "everyone" to believe that during that evacuation Waugh's commanding officer, Colonel Robert Laycock, behaved badly. Ordered to provide a rearguard and to leave after other fighting forces had embarked, Laycock (Mr. Beevor says or implies) led a third of his commandos to the beach "early," withdrew the rest of the troops from their defensive positions soon afterward, "lied" to colleagues that he had received relevant orders, and "jumped the queue" in front of higher-priority troops—all this despite Layforce's having received no orders to leave Crete. As for Waugh, Beevor claims that he "falsified the War Diary" to conceal Laycock's "arrogant disregard" of orders. The deceit allegedly caused him to develop a bad conscience, which led him to rail neurotically against the British effort on Crete and, later, to expose his own and Laycock's shame in *Officers and Gentlemen* (1955).

At the risk of appearing too sweeping, I am compelled to say that every accusation Beevor levels at Laycock is incorrect, as is each of the purported facts he adduces to support the charges. Nevertheless, Beevor reads well, and many Waugh biographers and some historians have embraced his thesis as a significant contribution to Crete's history and the key to *Sword of Honour*—although none has independently examined the military record. Admittedly, three aspects of Laycock's conduct warrant discussion, and they will be fully explored. But Beevor's starting point and central contention, that Laycock tried to get his men away "early" and without orders, has no basis in reality. This simply did not happen, and the many charges flowing from this premise are equally untrue. Multiple sources make clear that Laycock and his troops received orders to leave Crete.

Most contemporaries thought Laycock an exceptionally fine man and soldier, as his rapid promotions after Crete to command of the Special Services Brigade and to chief of combined operations demonstrate.[1] Some despised him as "over-promoted" and "too smart." Opinion remains divided.[2] But this essay is not concerned with personalities. It seeks only to establish the unvarnished truth about the conduct of Laycock and Waugh during the evacuation of Crete within the context of the orders, actions, times, troop movements, organization, and disorganization that did actually shape events.

Moreover, because Beevor and his followers denounce the Layforce War Diary kept by Evelyn Waugh as "distorted," "disingenuous," "falsified," "fiction," and "Waugh's playground," this chapter will nowhere rely on it as an authority. On the other hand, the facts established throughout this chapter will vindicate its honesty and basic accuracy.

Antony Beevor's sadly aberrant foray into this subject first appeared in 1991 in a prepublication article, "The First Casualty of Waugh," and then (slightly modified) in *Crete: The Battle and the Resistance.*[3] In 2000 this writer disputed Beevor's case, seeking not so much to engage in a point-by-point debate as to present all the facts relevant to a just conclusion.[4] Beevor replied shortly, avoiding most matters raised but reiterating certain charges.[5] In 2000 he wrote a piece about the Channel 4 *Sword of Honour* that may contain more realistic timings.[6] Since 2000 I have read the voluminous archive accumulated for the New Zealand official history of Crete, Laycock's papers, and other records. The new evidence reinforces my original contention that Laycock and Waugh did not commit the offenses Beevor alleges.

In fairness it must be said that "murmurings" to the effect that Laycock should have stayed behind on Crete predate Beevor's book, as do attempts to identify Laycock with Ivor Claire,[7] although no one before Beevor accused Laycock of trying to get his troops off "early" or contrary to orders. Moreover, the conflicting testimony of disoriented witnesses hampers every student of Crete.[8] But after making all due allowance, and happily acknowledging Beevor's distinction as a historian, the evacuation episode in *Crete* must be rated a mistake. For one thing, its impetus was a breathtaking leap from a novel to history: "The character of Ivor Claire [in Waugh's *Sword of Honour*] creates a moral mystery," writes Beevor, "that surrounds [Waugh's] time on Crete."[9] And again, "Mainly due to the diaries of Evelyn Waugh and his novel *Officers and Gentlemen,* interest [in the evacuation] has tended to focus on Colonel Laycock."[10] Any "focus" created by extraneous influences is bound to distort a historical study. In this case, "focusing" on Laycock through the lens of the newsworthy Waugh[11] blinds Beevor to crucial evidence and even distracts him from errors in Waugh's personal records.[12]

Thus, Beevor fails to notice self-contradiction in *The Diaries of Evelyn Waugh.* Waugh writes: "Bob ordered brigade HQ to embark. . . . We reached the destroyer *Nizam* at about midnight and sailed as soon as we came aboard."[13] What can one say to this? That *Nizam* was not at Sphakia on the night May 31st, that Waugh left on HMS *Kimberley,* and that *Kimberley* sailed at 3:00 a.m. Because the ship definitely sailed at 3:00 a.m., the two statements—(a) "we reached . . . *Nizam* at about midnight" and (b) the ship "sailed as soon as we came aboard"—cannot both be true. Beevor accepts the demonstrably incorrect first statement that Laycock and his HQ reached *Nizam* at midnight. Consequently, he places Laycock and his HQ on the beach "about 11 pm," waiting "for a landing craft to take them out to [a] warship" in which they will "ensconce" themselves.[14]

The fact is that at "about 11:00 p.m." the Navy had not yet arrived at Sphakia (the leading cruiser *Phoebe* dropped anchor at 11:20 p.m.) and all landing craft were, and would be for some time, fully loaded with New Zealanders. Moreover, as will be demonstrated, Laycock did not reach the beach until close to midnight. In isolation, such errors might be thought too trivial for comment, but here they expose Beevor's fatal lack of information about what the commandos actually did and when they did it.

Beevor is also blind to the determining features of the evacuation. He failed to read the War Diaries of "A" and "D" Layforce Battalions, whose movements are crucial to the argument. He does not even refer to the pivotal event of the night, the surprise 6:30 p.m. signal announcing that the Navy would not return but would lift 4,000-plus instead of 2,000 troops. And this despite the fact that after that signal had arrived, the single question crucial to this discussion became, *Did Layforce receive a share of the additional 2,000-plus places that became available after 6:30 p.m.?* Moreover, Beevor takes no real account of the chaos that developed at Sphakia after midnight, although it led directly to the capture of about 1,500 priority "fighting troops." Consequently, he blames Laycock for disasters in which he had no part. Ralph Bennett, who helped prepare the Ultra signals sent to Crete, and who "demolished" Beevor's misuse-of-Ultra case against General Bernard Freyberg,[15] points out that snippets of information (such as those Beevor took from Waugh) tend to be confusing in isolation from the wider picture. "Intelligence . . . however 'hot,'" he observes, "can only serve to mislead unless . . . firmly fitted into a known context."[16]

Read without reference to context, Beevor's story makes a vivid but indefinite impression. That is why, although so wrong, it has been so widely believed. And why biographers,[17] adapters for television,[18] critics,[19] historians,[20] and editors[21] have wildly inflated Beevor's claims without realizing they were doing so. One example of such inflation concerns the times (a) at which fighting ended and (b) when Layforce left its rearguard positions. The matter is important, because if Laycock withdrew when fighting was still going on, his crime would be black indeed. Conversely, if he withdrew long after fighting had ended and none was in prospect, he might be blameless. The times are in the record.

On the last night of the evacuation, May 31st, only two Allied units were in contact with the Germans, namely, 19 Australian Brigade and a battalion of Royal Marines, and in only one place, namely, around Vitsilokoumos, twelve miles northeast and high above Sphakia. Though ordered to begin withdrawing to the evacuation beach at 8:30 p.m., the Marines could not move until 8:45 p.m. when the Germans stopped "M.G. fire."[22] That machine-gun fire at 8:45 p.m. ended enemy shooting for the night, probably because sunset was at 8:20 p.m. and darkness fell soon after.[23] The last Australian company (under Major H. C. D. Marshall) withdrew at 9:15 p.m., reporting no recent gunfire.[24] Three German planes strafed Sphakia at 9:15 p.m., but no German troops harassed the rearguard or the evacuation in any way. This passivity was "most surprising," but it is relevant that the Germans were facing extremely rugged terrain in the dark.[25] The last shooting, therefore, was around 8:45 p.m., the last "contact" at 9:15 p.m.

Nevertheless, in order to convict Laycock of being "disingenuous" about the time shooting ended, Beevor hints at later contact. While admitting "the Germans did not fight at night," he refers to firing "at dusk" without putting a time on "dusk."[26] Two followers build on the hint. In a piece for his Channel 4 *Sword of Honour*, William Boyd says that Laycock ordered his men "to abandon their rearguard positions and escape *while serious fighting was still going on*."[27] But fighting ended at 8:45 p.m., and Laycock (as will emerge) ordered his men to "abandon their rearguard positions" at midnight, three hours *after* fighting ended. Professor D. L. Patey trumps Boyd with the even more egregious claim that "as [Laycock] left [Crete] *armed engagements could still be heard in the hills*."[28] Since Laycock left Crete on HMS *Kimberley* at 3:00 a.m., Patey's time for the end of fighting is six hours late. Neither Boyd nor Patey professes to know who was fighting whom or when or where—let alone the hour at which fighting ended or the hour at which Layforce withdrew. Rather, these exact writers and scholars believe they are reporting Beevor, when in fact they are unwittingly stretching his vague accusations beyond all reason—so myths are made.

Beevor's false charges and their ever more fanciful exaggeration, as in the examples cited, unjustly defame Laycock and Waugh and distort the historical record. Correction is obviously needed. Moreover, belief in these accusations has led Beevor et al. to imagine false motives for Waugh's intemperate criticism of the Crete campaign and, worse, to devise sadly limited readings of *Sword of Honour.* Making Laycock and Waugh's alleged personal dishonor on Crete its "crux" decenters the novel's profound moral and political themes. With all due regard to critical freedom in reading a work of imagination, an assertion that *Sword of Honour* reflects a historical crime is not a reading or interpretation. Rather it is a statement about history that must be open to the test of truth. Four questions, therefore, need to be asked:

(1) What did Laycock actually do, or fail to do, during the evacuation from Sphakia, and did Waugh truthfully record his actions in the Layforce War Diary?
(2) In the light of the facts established, is there merit in Beevor's charges?
(3) Why did Waugh react so intemperately to the Crete campaign?
(4) Does Beevor illuminate or impoverish *Sword of Honour?*

LAYCOCK, WAUGH, AND THE EVACUATION FROM SPHAKIA

The evacuation from Sphakia took place over four nights, May 28–31, 1941, and can best be described as a qualified success. Heroically, "11,973 troops plus 20 miscellaneous and a dog"[29] were taken off in the face of total German air supremacy, heavy Navy losses, difficult terrain, desperate shortages of food and water, and masses of unattached and demoralized troops impeding every movement. But failures in command made the operation less successful than it might have been. On the last night, May 31st/June 1st, difficulties multiplied because of unique events. Only at 6:30 p.m. did news arrive that this would be the last night on which ships would arrive and that double the expected number of troops would be embarked. Rearrangements had to be made in great haste. Problems fed on each other. The outer cordon around Sphakia withdrew early because of fears that disorder could lead to its being trapped, and the withdrawal made the disorder worse. And every officer with knowledge of the evacuation arrangements flew off before midnight, leaving no one at Sphakia to deal with the inevitable problems arising from disruption, disputed priorities, and unclear orders.

The evacuation on May 31st began well but ended badly. In round numbers this means that there were 4,000-plus places on the ships and 4,000-plus "fighting troops" scheduled to embark. At first, two heavily armed New Zealand cordons exerted strict control and enforced priorities. Then around midnight the New Zealanders withdrew and disorder followed. The result was that only 2,500 "fighting troops" got away while 1,500 failed. Conversely, 1,500 unscheduled troops got off.[30] This is the scale of the problem. Beevor nowhere acknowledges it. It follows that if Laycock took off "over 200" men "early" (as emphatically he did not do), he would have been one offender among many, not the "focus of the issue."[31]

Before going further, a word is needed to dispel myths about the commandos on Crete. In the first place they were quite unlike "X Commando" in *Sword of Honour*. Layforce consisted of a Brigade HQ (in which Waugh was intelligence officer) and four battalions, each of 400 men. Only Brigade HQ and "A" and "D" Battalions went to Crete, over 800 men in all. Part of "B" Battalion (on which "X Commando" is modeled) was engaged at Tobruk. "C" was on Cyprus preparing to attack Syria. The troops on Crete (despite the problems to be described) were keen and serious soldiers, not at all "smart," and "D" Battalion (the Middle East Commandos) was battle hardened. An Australian source ranks Layforce as "one of the few units to emerge [from Crete] with any reputation."[32]

May 26–30, 1941—Retreat and Rearguard

The retreat to Sphakia and the conduct of the rearguard lie outside the scope of this paper, except insofar as they relate to Layforce. By May 26th the Allies had lost the battle for northwest Crete. This meant loss of the campaign, for the area included the bases at Canea and Suda Bay, with all the "ammunition, supplies and food" needed to continue.[33] General Freyberg, whose first concern had always been to save his troops from capture, now sought permission to evacuate the island.[34] In London the defeat was a shock, because it was thought that exact forewarning of the attack through Ultra had given the Allies an insuperable advantage.[35] One result of the unexpectedness of the defeat is that the historiography of Crete has focused almost exclusively on the question, Why? Why was the battle lost? Why did Lt. Col. L. W. Andrew withdraw from the hill commanding Maleme airfield? Why was an immediate counterattack not launched? Thus preoccupied, major historians such as Dan Davin did not question informants about the evacuation and this chapter is of necessity exploratory.[36]

The troops from the northwest were ordered to retreat to the tiny fishing village of Sphakia on the south coast of the island, forty miles distant across the rugged mountains that traverse Crete. There the Navy would embark them. The retreating soldiers ranged from disciplined units of the rearguard to demoralized stragglers. But most were base troops from Suda Bay—cooks, clerks, storemen, mechanics, and Palestinian and Cypriot Pioneers who had never been armed. Traveling in blistering heat away from supplies of food and water, sleepless because German strafing by day forced them to move only at night, this stream of starving, parched, exhausted soldiers has become the defining image of the Crete campaign. To some witnesses it signified heroic endurance. But organized infantry tended to despise the "fear in the face of adversity" shown by what *looked* like a panic-stricken "rabble" that had thrown away its weapons.[37] Waugh wrote only briefly about the "pitiful spectacle," saving his scorn for the officers who had abdicated responsibility for their men (*DEW* 505, 503).[38]

Layforce mounted a successful, but troubled, rearguard. "A" and "D" Battalions of Layforce arrived at Suda Bay on May 25th and 26th respectively, in order to carry out Commando-type raids on German airfields. But by May 26th evacuation had been ordered and Freyberg instructed Layforce to act as a rearguard for the troops withdrawing to Sphakia. Laycock praised Freyberg's decision;[39] but when he went to General E. C. Weston's headquarters for orders, he found Weston "asleep on the floor" and "completely exhausted." Weston remained out of action for several days (*DEW* 499).[40] Fortunately Laycock met Brigadiers James Hargest (New Zealand) and George Vasey (Australia); they got on well,[41] and the three men "decided to fight [their] own battle."[42] Thus Layforce, with New Zealand and Australian units, improvised a rearguard. This typifies a campaign in which Layforce "did not once . . . receive an order from any higher formation without going to ask for it" (*DEW* 502).[43]

Another problem was that the commanding officer of "A" Battalion, Lt. Col. F. B. Colvin, cracked up and had to be relieved. Waugh's *Diaries* (502–4), Major F. C. C. Graham's "Cretan Crazy Week," and Laycock's letters record this sad event.[44] Colvin's personal qualities are irrelevant here,[45] but his actions are germane. Both Graham and Waugh describe a panic-stricken Colvin moving Brigade HQ far south without Laycock's knowledge. Laycock then sacked him (*DEW* 503–4).[46] Despite this, Colvin ordered "A" Battalion to withdraw while it was covering "D" Battalion's redeployment. Catastrophe could have followed.[47] Laycock was overheard to say that if Colvin and he returned to Egypt, he would "cashier" him.[48] But given the military's attitude to failure in battle, Colvin's return was unlikely.[49]

Desertion was also a problem. A group of Commandos was detected on a ship on the second night of the evacuation,[50] while both Waugh (*DEW* 507) and Anthony Cheetham name three officers who "disappeared" from Layforce headquarters. In a letter to Davin, Cheetham describes Laycock's reaction as "worried, and frivolous." Davin linked the desertions with *Sword of Honour* and wrote on Cheetham's letter above the name of a Hussar deserter: "Ivor Claire?"[51]

May 28th–30th—Embarkation Orders, Misleading Signals

Unable to evacuate all Allied troops, Creforce had to decide which units were to go and in what order. On May 28th, it set out a "programme" showing 15,000 troops being lifted from Sphakia over May 28th–31st. It ordered Layforce and the Royal Marines on "the night 31 May/1 June" to "hold an intermediate position" and then "disengage and embark": "It is intended to embark 5 NZ Inf. Bde and 19 Aust Bde on this night. Therefore the only troops available to hold an intermediate position will be the RM Bn and LAYFORCE. This they MUST do during 31 May and at nightfall they will disengage and embark night 31 May/1 June."[52]

Thus, Layforce was required to act as a rearguard for 5 NZ Infantry Brigade and 19 Australian Brigade on the last night of the evacuation, and then to "embark at nightfall." In the event, for reasons that will become clear, the Marine battalion with most of 19 Australian Brigade and the Commandos were left behind on Crete, but this does not alter Creforce's original intention that Layforce embark.

One reason for the failure to lift as many men as expected was lack of communication between the generals. Freyberg took charge of the evacuation and left Weston to organize the rearguard. But on May 29th Weston angrily protested against Freyberg's interference with his (Weston's) evacuation arrangements.[53] Far more serious were Freyberg's inaccurate and self-contradictory signals to General Headquarters Middle East, fatally understating numbers to be embarked and the troops' ability to resist. On May 28th Freyberg signaled: "It is most unlikely we shall be able to hold out here until night 31/1. . . . I am certain that tomorrow night [May 29th] will be the last that we can hope to get our people away."[54] This pessimism sharply contrasted with Navy reports that on the same night "up to 10,000 troops [would] be available for evacuation." So disturbed was Admiral

Cunningham by the Creforce signals, which made the Navy's job "most difficult," that he collected the signals and attached them to his narrative as an appendix.[55] The Admiralty declined to print the appendix, but there is no doubt that misinformation from Creforce helped convince the Navy that a small lift of 2,000 on May 31st was all that was required.

May 30th—German Action; May 31st—German Inaction

On May 30th, the Germans reached Vitsilokoumos, a mountainous area twelve miles northeast of Sphakia. There they were held by a well-situated 19 Australian Brigade (HQ, 2/7, and 2/8 Battalions) and a Marine battalion. In addition, 5 NZ Infantry Brigade and Layforce created a perimeter (*not* an "inner" line) along the mountain ridges north of Sphakia and across open areas to the west and east. The Germans immediately tried to move around the defenses in order to encircle Sphakia. But heavy casualties "convinced [them] the position was strongly defended," and, as a result, there was "no [significant] enemy activity on 31 May."[56] The Germans prudently settled for an attack on June 2nd, when air support would arrive.[57] Light German patrols did reach the coast many miles to the east and west of Sphakia but "created no pressure."[58] Consequently, on May 31st the Germans were not an immediate threat to Sphakia. Eminent historians have long agreed on these facts.[59] But Beevor, determined to convict Laycock of failing to shield Sphakia, repeatedly claims that by May 31st "detachments of mountain troops had . . . surrounded the beachhead."[60] This is simply not true.[61]

On the night of May 30th, Freyberg and his entire staff, including those organizing the evacuation, flew to Alexandria. This left Weston in command. The last signal from the Navy that night was ominous. It indicated that the Navy would send all "available" ships but the number lifted would "not exceed" 2,000.[62] Weston's first act was to send out trusted officers to establish the number of troops actually at Sphakia.

May 31st, Morning—Uncertainty, Hopes
for Evacuation on Two More Nights

As this fateful day began, Weston, lacking definite information, had to *assume* the Navy would arrive that night and pick up 2,000 men. He hoped it would return on the next night, June 1st, and possibly on June 2nd. Orders required him to embark "fighting troops" (those still organized to fight) first. He made a list of twelve such units, each with its quota of places, 4,000 men in all. Fifth on the list was "LAYFORCE 500."[63]

Weston then gave orders to the 2,000 who were to leave that night: 5 NZ Infantry Brigade, 1,100; 2/8 Australian Battalion, 203; Landing and Maintenance Marines, 200; walking wounded; and other small quotas.[64] The New Zealanders would provide perimeter defense during the day; then Layforce, 17 Australian Battalion, 1 Welch Regiment, and the Rangers would take over their positions at 6:30 p.m.[65] The Marines and 19 Australian Brigade would remain in place at Vitsilokoumos at least until the next night, June 1st, when (Weston hoped) they and the perimeter troops would be embarked. Thus, on the morning of May 31st there was no question of Layforce's leaving that night.

The Navy confirmed that it would pick up 2,000 men as forecast. But Weston's officers now reported many thousands more troops at Sphakia than had earlier been believed. At 11:51 a.m. Weston therefore signaled: "Request anticipated operations tonight *and* subsequent nights. Approx. 9000 still remain. . . . Have every hope of using Spharkia [*sic*] again tomorrow night." He also cabled a "plan for evacuation" for the nights June 1st/2nd, 2nd/3rd in which he himself would embark June 1st/2nd.[66] Consternation followed. The heavily depleted Navy had other vital tasks. Now it faced an unexpected further effort. But the Naval Staff History reveals that political pressure led the Navy over the course of the day to add a cruiser and allow the ships to fill "to capacity," thus boosting the lift from 2,000 to more than 5,000.[67]

2:00 p.m.–6:00 p.m. May 31st—Brigadier
Hargest Takes Charge of Embarkation

The personal dynamics involved in deciding which units would get away from Crete are revealed in only one source, a letter by a "close associate" of Brigadier Hargest, Wynne Mason, who reveals how far Hargest took over arrangements. Having "little confidence in Weston," Hargest "determined" to ensure that his troops "would not take second place to those who had been at the evacuation point for some time and should (on the face of it) have had an opportunity to be evacuated." To be on the spot, he "moved his troops down from [above Sphakia] to the beach" without an order from Weston. "Hargest or Dawson or I," writes Mason, then "haunted [Weston's] HQ all day."[68]

During the afternoon, Hargest personally ordered Sphakia cleared at bayonet point, fearing that Palestinians, Cypriots, Greeks, and "Cretan civilians in battledress" might "crowd the evacuation beach" and "create a rabble."[69] Later he set up two heavily armed cordons around Sphakia, supported by machine-gun posts. All New Zealanders detailed to leave were to be lined up on the track to the beach by 10:00 p.m. It was Hargest's "persuasion," says Mason, that "made Weston give preference to [his] troops." His ruthless determination ensured that his men got away when so many other priority troops did not.

Sometime during the afternoon Laycock met with Weston, who proposed that Laycock surrender. Laycock refused the "offer" and Weston "ordered" Laycock to choose an officer to carry out the task. This matter will be fully discussed in the following.

6:30 p.m. May 31st—Final Signal; Last Ships; Numbers Doubled; Fresh Orders

At 6:30 p.m. Weston received a shocking signal that had been long delayed. It revealed that this was the last night on which the Navy would arrive. However, the blow was softened by the news that the ships would pick up, not 2,000 as forecast, but 3,600 (later revised to "ships' capacity," i.e., around 5,000).[70] Clearly, the decision to end the evacuation leaving thousands of troops behind was potentially catastrophic. If word spread, the "rabble" could become violent. And even the additional places created problems: recent orders and arrangements had to be reversed, and Brigadiers competed fiercely for larger quotas for their troops.

A conference was held. Hargest has left the only account of it. He boasts of "forcing up" the already large New Zealand quota from 1,100 to 1,400 and "getting off 1,500 actually" (an understatement).[71] He adds only that "the staff arranged increases all round."[72] But as will emerge later, there were also private arrangements.[73] Weston says nothing about a conference, but so concerned was he about the Australians and Marines at Vitsilokoumos that he personally climbed to Vasey's headquarters and at 8:00 p.m. reversed recently reiterated orders to stay in place until the next night. He gave 500 places to the Australians[74] and 300 to the Marines (which he later reduced to 100).[75] Vasey ordered the troops to hurry to Sphakia, beginning from 8:30 p.m.

But the question now arises, Did the conference, or did Weston, give any of the additional places to Layforce? Davin, following Hargest, hints that the conference did not: "Layforce had been the last troops to arrive. There would be no room for all who had fought. Some would have to stay."[76] But the conference decisions did not, apparently, bind Weston, who reduced the Marine battalion's quota from 300 to 100 as late as 10:30 p.m. It must also be remembered that at 6:30 p.m. it was impossible to give Layforce *time-specific* orders. As the final rearguard, it could embark only if the Germans remained inactive. At 6:30 p.m. no one *certainly* knew what the Germans would do. Moreover Davin, publishing in 1953, did not know the Naval Staff History published in 1960 and believed that the Navy was to lift only 3,500. Weston learned of the Navy's decision to fill "to capacity" only later in the evening, and that gave him a flexibility about numbers of which the conference and Davin were unaware.

6:30 p.m. and 11:30 p.m. May 31st—Weston Orders
Laycock and His Battalions to Embark

Very strong evidence suggests that during the evening of May 31st Weston gave Laycock and his men orders to leave Crete. Beevor denies that Weston gave the battalions such orders, but at this point I shall confine myself to setting out the events leading to the issuing of embarkation orders. A full discussion of the Creforce orders of May 28th and 30th, of the post-Crete documents (which strongly support Laycock), of related proposals that Laycock surrender and of Beevor's objections appear later.

It is certain from Waugh's *Diaries* and Davin's *Crete* that Weston met Laycock (with Waugh) to discuss "further orders."[77] The meeting must have taken place after 6:30 p.m. because the radio had failed, Weston already knew that this was the "last night for evacuation," and he was still advising "those who were left behind . . . to drift eastwards and look for boats" (*DEW* 508).[78] Only Waugh relates firsthand—albeit elliptically—what was said at this meeting. He has Weston repeat Freyberg's "order of priority for disembarkation which said Layforce was to be last, but all fighting troops had precedence over others." After a digression, Waugh goes on, "Weston said that we were to cover the withdrawal and that a message would be sent to us by the embarkation officer on Sphakia beach when we could retire" (*DEW* 508–9).[79]

Later, around 11:30 p.m. (the time is crucial and will be established later), Laycock hurried to Creforce headquarters to meet his brigade major, F. C. C. Graham, whom he had not seen all day. Graham reports Laycock's blurting out on arrival that Weston had given him "counter-orders": "We are to take *as many of our troops with us as we can.* . . . General Weston said *my staff will see to it,*"[80] which is different from, but not inconsistent with, Waugh's version. Graham's report is, of course, secondhand, but Beevor does not question Graham's reliability. Instead, he claims that Laycock invented the order and "lied" about it to Graham.[81] In light of all the known facts, Beevor's accusation is untenable. Graham was a no-

nonsense professional soldier who went on to a distinguished command; he was outside Laycock's social set, and no dupe. Moreover, Graham lodged Laycock's version of Weston's order in the Imperial War Museum and later reaffirmed its truth when replying to pointed questions from the editor of Waugh's *Diaries*.[82]

Four facts make it credible that Weston issued an embarkation order to Layforce. First, early on May 31st Layforce expected to embark, if at all, on June 1st or 2nd. Once it was known that the Navy would not return after May 31st but would double the number to be lifted that night, Layforce, a "fighting" unit, could reasonably expect a quota of the new places. Second, Laycock's report had a ring of truth, for no clever liar would invent a promise like "my staff will see to it," making his fate dependent on an unreliable third party. Third, Weston's "counter order" was plausible in the light of Weston's "casual" style and his propensity to reverse orders.[83] But the fourth consideration is compelling. Weston's directive as reported by Waugh and Laycock—"Weston said that we were to cover the withdrawal and that a message would be sent to us by the embarkation officer on Sphakia beach when we could retire"; "take as many of [your] troops with [you] as [you] can . . . my staff will see to it"—contains, on inspection, all the crucial elements found in the written Creforce order of May 28th, discussed earlier, which directs Layforce on "31 May/1June" to hold an "intermediate position" covering "5 NZ Infantry Brigade and 19 Australian Brigade" and "at nightfall . . . embark." On May 30th, Freyberg repeated that order to Laycock verbally: in Waugh's elliptical diary it comes out as "You were the last to come so you will be the last to go" (*DEW* 507).

In summary, then, Layforce received orders during the evening of May 31st that required it to do four things:

> (1) adopt an "intermediate position" / "cover the withdrawal"
> (2) retire "at nightfall" / "after a message from the embarkation officer"
> (3) leave "last of the [designated] fighting forces"
> (4) "embark" / "take as many of [your] troops with [you] as [you] can"

9:30 p m.–10:00 p.m.—Weston Orders Surrender

At 9:30 p.m. Weston returned to his headquarters, where authorization for troops left behind to surrender next morning had presumably been received.[84] He shouted for Laycock, who was not present, and Major Graham, who was, went in. There he found Lieutenant Colonel Colvin with Weston, and Weston dictated the surrender order to Graham, addressing it to "the senior officer available Lt. Col. Colvin." Graham kept one of the three copies.[85] Among the five extant versions of the surrender order, this one is unique. Other versions instruct the bearer to pass the order to the "senior officer left on the island." This one orders Colvin to surrender in person.[86] The difference occurs because if the evacuation had gone as planned, every lieutenant colonel commanding a "fighting" battalion would have left Crete—unless one was personally ordered to stay. The propriety of choosing Colvin to conduct the surrender is fully discussed later.

10:30 p.m–Midnight—Laycock at Creforce HQ;
Finds No Beach Officer; Withdraws Troops

Weston and the embarkation staff left the headquarters cave around 10:00 p.m. to join the Sunderland seaplane taking off at 11:50 p.m.[87] Later, after 11:35 p.m., Laycock "panted up" seeking "the embarkation officer" for orders to withdraw.[88] The time of Laycock's arrival is in dispute because Beevor says Weston summoned Graham into his cave "at about nine o'clock"[89]—which is half an hour earlier than Weston says he returned there; he has Weston leave immediately, Laycock arrive "shortly after" and "sweep . . . any Layforce personnel he could find down to the beach." Since the distance from cave to beach was about thirty minutes, Beevor's narrative puts Laycock on the beach by 10:30 p.m., certainly before "11:00 p.m.," which Beevor nominates as the hour at which Laycock sent for his other troops.[90] But Beevor cannot be right because, *before* Laycock "panted up," Graham had "*already*" heard "the ships . . . filling."[91] Since the leading cruiser *Phoebe* began loading at 11:35 p.m., Laycock arrived at headquarters after 11:35 p.m.[92]

Laycock now blurts out (as Graham, who had not seen Laycock since morning, relates) that Layforce had received orders to leave Crete but still needed permission to withdraw from its defensive positions. Gathering a few nearby colleagues (some who were asleep complained later about not being wakened[93]), Laycock "set off hot foot to Sphakia"[94] to find the "embarkation officer on [the] beach" (*DEW* 509). (Beevor wrongly implies that the party Laycock led to Sphakia numbered "over 200": he nowhere mentions any other large party of Commandos to reach the beach but claims that "*over 200 men of Layforce* slipped in ahead of the Australians."[95] Thus he must be saying that the Laycock party numbered "over 200.") As had Major Ralph Garrett RM earlier, Laycock found "no staff officer" on the beach.[96] Beevor claims that this was pretense, because Laycock must have known that the staff was going to depart,[97] but Garrett and Laycock had no reason to suppose that every embarkation officer would leave and not be replaced.

That no responsible staff officer was present is confirmed by Lt. Col. W. R. S. Windham, Royal Signals. His Minute sent to the Inter-Services Committee investigating Crete angrily protests that a young lieutenant on the beach on Signals business, who did not know that Crete was to be surrendered, had been "left to run the whole evacuation."[98] This lack of Creforce staff moved the Inter-Services Committee to insist that during evacuations a "Beachmaster" be appointed with "full knowledge of the local situation on shore."[99] A submission to the Committee asserted that the Beachmaster ought not to be anyone "raked up from the base" but an officer capable of handling men, making "difficult decisions," and taking "stern measures."[100]

In the absence of staff, Laycock now took drastic action. Time was running short for troops in distant positions to reach the beach by 2:30 a.m. Laycock therefore sent Private Ralph Tanner with a verbal message to Lt. Col. George Young, then commanding both Layforce battalions: "If [Layforce] *could* get away, they *were* to get away."[101] Beevor says this message is a "direct contravention of . . . orders"[102] and that it damns Laycock "straight from the horse's mouth."[103] In fact, as will be demonstrated, Laycock's withdrawal order was lawful and proper.

12:30 a.m.–2:30 a.m. June 1st—Layforce
Withdraws, 120 Commandos Escape

After receiving Laycock's order and having determined that German inactivity meant that the troops "could get away," Lieutenant Colonel Young began the lengthy process of withdrawing his two battalions. Captain Jocelyn Nicholls and his men were typical of the Commandos. In "excellent spirits" while mounting perimeter guard in the west, they had been observing the shadowy Navy ships, believing their own chances of getting off "almost nil."[104] Then "around midnight" came the order to withdraw "if possible."[105] The enemy had not moved since the rearguard withdrew from Vitsilokoumos, so "getting away" was "possible," and the troops raced in from distant posts to Sphakia, but the majority suffered bitter disappointment.[106] Beevor says that the Commandos were "too dispersed to react in time" to reach Sphakia. In fact, the bulk of "D" and "A" Battalions, who were centrally located, reached Sphakia around 2:00 a.m.,[107] where the crush prevented their getting through to the beach.[108] Those watching the eastern perimeter had so far to travel that they arrived only after the ships had left.[109] Perhaps some Commandos "made their own way" to the boats.[110] But—and this fact is central to the entire discussion, although Beevor completely misses it—120 members of "A" Battalion located on the western perimeter ran onto the beach from that direction at 2:30 a.m. and just got away on the very last landing craft to leave the shore.

This last-minute escape of 120 Commandos, unnoticed by Beevor, is fully explained in the "A" Battalion War Diary and is clearly noted in the Layforce War Diary, in Waugh's *Diaries,* and in other records.[111] Troops "A, B, part of E and G" had been covering the west. Running to Sphakia from that direction, they did not encounter the crowds blocking the east. Moreover, as it was 2:30 a.m., the pickets had already embarked. Thus the 120 men got through the village streets and by "sheer luck" and amid "great confusion" were taken aboard the last assault landing craft (ALC).[112] Letters to parents reveal how close a shave it was: the men "climbed down a cliff and by running . . . got on the very last boat to leave."[113]

For the 120 Commandos, their escape was "sheer luck." But while they got away, around 550 higher-priority Australians and Marines were captured. Why?

11:30 p.m.–2:30 a.m. May 31st /June 1st—How Priority Fighting Troops Were Prevented from Embarking

The full complexity of what went wrong with the later stages of the evacuation is beyond the scope of this chapter to explain. Suffice to say that over 9,000 British and Empire troops, as well as many Greeks and Cretans, were at Sphakia, most spread around the rough plateau high above the beach. Everyone was confident of being evacuated. But only 4,000-plus British and Empire "fighting troops" could be taken off. Of the 5,000 troops who would be left behind, some were specialists (e.g., artillery, engineers) or members of officered groups of fifty; but many were "unattached," and some were lawless and desperate.

The selective embarkation of 4,000-plus "fighting troops" in the dark and over difficult terrain was inherently difficult. The "road" to Sphakia ended in a goat track down a 500-foot escarpment. The path to the beach was sunken and narrow, fatally easy for truculent stragglers to block. The beach was minuscule. And thousands of unattached troops milling about and desperate to get away compounded the other difficulties. Even Major A. S. Keyes, whose 2/8 Australian Battalion followed the New Zealanders to the beach and got off at 1:30 a.m., complained bitterly of "practically non-existent control" and the "necessity for units . . . to take measures to secure a passage down to the beach."[114]

In spite of the difficulties, the evacuation began extremely well. The New Zealanders, who had the lion's share of places, were determined not to be stopped. Brigadier Hargest ordered Sphakia cleared at bayonet point.[115] Then at 8:00 p.m. he set a shoulder-to-shoulder cordon of Maori around the village and the beach, and another cordon of 22 NZ Battalion two miles inland. Armed with grenades and supported by machine-gun posts, the cordons strictly controlled access.[116] By 10:00 p.m., well over 1,500 New Zealanders were lined up on the track leading to the beach. At 10:30 p.m. 540 men boarded three ALCs ready to go out to meet the ships when they arrived at 11:20 p.m.; lifts continued until, shortly after midnight, the majority of the New Zealanders were aboard. Then, shortly after midnight, the New Zealand cordons withdrew and embarked, having handed over to 64 Medium Regiment Royal Artillery.

No history records, and only one draft Narrative[117] briefly mentions,[118] the withdrawal of the New Zealand cordons and the handover to 64 Medium Regiment (or even the presence of the 64th at Sphakia).[119] Fortunately, the War Diary of 28 NZ (Maori) Battalion, the War Diary of 64 Medium Regiment, and a long letter to his unit historian by Major Dyer, who commanded the cordon, establish that the Maori guarded the beach only "till about 2400 hrs when its duties were taken over by 64 Medium Bty [sic]."[120] Dyer's letter also describes violence that erupted during the handover. Before the new cordon could settle, "rabble" poured down the hill on top of it. The Maoris raced back with fixed bayonets and, amid "sights best forgotten,"[121] restored the line. But from that point onward, troops scheduled to embark found access to the beach extremely difficult. Resentful stragglers, many of whom had been at Sphakia longer than the rearguard troops, sat down in the track to stop them from passing. "Movement control officers" with incorrect orders forbade the Australians to move forward. And because *every* Creforce officer had decamped by seaplane before midnight, no one on the island possessed the knowledge or authority to enforce priorities.

By contrast, because the outer cordon withdrew "too early,"[122] the beach lay open to intruders using unofficial routes. Universally respected witnesses such as Major Burston observed that "by nightfall organization had completely broken down at Sfakia . . . and troops were reaching the beach across country."[123] Ralph Tanner, who carried the withdrawal order from Laycock to Young, remembers no cordons "going or coming,"[124] potentially confirming that the withdrawal order was issued after midnight. The Australian Official History praises Captain Forbes, who led a "disciplined party across country" onto the beach "at 1.00 am" and embarked.[125] The Narrative of the New Zealand Artillery (which was not scheduled to leave) explains the circumstances in which a party of gunners was taken aboard: "After the organized groups . . . had been taken off (the rest of the fighting units could not get through the crowds on the paths down to the beach) the last flight of landing craft was loaded with any troops at hand. Captain Bliss took good care that his men were among those duly embarked."[126] Thus, at the end of the evacuation the Navy was loading nonscheduled gunners and "any troops at hand." Since this anomaly arose because the "fighting units" were prevented from "getting through the crowds on the path leading to the beach," the narrator is rightly proud of Captain Bliss's initiative. Clearly, the facts that justify the gunners' escape ahead of the priority Australians and Marines also justify the Navy's embarking the 120 Commandos—who were scheduled "fighting troops"—when they ran onto the beach at 2:30 a.m.

2:15 a.m.–2:30 a.m—Did the 120 Commandos Who Escaped at 2:30 a.m. "Jump the Queue" in Front of the 550 Higher-Priority Australians and Marines?

To answer this question we must return to the Australian and Marine rear-guard leaving Vitsilokoumos about 9:00 p.m. to go to Sphakia and embark. After superhuman effort,[127] they arrived at the approaches to the village before 11:30 p.m.[128] Bitter disappointment awaited. A turbulent throng blocked the path. Forming single file, each man clutching the belt of the man in front, the Australians followed by the Marines worked their way through the crush. Then stragglers sat down in the track to prevent their passing. Worse, "movement control officers," presumably members of 64 Medium Regiment with incorrect orders, instructed the Australians to halt.[129] Eventually the Australians took matters into their own hands, but the delay meant that these troops took over three hours to cover the short distance to the beach and arrived too late to board. Of the 500 Australians and 100 Marines from Vitsilokoumos ordered to embark, only 50 from 19 Brigade HQ and 16 from 2/7 Battalion got away. The remaining 534 Australians and Marines were left behind.

The best explanation of the tragedy is found in the complementary narratives of the 2/7 Australian Battalion War Diary, Brigadier Vasey's "Account of the Operations of the AIF on Crete," and David Horner's *General Vasey's War*.[130] After reaching Sphakia and being held up, Vasey went to the beach and waited anxiously for his troops. At 2:00 a.m., two ALCs became available for the Australians. At "0215 hrs" Vasey's headquarters "arrived on the beach" and boarded. But the 450 men of 2/7 Bn "had been delayed longer." Eventually, Lt. Col. T. G. Walker "took command of the [2/7] column" and "pushed on past armed parties to the beach." But it was too late: sixteen leading soldiers boarded the last landing craft; the rest were left behind. The tragedy has several explanations. The 2/7 Battalion's War Diary forthrightly complains that "large numbers of rabble were taken off and no effective control was attempted or maintained." Vasey says that movement control was not told that "my HQ and 7 Bn were included in the troops to embark that night . . . and this accounted for the delay of my own HQ and the loss of 7 Bn."[131]

In light of the preceding, Beevor's story of Laycock's leading "over 200" Commandos to the beach before 11:00 p.m., thus "jumping the queue" in front of the Australians and Marines, is pure fiction. The truth is that 120 Commandos ran onto the beach at 2:30 a.m. The Navy embarked them because 2/7 Battalion had not arrived, having suffered a "longer delay" than 19 Brigade HQ, which arrived at 2:15 a.m. and got off. That fifteen-minute gap was decisive. The Navy had a strict timetable and was almost certainly exasperated by the hold-ups that had so far stopped the ships from filling to capacity.[132] When the anxiously awaited 2/7 Battalion did not appear, the Navy, given the need to sail on time, presumably felt obliged to load the waiting boats with "anyone at hand." Nonscheduled parties like Captain Bliss's were "at hand." And then 120 Commandos, who were scheduled "fighting troops," ran onto the beach.

BEEVOR'S ACCUSATIONS

Beevor's case against Laycock is not systematically argued. Rather, it creates a vivid impression through selected detail, anecdote, and camouflaged guesswork—"must have," "more likely," "perhaps," and "seems to have" occur with astonishing frequency. It may seem ponderous, therefore, to counter this lively story with documented argument. Nevertheless, the following pages will analyze nine charges that Beevor levels at Laycock, as well as certain claims he makes about the evacuation that are material to the charges. In the light of the previous narrative, it will become evident that charges (1)–(6) have no foundation in reality, while (7)–(9) connect with real events. These three matters will be fully discussed.

(1) *"Laycock Swept [Over 200 Men]*
Down to the Beach" at About 10:30 p.m.

Beevor says Laycock "swept Graham and any other Layforce personnel [he] could find down to the beach" around 10:30 p.m.[133] But how many men does Beevor imagine were "swept down" at this time? The answer must be "over 200," because Beevor makes no further mention of Commandos arriving at the beach until he claims that "over two hundred men from Layforce slipped in ahead of [the Australians trying to embark]."[134] He is of course wrong. The New Zealand pickets then operating would never have allowed 200 troops near the beach without written orders (see note 116). Moreover, "over 200" Commandos could not have left on the last night. The official total of Layforce personnel returned from Crete is *209*. The bulk of the total is the *120* who escaped at 2:30 a.m. on the last night under Captain Nicholls (never mentioned by Beevor) with about *12* HQ. Around *35* wounded and *35* deserters left on previous nights; *7* escaped after the surrender.[135] Obviously, the number who escaped on the last night was about 130. And there is no room in the total *209* returned for an added "over 200" men that Beevor imagines Laycock "swept" to the beach.

(2) *Laycock "Brought [the Rest of Layforce] Down to Sphakia"*
before "the Marines and 2/7 Australian Battalion Had Arrived"

Beevor says that Laycock reached the beach around 10:30 p.m. and at "about 11:00 p.m." issued an order to the rest of his troops to leave their perimeter positions and go to the beach, and that he did this *before* the Australians and Marines from Vitsilokoumos had arrived at Sphakia.[136] He is wrong on each count. Graham's memoir and the log of the *Phoebe* show that Laycock arrived at Creforce HQ after 11:35 p.m. and at the beach close to midnight, one and a half hours later than Beevor alleges. Only after that did he send for his troops. Nor does Beevor so much as guess at the time the Australians and Marines arrived at Sphakia. Major Madoc's journal shows that the Marines (who followed the Australians) had "moved on by slow stages with frequent halts" for quite some time before they heard General Weston's Sunderland taking off at 11:50 p.m. (see note 128). Thus, the Australians and Marines were in front of Sphakia at 11:30 p.m., and Laycock issued his withdrawal order around midnight. Laycock's order was issued *after*, not before, the Australians and Marines arrived. Thus it is evident that Laycock carried out his orders to cover their withdrawal.

(3) *Orders Required Layforce to "Stay in Position"*
Until Other Fighting Forces Were "Safely Away"

Beevor asserts that orders required Layforce "to stay in position until ['the Marines and 2/7 Australian Battalion'] were safely away,"[137] or "until after their embarkation."[138] But these assertions misrepresent the orders given to Laycock. Even granted orders to leave literally "last" of all fighting forces, no version of any order required Layforce to "stay in place" until other fighting troops were "safely away."

An order to remain in place many rugged miles from the evacuation beach until other troops had actually boarded was tantamount to requiring Layforce to remain behind on Crete. And that would have contradicted the written Creforce order of May 28th, which directed Layforce to cover two designated units—5 NZ Infantry Brigade and 19 Australian Brigade—and then "disengage at nightfall and embark," which they could not do unless they left their positions in time. The Layforce War Diary states matters accurately: "Layforce positions to be held . . . *only as long as was necessary* to *cover other fighting forces.*"[139]

(4) *Laycock Claimed to Have Orders for Layforce to Leave "Early" and Tried "to Leave in Front of Other Fighting Troops"*

Central to Beevor's case is the notion that Laycock tried to get his troops away "early." It grows out of the demonstrably incorrect claim that Laycock led a large body of troops to the beach before orders permitted, and that he instructed the rest of his troops to withdraw from their defensive positions before other fighting forces had reached Sphakia. It also depends on putting words in Laycock's mouth. Thus, Laycock reported Weston as saying, "As many of your men as you can get away must go tonight—my staff will see to it." Beevor, without explanation, turns this cautious permission to embark, if possible, into a claim that Weston had allowed "Layforce to jump the queue in front of his own Marine battalion and the two Australian battalions."[140] He makes the repeated allegation that Laycock claimed to have orders to leave "*in front of*" or "*before*" other "fighting forces."[141]

But nowhere is there a trace of such a claim by Laycock; nor did Laycock act as though he had received orders to leave "*in front of* other 'fighting troops.'" On the contrary, all Layforce personnel—Laycock, Graham, Young, Waugh, Nicholls, et al.—express the need for extreme haste if *any* Commandos are to reach the beach *before the ships leave*. Because the night was such a "hell of a rush," Laycock did not even wait to rouse his headquarters staff before "hot footing" it to Sphakia to find a beachmaster. He managed to persuade the Navy to hold back "the last boats . . . to allow 'Layforce' an extra chance of getting aboard."[142] The fact is that the bulk of Layforce reached Sphakia after 2:00 a.m., three hours later than the Australians and Marines. The 120 who escaped scrambled onto the last ALC at the last minute. Commandos from more distant positions arrived only after the ships had sailed. The notion that Laycock claimed to have orders to leave "early" is therefore sheer fantasy.

(5) *"Detachments of Mountain Troops Had by Then
Surrounded the Beachhead and Waugh Himself Had
Recorded Firing at Dusk. There Was No Enemy Contact
Only Because the Germans Did Not Fight at Night"*

In trying to convict Laycock of shirking his duty to guard Sphakia, Beevor insists that the Germans had "surrounded the beachhead" and continued fighting longer than the Layforce War Diary admits. Both assertions are false. The Germans reached Vitsilokoumos, twelve miles northeast and high above Sphakia, on May 30th. There, well-situated Australian and Marine units blocked their advance. The Germans *tried* to encircle Sphakia on May 30th, but heavy casualties forced them to desist. Instead, they opted to wait for air support on June 2nd. Thus, the fact that a party of Germans were, in Beevor's words, "annihilated"[143] in a ravine close to Sphakia on May 30th does not prove, as Beevor imagines, that Sphakia was under threat on May 31st.[144] Rather, the "annihilation" was another reason for German inactivity on May 31st. They did send light patrols to the coast many miles to the east and west of Sphakia, but these created no pressure. Furthermore, on May 31st New Zealand units and Layforce threw a wide screen around Sphakia. It is nonsense to imply that "detachments of mountain troops" were inside the screen. Nor, *pace* Beevor, was there "scattered firing around the perimeter that evening."[145] The last shooting occurred at 8:45 p.m. just before the Marines pulled out. All contact ended at 9:15 p.m., when the last Australians withdrew without incident. No other unit came into contact with the Germans that night.

(6) *Laycock "Lied" and "Directed Waugh to Falsify the War Diary"*

If Laycock had received orders to embark "last" of the fighting troops but had instead swept 200 Commandos to the beach around 10:30 p.m., thus jumping the queue ahead of other fighting forces; and *if* Layforce had instructions to remain in place until other fighting troops were "safely away" but instead withdrew to Sphakia before the Australians and Marines arrived; and *if* Laycock and his men had attempted to leave Crete without orders; and *if* Laycock failed to protect the evacuation from the Germans who were "surrounding" it—then Beevor could reasonably have argued that Laycock "must have lied to justify himself,"[146] that "Laycock's lies . . . must have troubled [Waugh's] conscience," and that Laycock "directed Waugh to falsify the War Diary."[147] But Laycock *did* have orders to leave Crete, he and his men did *not* have orders to remain in place until other fighting troops were "safely away," he did *not* take his men to the beach "early," and Sphakia was *not* "surrounded." In short, Laycock had no need to "lie to justify himself," and Waugh had no need to "falsify the War Diary" to protect Laycock.

(7) *Laycock's Personal Escape from Crete Was "Morally Doubtful" Because He "Passed On" the Surrender to Colvin*

Beevor's treatment of Laycock's personal escape from Crete is mystifying. He acknowledges the Creforce order that the "HQ of each unit must be embarked."[148] He records the fact that General Weston "allowed Layforce Brigade Headquarters to leave."[149] He admits that Lieutenant Colonel Young, who commanded "D" Battalion, "never blamed Laycock" for leaving,[150] a very pale reflection of Young's actual words. In fact, Young was "strongly of the opinion" that Laycock's departure was "justified" and "required."[151] Beevor even quotes Waugh's approval of Weston's decision that Colvin surrender: "He [Weston] . . . realized that it was foolish to sacrifice a first-class man [Laycock] for this and chose instead [Colvin]" (*DEW* 509).[152] And yet, having agreed that Laycock's departure was "legitimate," *and* that Waugh welcomed the substitution of Colvin for Laycock, Beevor asserts—guided only by nebulous intimations from the novel *Officers and Gentlemen*— that "the passing on of the surrender order . . . raised more than a doubt in Waugh's mind."[153]

The probity of Laycock's "passing on the surrender order" to Colvin is worthy of discussion, though not for Beevor's reasons. The known facts are few: namely, Weston proposed that Laycock surrender, a proposal Laycock "frankly refused,"[154] and Weston ordered Colvin to surrender.[155] Beyond this, all we have are two secondhand accounts of a conversation between Weston and Laycock, Davin's report of a subsequent order by Weston, and Christopher Sykes's denial that GHQ Mid-East was disturbed by Laycock's actions.

One secondhand account is from Major Graham. Laycock told Graham that Weston had "ordered" him (Laycock), as "the Junior Brigade Commander on Crete," to surrender next morning and that he accepted the order. But "Weston's staff officer" pointed out that Laycock had two battalions elsewhere. After that, no more is said about Laycock's surrendering. Instead, Weston ordered Laycock to leave Crete with "as many of his men as he could get away."[156] Weston's change of mind is credible because the staff officer had indicated what Weston probably did not know, that Laycock, though a colonel, was responsible for a full brigade with two battalions on Crete, one on Cyprus preparing for Syria, and one partly engaged at Tobruk. Graham's account is consistent with the Creforce policy of evacuating all brigade headquarters.

Professor G. C. Kiriakopoulos gives a dramatized, seemingly eyewitness account of a meeting during which Weston tells Laycock that he (Weston) is leaving that night and that he has been instructed to "pass the command to the next senior officer." Weston then "*offers* Laycock command," and Laycock "respectfully declines the *offer*."[157] (Christopher Sykes, who was on the staff of GHQ Mid-East at the time, independently gave a similar explanation to a correspondent: Laycock was not "ordered" but "urged" to surrender "with the right of refusal.")[158] But "declining the *offer*" did not end the matter. Kiriakopoulos says that Weston now *"ordered"* Laycock to "pick the officer" to capitulate.[159] This part of the account is corroborated by Davin, who writes that after 6:30 p.m. Weston sent for Laycock, who "was to nominate an officer" to capitulate.[160]

The "command" that Laycock "nominate an officer" to capitulate could, of course, imply that Weston believed the task of capitulating belonged to Laycock, or at least to Layforce. During the afternoon, when only 2,000 men were to leave that night and it was clear that Layforce would have to stay behind, Laycock was the first choice for surrender; although Weston may well have "offered" rather than "ordered" surrender to give the adventurous young officer a chance to take to the hills rather than be captured. On the other hand, after 6:30 p.m., when 4,000-plus were scheduled to leave, the responsibility for surrendering no longer fell on Laycock. His departure was consistent with the Creforce policy of evacuating all brigade headquarters, and not inconsistent with General Wavell's message to "pass the command" to the "Senior British Officer *remaining behind*."[161] At 9:30 p.m. Weston ordered Colvin to remain behind and surrender.[162] Presumably he judged Colvin capable of the task, for, when not under fire, Colvin still cut a "soldierly figure" (*DEW* 502), and on the morning of surrender he was seen presciently urging troops away from Sphakia to avoid bombing.

In summary, Lieutenant Colonel Young's judgment, quoted previously, appears definitive: as he was brigadier, Laycock's departure was "justified" and "required." If that was so, then some other senior officer had to remain and surrender. Hard military logic dictated that the choice fell on the man who would be "of less value to the war effort."

(8) *"On the Basis of All the Evidence, Laycock Did Not Receive
'a Counter-Order' Allowing Layforce to Depart en Bloc"*[163]

Beevor several times denies that General Weston gave Laycock an order
allowing Layforce to leave Crete. But his denials about orders to *leave* are
always muddled with a claim that Laycock tried to leave "*in front of*" other
fighting forces, and they are further confused by his conflating the order to
leave, which had been issued by Weston, with the order to *withdraw,* which
Laycock was compelled to issue on his own responsibility. Nevertheless,
the first and most essential task is to answer the straightforward question,
Did Weston give Laycock and Layforce orders to leave Crete?

To support his denial, Beevor correctly points to the fact that there is no
evidence of a written order issued by Creforce on the night May 31st directing Layforce to embark. But against that gap in the evidence must be bal-
anced the compelling weight of the written and verbal orders of May 28th,
30th and 31st (cited previously) and of every post-Crete official record.

To recapitulate: On May 28th, Creforce instructed the Commandos in
writing to "hold an intermediate position" on "night 31 May/1 June" (then
envisaged as the last night of evacuation) and "at nightfall disengage and
embark." Thus, *pace* Beevor, "an order allowing Layforce to embark *en
bloc*" was in force from May 28th onward. On May 30th, Waugh records
Freyberg's saying to Laycock, "You were the last to come so you will be
the last to go" (*DEW* 507), presumably elliptical shorthand for Creforce's
written order of May 28th. And on May 31st, Weston repeated to Laycock
Freyberg's "order of priority for disembarkation which said Layforce was
to be last but all fighting troops had precedence over others" (*DEW* 508). In
Major Graham's account, Laycock said he had received a "counter-order,"
presumably because the order to leave that night (May 31st / June 1st) reversed the order given in the morning that Layforce leave on June 1st or
2nd, and Graham recalled the order as indefinite (take as many troops "as
you can"). Finally, Weston indicated how Layforce's withdrawal was to be
facilitated: "My staff will see to it" (Graham's version), and an "embarkation officer" would send a message when Layforce "could retire" (Waugh's
diary version).

Typing up the Layforce War Diary in Egypt, Waugh had no written
evacuation order dated May 31st to transcribe. Instead, he must have put
into formal language the various verbal orders Laycock had received and
entered them as "final order for evacuation" at "31 May, 1400 hrs": "Final
order from CREFORCE for evacuation. (a) Layforce positions not to be
held to last man and last round but only as long as was necessary to cover

withdrawal of other fighting forces. (b) No withdrawal before order from H.Q. (c) Layforce to embark after other fighting forces but before stragglers."[164] It is difficult to understand how an embarkation order issued at 2:00 pm could be "final," because at 2:00 p.m. there was no question of Layforce's leaving that night. One explanation for the timing at 2:00 p.m. is that the order sets out the conditions for Layforce to embark irrespective of when it might happen. At 2:00 p.m. Weston still hoped the ships would return on June 1st and 2nd, and the order applied to *any* night, whether May 31st or June 1st or 2nd. As it turned out, Layforce covered the withdrawal of other "fighting forces" on May 31st as ordered, and about 120 Commandos embarked absolutely "last" of the "fighting forces" who got away.[165]

That Weston gave Layforce an order to leave Crete on the night of May 31st is put beyond doubt by a wealth of post-Crete documents: (a) Weston's Despatch and War Diary place "LAYFORCE 500" fifth on a list of the twelve "fighting" units that Weston says he was "required by orders to get away," and the list, when it includes Layforce, makes "approximately equal allocations for Australians, N.Z. and British troops."[166] (b) The British Narrator, Colonel E. E. Rich, twice says, "Layforce was ordered late in the evening to embark." He also regrets Layforce's failure to "penetrate the rabble" and reach the boats. This evidence is crucial, because the narrator submits a draft to all senior officers involved in a campaign, and they *do* comment. If Laycock had disobeyed an order to remain behind, or if he had received no order to leave, Freyberg or Weston would have quietly told Rich to drop the references to "orders to embark."[167] (c) Winston Churchill was furious about the Crete debacle, and an Inter-Services Committee chaired by the outspoken Brigadier Guy Salisbury-Jones was set up to investigate.[168] Beevor blusters that the committee was "well known to be an exercise in buck-passing and umbrella opening."[169] In fact, the committee's report was so "controversial" that it circulated only at the highest levels; Brigadier Erskine was ordered to expurgate it; and the document, and its author, were then buried.[170] Brigadier Vasey and General Weston, whose troops Beevor says were captured because of Layforce, gave evidence to the committee. And yet the report treats Layforce and the Australians, in the same paragraph, as equally unfortunate victims of disorder. It also "regretted the misunderstanding" that led to "the bulk of Layforce being left behind" and excused the failure by allowing for "great distances" and "no means of communication."[171] This implies that Weston intended the Commandos to be sent an order to withdraw, but that the staff failed to carry it out because of the practical difficulties involved. (d) Ralph Tanner, Waugh's soldier servant, carried the withdrawal order from Laycock to the battalions,[172] and Weston recommended him for a "C. in C's Award."[173] Weston would not have recommended a decoration for carrying an order that contravened his own instructions.

In short, the evidence provided by Laycock, Graham, and Waugh that Weston permitted Laycock and Layforce to leave Crete is corroborated by the War Diary/Despatch of the Officer Commanding Crete, General Weston; by the British Narrator, Colonel Rich; and by the Inter-Services Committee. These authorities had access to every relevant document and witness, friendly and hostile, immediately after the campaign. Their testimony leaves no doubt that Weston gave Laycock and the Layforce battalions orders to leave Crete.

(9) *There Was No "Specific Counter-Order Allowing Layforce to Abandon Its Defensive Positions. . . . The Key Phrase Is 'Col. Laycock on Own Authority.' This Demonstrates Straight from the Horse's Mouth That Laycock Had Not Received Permission to Embark His Men Before Other Fighting Forces"*[174]

Nothing better illustrates Beevor's confusion than this passage, because it asserts, as if Laycock claimed the opposite, that "there was no specific order allowing Layforce to abandon its defensive positions." Of course there was no such order. The Layforce War Diary itself explains that Creforce staff left *without* giving an order allowing Layforce to abandon its defensive positions, and that, because Creforce *failed* to issue this order, Laycock issued it himself. "22 hrs, 31 May: On finding that the entire staff of CREFORCE had embarked, in view of the fact that all fighting forces were now in position for embarkation and that there was no enemy contact, **Col. LAYCOCK on own authority, issued orders to Lt. Col. YOUNG to lead troops to SPHAKION** by route avoiding the crowded main approach to town and to use his own personality to obtain priority laid down in Div. [Creforce] orders" (Emphasis added). Quite obviously, the point at issue is not whether Creforce issued an order "allowing Layforce to abandon its defensive positions"—the Layforce War Diary makes clear that it did not—but whether Laycock was legally and morally entitled to issue the withdrawal order "*on own authority.*"

At the post-6:30 p.m. meeting between Weston and Laycock (with Waugh present), Weston (in Laycock's report to Graham) allowed Layforce to leave Crete and added, "My staff will see to it." In Waugh's account: "We were to cover the withdrawal and . . . a message would be sent to us by the embarkation officer on Sphakia beach when we could retire." Thus

Weston, in effect, attached a directive to his order: "Wait for a message from staff before withdrawing." But at 11:50 p.m. Weston and the embarkation staff flew off without having sent a message to retire, and without having appointed a replacement embarkation officer. Laycock therefore sent the message to retire himself. Was he guilty of disobedience?

A simplified example drawn from an incident on Crete will illustrate the principles involved in an answer. Brigadier X ordered Captain Y to go to a certain place; confer with Major Z, who was in command there; and attack a position. Captain Y went as ordered but found Major Z gone. Nevertheless, he attacked. Was it disobedience to carry out the order to attack without having conferred as directed? This writer does not pretend to expertise in the relevant military law beyond knowing some basic principles and famous cases. But it is safe to say that this case involved an order to attack with an attached directive to confer. In many situations it would, of course, be essential that the captain confer with the local commander before attacking in his area, and the directive would then state or imply that the attack could take place *only* after a conference. But in the case of Captain Y, because it was "physically impossible" to confer with an absent officer; because he reasonably "understood" that the conference with Major Z was intended to facilitate, not limit, his operation; and because "circumstances" permitted, he was not disobedient. In recording the incident, the unit War Diary did not say that the officer acted "on own authority"—which is pure Waugh-speak. Rather it used the standard formula: "Being unable to confer with Major Z as directed, Captain Y carried out the attack in conformity with Brigadier X's prior instructions."

Laycock's case is similar. Weston gave Laycock and his men an order to embark but attached to it a directive to wait for a message from staff before withdrawing. By midnight, no staff remained on the island to give the order to withdraw, and Laycock issued the order himself. Whether he was disobedient depends on the three considerations outlined.

First, it was *physically impossible* for Laycock to obtain an order from staff who had already left Crete. Second, if Weston had specified that Layforce withdraw *"only"* after staff sent a message (as he might well have done if the Germans had been active), then Layforce would have been obliged to stay in place. But Laycock correctly *understood* that Weston's directive was facilitating: it basically indicated the manner in which the primary order to leave Crete was to be carried out ("my staff will see to it"). This understanding is confirmed by the Inter-Services Committee. It "regretted" that Layforce failed to embark because of a "misunderstanding" and excused the failure of staff by citing "difficulties" and "no means of communication."[175] In short, the staff would have delivered the order to withdraw if they had had some means of communication.

And third, *circumstances* permitted. When Laycock issued his withdrawal order around midnight, there was "no enemy contact"—the Australians and Marines had disengaged by 9:15 p.m., while the Germans had stayed in place. Moreover, "all fighting forces were in position for embarkation," namely, on the track leading to the beach. And the Commandos were so dispersed that, unless withdrawal began around midnight, most would have had no chance of reaching Sphakia. In summary: it was impossible to obtain a withdrawal order from absent staff, Weston's directive allowed discretion, and circumstances permitted. Laycock therefore acted lawfully in ordering his troops to withdraw when he did.

RECKONING

Beevor's argument distills to a contention that Laycock "lied" that he had orders allowing Layforce to "leave in front of other fighting troops." Indeed, he promises "to eat humble pie" if anyone "manages to produce a specific counter-order allowing LAYFORCE to . . . leave in front of other fighting troops," a point he immediately reiterates, twice.[176] This echoes *Crete:* "One can hardly imagine [Weston's staff giving] priority to Layforce when they had their own Marine battalion to get off,"[177] and "First Casualty": "Laycock's story [was] that Weston was allowing Layforce off early."[178] But the allegation that Laycock claimed to have an order allowing Layforce to embark "*in front of*" other fighting troops is a fundamental misconception, literally non-sense. For no one connected with Layforce— Laycock, Graham, Young, Nicholls, Waugh, Stewart—ever claimed, or acted as if he believed, that Layforce was allowed to leave "*in front of*" other fighting troops. On the contrary, every scrap of evidence proves that the primary anxiety of Laycock and his colleagues was that they would not reach the beach before the last boats left.

Beevor's argument is nonsense mainly because at the time of writing he did not know where the Commandos were positioned or the times at which they moved. He did know that 209 of 800 Commandos returned from Crete, but not that around 35 wounded and 35 deserters had left before May 31st and that some Commandos got off after the surrender. More importantly, he failed to notice the well-documented fact that 120 Commandos under Captain Nicholls went in from the west and boarded the very last ALC at the very end of the evacuation. And he did not appreciate that the 550 Australians and Marines of the rearguard, who had higher priority than the Commandos, could not reach the beach before the evacuation ended. Consequently, to account for the escape of 209 Commandos, he guessed, bizarrely, that Laycock "must have" led "over 200" men to the beach "early," and they "jumped the queue" in front of the Australians and Marines. The truth is that it was only because disorder made it impossible for the higher-priority fighting forces to reach the beach that 120 Commandos embarked "in front of" them.

If Layforce had tried to leave "in front of" other fighting troops, it would be reasonable to conclude that it "arrogantly disregarded" orders to cover the withdrawal of the rearguard. But because Layforce did *not* leave its positions "early," and because Sphakia was not at all threatened by the German forces at Vitsilokoumos, Layforce did *not* fail in its duty to cover the withdrawal of the fighting units that orders designated.

Unfortunately, Beevor did not know the principal written order governing the Commandos' embarkation, while he did know Waugh's elliptical diary accounts of conversations between Freyberg and Laycock. The result was deep confusion. The essential facts, set out principally in (8), leave no doubt that Creforce ordered Layforce to *embark*. But on May 31st Weston, having repeated embarkation orders to Laycock, attached a directive that Layforce stay in its defensive positions until Creforce staff sent a message to *withdraw*. The entire staff then flew off at 11:50 p.m., without being able to send the message to withdraw, which they regretted. In the circumstances set out in (9), Laycock sent his troops a message to *withdraw*—an initiative that the Layforce War Diary records with impeccable frankness. Beevor's inability to distinguish between the order to *embark* and the order to *withdraw* obfuscates his entire argument. The fact is that in ordering his troops to *withdraw*, Laycock acted legally and properly and in accordance with Generals Freyberg and Weston's prior instructions that they *embark*.

The Inter-Services Committee of Enquiry into Crete, the British Army narrative, and General Weston's War Diary make it plain that Layforce had orders to leave Crete.

Beevor's treatment of evidence is simply incomprehensible. On the one hand, he assails the Layforce War Diary as "definitely false" and "disingenuous,"[179] designed to "bury the truth" about Laycock, and so dishonest that "it would have been hard to compress more distortions of the truth into a single sentence."[180] But on other occasions he declares the same War Diary "the key contemporary document."[181] This chapter, therefore, refrains from citing the Layforce War Diary as an authority, but the evidence it offers shows that the War Diary is substantially accurate and, more than that, unconventionally frank.

Beevor relies on an exchange of telegrams between Ann Fleming and Waugh and an entry in Waugh's diary to clinch the argument that Ivor Claire's dishonor mirrors Laycock's. The exchange and the diary raise issues too complex for this space. But briefly, Ann Fleming teasingly identified Laycock with Claire, and Waugh very violently denied the identification. Beevor and many others see the violence of Waugh's denial as proof that Fleming had touched on a sensitive truth. And an apparent inconsistency between Waugh's denial to Fleming ("no possible connection") and his diary entry ("this cruel fact") seems confirmation. My tentative suggestion is that Waugh already knew the gossip about Laycock's "take-off" from Crete, and that it was baseless. He also knew that Fleming (a mischief maker as he was) would enjoy spreading the rumor that *Officers and Gentlemen* endorsed the gossip, which could destroy his friendship with Laycock and his wife. He therefore boiled over. Rage caused incoherence, as did old-fashioned use of the word *fact* as *alleged fact*. (Even today, *fact* is used to mean "untrue" fact. In response to a claim that he had made a certain payment, a modern editor retorted, "This fact is not correct.")[182] In short, I explain Waugh's incoherence as the effect of his knowing that the gossip about Laycock's departure from Crete was a cruel and potentially very damaging reversal of the truth, a truth most lucidly stated by Lt. Col. George Young: Laycock's departure from Crete was both "justified and required."

"BLOODY FIASCO!"[183]

When Waugh railed against the conduct of the Crete campaign in so-called extreme[184] and even "childish"[185] terms, he was not sublimating neurotic guilt about his own and Laycock's escape. He was voicing the frustration felt by many (but by no means all) fellow soldiers. A sample of comments from a range of ranks and political backgrounds shows that these men believed they had taken part in a disgrace and were tainted by it. They felt the Allies had run away when, with a little resolution, they could have won. Brigadier H. K. Kippenberger sums up this feeling when he says that the Allied commanders were "utterly without offensive spirit."[186] Other ranks were harsher. A New Zealand Intelligence debriefing revealed that soldiers "considered that the Germans bought high officials on British side as was the case with France," felt "badly let down by the authorities," and were "disgusted" by organization that was "either extremely bad or completely non-existent."[187] A communist poet writes of "muddle tall as treachery."[188] A private in 1 Rangers, a self-styled "former Commie," writes in terms close to Waugh's: "There are times when I feel I do not like my fellow countrymen." He curses the "strange lethargy . . . cravenness of spirit [and] blind incompetence" that held his unit back from attacking vulnerable German paratroopers.[189] The widely admired Major Madoc RM, learning in prison that General Freyberg had been knighted for Crete, wrote: "It made me want to vomit."[190] Gunner J. C. Whelan writes: "In retrospect I think our officers were nearer to the present day ethos of 'opting out' than the people they were supposed to be leading."[191] C. J. Hamson, an Oxford don, found Crete "a *shaming* and profoundly disgraceful *flight.*"[192] A typical private writes after Crete: "I felt . . . shamed—above all ashamed."[193] Shame at being taken prisoner was also common. Soldiers knew what a common reaction at home would be: "Who would have thought *that* boy would shove his hands up?"[194] To some ordinary soldiers, surrender—and "doing a bunk"—also "smacked of treachery."[195]

This widely shared shame was exacerbated by Waugh's personal experiences. He saw General Weston "completely exhausted" on the floor. Several Layforce colleagues deserted. Lieutenant Colonel Colvin forced Layforce Headquarters into an ignominious flight. Weaponless, panic-stricken base troops, easily mistaken for fleeing combatants, jammed the road that Waugh crossed and recrossed delivering orders. On the other hand, Waugh observed that "D" Battalion of Layforce was "in the steadiest condition" (*DEW* 505), and he wrote admiringly of seeing 1 Welch "marching [into Sphakia] with their equipment in perfect order."[196] The Maori troops also won unqualified praise. But the overwhelming impression Waugh (and many others) took away from the battle was disillusioning. He had no need to be party to a crime committed by Laycock to feel deflated after Crete.

CRETE AND *SWORD OF HONOUR*

Like most major war novels, *Sword of Honour* is not about fighting per se but about men and women at war. It is a daring mix of army life, wartime England, love, farce, class conflict, and deeply personal religious exploration. It is also confrontationally political in the way it construes England's wartime alliance with Russia. The brilliantly personalized image of a Stalinized Eastern Europe that ends the novel will obviously anger "good war" believers like the followers of A. J. P. Taylor who have never regretted Yalta. But even readers sympathetic to the "How-we-won-the-

war-but-lost-the-peace" thesis will be shocked, as was Guy's father, to find
Guy Crouchback after the alliance temporarily losing interest "in victory
. . . it doesn't seem to matter now who wins. When we declared war on
Finland . . ."[197]

The Crete episode prepares for this pivotal disillusion by setting up a
crime, a possible court-martial, and a debate about pragmatism and justice.
Ivor Claire commits the crime of disobedience by escaping from Crete
instead of surrendering as ordered. Guy and Tommy Blackhouse, back in
Egypt, think differently about whether Claire should be court-martialed.
Tommy, the pragmatist, thinks it would be a "bloody hell of a thing" (SoH
527) and cause "trouble" for "no advantage" (SoH 529–30). Guy, the an-
guished believer in justice,[198] preserves the evidence of Claire's crime for
a possible trial. If "advantage" rather than "justice" is to be the rule, he
muses, why endure the horrors of war?

When Germany attacks Russia on June 22, 1941, all Guy's decent English friends, buoyed by hope of victory, are "unworried by issues of right
and wrong" (SoH 532). But in Guy's abstract and lonely mind, Joseph
Stalin is an aggressor on whom England should have declared war. Stalin
has subjugated the Baltic states, Finland, and part of Poland; his trains are
"rolling east" from "Poland and the Baltic" with their "doomed loads,"
just as Hitler's are rolling west to German slave camps (SoH 87, 141). Two
million Poles, we now know, were deported to the Arctic and Central Asia,
half doomed to die within a year. Guy's sense of justice is destroyed by
England's warm welcome of one of the two oppressors of the country that
England went to war to defend.[199]

Few present-day readers of Sword of Honour are likely to be aware
of the moral dilemma that a Russian alliance posed for a Tablet-reading
Catholic like Guy. Before 1939, he would have seen many forecasts (correct, as it turned out) that alliance with Russia would lead to the Sovi-
etization of Eastern Europe and the systematic suppression of Christian
communities.[200] Many prewar Catholics therefore opposed an alliance and,
like Guy, were euphoric when Germany and Russia signed a nonaggression
pact. They could now support the war against Hitler unreservedly. When
on June 22, 1941, "a day of apocalypse for all the world for numberless
generations," England did an about-face and embraced Russia as an ally,
Guy inevitably felt "awfully low" (SoH 530–31).

Numbed by the voiding of justice on a world scale, Guy no longer has
the will to bring one minor delinquent to justice. He therefore thrusts the
evidence against Ivor Claire into the fire (SoH 532). Beevor says that Guy
is here trying to "bury the truth." Rather he is acting like the soldier at

Sphakia who, in a carefully crafted parallel, throws the parts of his gun one by one into the sea. The soldier is making a ritual farewell to arms. Guy is making a ritual farewell to a war no longer fought for justice. This is his low point.

Of course Crete begins Guy's disillusion, and "the shadow of Ivor Claire lay dark and long over the Commandos" (*SoH* 543). But Crete not only dispels the glamour with which Guy and others had invested war; it destroys his trust in "gentlemen." It is not the lower-middle-class Hooper or Trimmer but the quintessence of upper-class Englishry, Ivor Claire, who "turns traitor" and takes the easy downward path to escape and dishonor—the same easy path England's ruling class will take when it blunders into the "dishonour" of the Soviet alliance (*SoH* 532). Tommy Blackhouse (an acknowledged portrait of Laycock) shares in the dishonor of his class to the extent that he pragmatically supports the Russian alliance.

But *Sword of Honour* cannot be read as reliably encoding historical crimes committed by Laycock. Of course it brilliantly creates the atmosphere of an army in retreat, attributes some of Colvin's actions to Hound, and draws vignettes (like the young girls watching over the dead soldier) from life. But as do all great novels, *Sword of Honour* shapes raw material and invents. The fictional Hookforce (of four battalions) begins its Crete campaign by getting "right onto the [Maleme] aerodrome" (*SoH* 451). The historical Layforce (only two battalions present) did not get within twelve miles of the aerodrome, which was lost before Layforce landed. In the novel, the Halberdiers, modeled on the Marines, are the main rearguard; in reality only one battalion of Marines fought with the rearguard and then only on the last two days.[201] In short, Christopher Sykes reverses the truth when he asserts that "the whole story of Crete" is told in *Officers and Gentlemen*: "To indicate how [the diary and the trilogy] diverge is to deal in minutiae."[202] The truth is that the fiction differs so widely from fact that it cannot be used as a source of information about any specific event.

Ivor Claire's desertion does not mirror Laycock's conduct, however obliquely, because Claire is ordered to remain on Crete, while Laycock was ordered to leave with as many of his men as he could get away. Nor does Guy's burning his notebook mirror Waugh's "falsifying the War Diary" to protect Laycock, for Laycock did not commit crimes that Waugh needed to cover up. Most importantly, Claire's desertion and Guy's burning his notebook are not the "crux" of the novel, for, resonant as these events are, they lack the special resonance that Beevor and his followers ascribe to them on the false supposition that they reflect defining moments of dishonor in the lives of Laycock and Waugh.

Waugh published *Put Out More Flags* (1942) soon after Crete. Despite that grim experience, he was still buoyed by the "Churchillian Renaissance" and believed that "a great injustice in the world" could be "drowned by the sword."[203] Yalta was still three years away. But when writing *Officers and Gentlemen* ten years later, having watched a war to right a wrong turn into a gross betrayal of the nation England had gone to war to protect, Waugh strips his central character of chivalrous "hallucinations." At one point Guy is close to losing interest in winning the war in which he is engaged. But over time he learns to see the ambiguous morality of the war as part of the ineradicable corruption of the world: a world in which priests spy, gallant friends turn traitor, and well-intentioned nations blunder into dishonor. Mme. Kanyi articulates the final truth that Guy has been so slow to admit to himself, that war itself is no answer to the world's evil; that the sword cannot drown injustice or restore jaded men to manhood. Salvation is personal.

NOTES

1. The promotions indicate that the military authorities accepted Laycock's departure from Crete as proper. E. H. Hanson wrote to Christopher Sykes on June 6, 1976 suggesting that the authorities disapproved of Laycock's conduct. Sykes, who had been on the staff of General Headquarters Middle East (GHQ Mid-East) at the time, replied on June 13, 1976 that "there was no question of [Laycock's] being in bad odour with the authorities when he returned to Egypt." He pointed to Laycock's employment by successive commanders in chief and to his rapid promotions. See Christopher Sykes Papers, Box 25, Folder 11, Special Collections Division, Georgetown University Library (hereafter cited as GU).

2. Christopher Sykes summarizes the laudatory opinion of Laycock in the *Dictionary of National Biography: 1961–1970.* An officer who served briefly with Laycock made the critical comments quoted earlier. Michael Asher attacks Laycock's character and abilities throughout *Get Rommel: The Secret British Mission to Kill Hitler's Greatest General* (London: Weidenfeld & Nicolson, 2004). G. C. Kiriakopoulos praises Laycock highly in *The Nazi Occupation of Crete, 1941–1945* (Westport, CT: Praeger, 1995), 153–66.

3. Antony Beevor, "The First Casualty of Waugh," *Spectator,* April 6, 1991, 25–26; Antony Beevor, *Crete: The Battle and the Resistance* (1991; rep., Harmondsworth, UK: Penguin, 1992), 218–23.

4. Donat Gallagher, "Sir Robert Laycock, Antony Beevor and the Evacuation of Crete from Sphakia," *Journal of the Society for Army Historical Research* 78, no. 313 (Spring 2000): 38–55.

5. Antony Beevor, "Note: Colonel Laycock in the Evacuation of Crete," *Journal of the Society for Army Historical Research* 78, no. 315 (Autumn 2000): 226–27.

6. Antony Beevor, "Officers, but Not Gentlemen," *Sunday Telegraph,* December 31, 2000: review 2. This piece indicates that Beevor now places a meeting between Laycock and Gen. E. C. Weston hours later than he once did. See note 90 for detail. Since the followers of Beevor draw on *Crete* (1991), it must remain the focus of discussion.

7. I. McD. G. Stewart, *Struggle for Crete, 20 May–1 June 1941: A Story of Lost Opportunity* (London: Oxford University Press, 1966), 471, contains the sentence: "[Weston's last order] was addressed to 'The Senior Officer Left on the Island', a post which Laycock had declined" (a fact found in a letter Laycock wrote to Dan Davin—see note 154). Stewart (February 3, 1976) told Davin that the second half of this sentence was a hint that "the manner of [Laycock's] take-off from the island had led to murmurings." See D. M. Davin (Davin Papers), MS Papers 5079–167, Crete Correspondence, Alexander Turnbull Library (hereafter cited as ATL), Wellington, New Zealand. Citing Stewart's innuendo, E. H. Hanson in a letter (June 6, 1976) to Sykes likened Laycock to Ivor Claire. Sykes replied (June 13, 1976) that Laycock had a "right of refusal" (Sykes Papers, Box 25, Folder 11, GU). Similarly, Kiriakopoulos claims that General Weston did not "order" Laycock to surrender but "offered" him the task. See note 157. The matter is more fully discussed in "Beevor's Accusations (7)."

8. Disorientation was common on Crete. Davin, MS Papers 5079–202, Reports Relating to Crete Campaign, 7, ATL: "Capt Smithson gave a straightforward story without claiming to remember many details. . . . Like all or most Crete soldiers he found it difficult to distinguish one day from the other." In his introduction to Christie Lawrence, *Irregular Adventure* (London: Faber, 1948), 11, Waugh eloquently describes the way "Hunger and exhaustion . . . produced a dream-night condition when people seemed to appear and disappear inconsequently and leave unconnected fragments of memory behind them."

9. Beevor, "First Casualty," 25.

10. Beevor, *Crete*, 219. "The First Casualty of Waugh," the *Spectator's* title, suggests that Waugh incriminates Laycock.

11. Ann Fleming in a telegram to Waugh "presumed" that the dedication of *Officers and Gentlemen* to Laycock was "ironical." Waugh denied this violently: see Mark Amory, ed., *The Letters of Ann Fleming* (London: Weidenfeld & Nicolson, 1985), 155–56. Waugh wrote, "I replied that if she breathes a suspicion of this cruel fact it will be the end of our friendship." See Evelyn Waugh, *The Diaries of Evelyn Waugh*, ed. Michael Davie (London: Weidenfeld & Nicolson, 1976), 728. Fleming retracted in David Pryce-Jones, ed., *Evelyn Waugh and His World* (London: Weidenfeld & Nicolson, 1973), 236. These matters are more fully discussed in "Reckoning."

12. The worst effect of the Waugh-inspired "focus" on Laycock, who had nothing to do with organizing the evacuation, is that it led Beevor to ignore the main events and actors.

13. Evelyn Waugh, *The Diaries of Evelyn Waugh*, ed. Michael Davie (London: Weidenfeld & Nicolson, 1976), 509. Hereafter cited as *DEW*.

14. Beevor, *Crete*, 220–21; "First Casualty," 26.

15. Ralph Bennett, "Ultra and Crete," in *Intelligence Investigations: How Ultra Changed History* (London: Frank Cass, 1996), 195–203. Beevor, *Crete*, 88–91, claims that General Freyberg did not take proper advantage of Ultra.

16. Bennett, *Intelligence Investigations*, 6.

17. Selina Hastings, *Evelyn Waugh: A Biography* (London: Sinclair-Stevenson, 1994), 427–31; Douglas Lane Patey, *The Life of Evelyn Waugh: A Critical Biography* (Oxford: Blackwell, 1998), 187–89.

18. William Boyd, "A Hero Fit for Waugh," *Sunday Times*, News Review, December 24, 2000, 6.

19. David Cliffe, *A Companion to Evelyn Waugh's* Sword of Honour, *An Introduction to Section 2,* Officers and Gentlemen: http://www.abbotshill.freeserve.co.uk/OGIntro.htm;

Alan Munton, "Evelyn Waugh's *Sword of Honour*: The Invention of Disillusion," in Carlos Villar Flor and Robert Murray Davis, eds., *Waugh without End: New Trends in Evelyn Waugh Studies* (Bern: Peter Lang, 2005), 225–46.

20. Julian Thompson, *The Royal Marines: From Sea Soldiers to a Special Force* (London: Sidgwick & Jackson, 2000), 261. (Beevor correctly notes that of the 800 Commandos who went to Crete only 209 returned. Thompson says that "Laycock, his headquarters, *and most of his men* [got] away," emphasis added).

21. In his edition of Evelyn Waugh, *Sword of Honour* (London: Penguin, 1999), x–xi, Angus Calder claims that Laycock "cheated" by "barging . . . through the rabble with some, though not all, of his commandos." Nothing could be further from the truth.

22. Major Ralph Garrett's Report on R.M. Battalion formed for Rearguard Duties in the Withdrawal from Suda Bay, Crete, 2, Box 7/19/7, Crete 1940–1941, Royal Marines Museum (hereafter cited as RMM), Southsea, United Kingdom.

23. *Naval Operations in the Battle of Crete: 20 May–1 June 1941, Battle Summary No. 4*, Naval Staff History Second World War (Historical Section, Admiralty, 1960), 8. Many soldiers record the sudden onset of darkness. Later, there was a good moon.

24. Major H. C. D. Marshall, 2/7 Aust. Inf[antry] B[attalio]n, Diary, 36, Item 255/4/12, Australian War Memorial (hereafter cited as AWM) 54, Campbell, ACT.

25. For strafing, see War Diary, 5 NZ Inf. B[riga]de, Sat. May 31, 2115 hrs., Public Record Office (hereafter cited as PRO) WO 201/2662, Richmond, United Kingdom. For "surprising," see Admiral Lord Cunningham's Papers Add. 52573, Folios 128–29, "Report of the Evacuation of Crete," British Library (hereafter cited as BL): "The enemy's failure to interfere . . . was most surprising." Regarding terrain: despite having guides posted, Marshall's company became lost. See Marshall, Diary, 37, AWM 54.

26. Beevor, *Crete*, 220. Beevor, "Note," 227, vaguely refers to "reports of scattered firing around the perimeter."

27. Boyd, "Hero Fit for Waugh," 6. Emphasis added.

28. Patey, *Evelyn Waugh*, 188. Emphasis added.

29. Qtd. in Dan Davin, *Crete: Official History of New Zealand in the Second World War 1939–1945* (Wellington: War History Branch with Oxford University Press, 1953), 458.

30. These totals are approximate. General Weston lists 4,000 "fighting troops" entitled to embark, but the list omits, for example, the 243 men from 64 Medium Regiment (Med. Rgt) who had orders to leave and embarked. As late as 10:30 p.m. Weston reduced the Marine battalion's quota from 300 to 100. Unit War Diaries reveal that the main bodies of "fighting" troops to leave, mainly before 1:30 a.m., were 5 NZ Inf. Bde, 1,500–plus; 2/8 Aus. Bn, 208; L & M Marines, 200; 19 Aus. Bde HQ, 50; 64 Med. Rgt, 243; "A" Bn Layforce, 120; wounded and various smaller groups make up the total. The largest scheduled units that failed to embark were 2/7 Aust. Bn, 450; RM Bn, 300; Layforce, 470.

31. Beevor, *Crete*, 219.

32. For the Commandos on Crete, see Charles Messenger, with Col. George Young DSO and Lt. Col. Stephen Rose OBE, *The Middle East Commandos* (Wellingborough, UK: William Kimber, 1988), 73–95. Roland Griffiths-Marsh, *The Sixpenny Soldier* (Sydney: Collins/Angus & Robertson, 1990), 205.

33. General Freyberg, letter to Maj. Gen. H. K. Kippenberger, January 3, 1952, ATL.

34. General Freyberg, Memorandum of 27 Aug. 1948 to Director of Public Relations, War Office, National Archives of New Zealand (hereafter cited as NANZ) DA 491.22/10,

commenting on a draft of Christopher Buckley's popular official history of Crete. This is an exceptionally useful exposition of the Crete campaign.

35. Beevor, *Crete*, 89. But Bennett, *Intelligence Investigations*, 197–203, explains the gaps in signals that could have misled Freyberg.

36. Davin did not question his correspondents about the evacuation, nor did the historians who drew on Laycock. See Davin, letter to Evelyn Waugh, September 5, 1951, BL; Davin, letters to Laycock, November 8, 1949 and August 17, 1951, and Laycock, letter to Davin, September 17, 1951, ATL. Lt. Col. G. Young's long memorandum to Davin, February 12, 1950, ATL, contains only one (uninformative) sentence about the evacuation. See also John Spencer, letters to Laycock, December 4 and 14, 1959, and Laycock, letters to Spencer, December 8 and 20, 1959, Laycock Papers, Liddell Hart Centre for Military Archives (hereafter cited as LHC), London. One exception is Tony Simpson, *Operation Mercury: The Battle for Crete, 1941* (London: Hodder & Stoughton, 1981), 271–72, who presents eyewitness accounts of attempts to "break" the cordons and "rush the boats."

37. Griffiths-Marsh, *Sixpenny Soldier*, 198–99. Like most disciplined soldiers, Griffiths-Marsh (2/8 Aus. Bn) was shocked at the "chaos and flight" that developed behind the rearguard.

38. By the time he wrote *Officers and Gentlemen* Waugh better understood the makeup of the "rabble."

39. Laycock, letters to Spencer, December 8 and 20, 1959, LHC.

40. Laycock, letter to Davin, September 17, 1951, LHC.

41. Laycock, letter to Spencer, December 20, 1959, LHC. Spencer sympathized with Laycock's having to deal with "Dominion officers," but Laycock explained that he got on well with them and became "great friends" with Vasey. An Australian source says that Dominion officers "trusted" Laycock because he was "entirely free of the unconscious hauteur of the English Officer *vis à vis* Colonials."

42. Laycock, letter to Spencer, December 20, 1959, LHC. Weston handsomely acknowledged the situation: "The fact that the rearguard op[eration]s were successfully conducted was due mainly to the excellent cooperation between the Australian and New Zealand Brigadiers and Col. Laycock." See Despatch by Major-General E. C. Weston . . . 22 April–31 May, 1941, para. 32, PRO ADM 202/442.

43. See also Papers of Major F. C. C. Graham, CB, DSO, DL, "Cretan Crazy Week," 5, 76/180/1 Imperial War Museum (hereafter cited as IWM), London: "It became urgent that we tried to find General Freyberg and get some orders—there was only one way to do this, one of us had to go and find him."

44. Graham, "Cretan Crazy Week," 5, IWM. Laycock, letter to Davin, September 17, 1951, ATL.

45. Anthony Cheetham, letter to Davin, undated, ATL. In reply to a request from Davin for some "gossip" about Colvin, Cheetham relays many pungent assertions by members of "A" Bn. that Colvin, even before he went to Crete, lacked fighting and Commando qualities. Laycock, letter to Davin, September 17, 1951, ATL, says Colvin was "such a nice chap."

46. Graham, "Cretan Crazy Week," 5, IWM: Graham remembers Laycock's "good round swearing" on this occasion.

47. Laycock, letter to Davin, September 17, 1951, ATL, explains that he relieved Colvin of command because he "lost his nerve" and did not understand rearguard fighting. Laycock, letter to Spencer, December 20, 1959, LHC, refers to an unnamed "bomb-happy officer" who retreated "before the appointed time," creating a "very uneasy" situation.

48. Cheetham, letter to Davin, undated, ATL.

49. Maj. R. W. Madoc, Journal, Box 3, 101, LHC. The policy of leaving behind failed personnel emerges when 300 Marines were drawing lots for 100 places on the ships. Madoc recalls that "[Maj. Garrett] said that [Capt. X, who had delayed going to their assistance] was to be left out of the draw, owing to the incident of the wounded men after the shelling."

50. Geoffrey Cox, *A Tale of Two Battles* (London: William Kimber, 1987), 105: "We took a muster roll of the men crowded on the decks. . . . Amongst them were a number from the Commando units."

51. Cheetham, letter to Davin, undated, ATL.

52. D. M. Davin, Official Files re Crete Campaign, MS Papers 5079–229, Operational Directive to Maj-Gen. Weston, No. 6, (Sgnd) R. C. Querie, Major for HQ British T[roo]ps on Crete, 28 May 41, ATL.

53. Official Files, Weston to Freyberg 0730 hrs, 29 May, ATL.

54. Official Files, Sig. 0 672 28 [May], To MIDEAST from CREFORCE, MOST SECRET . . . for C[ommander]-in-C[hief], ATL.

55. Cunningham's Papers, Add. 52573, "Narrative," folios 126–29, BL. The printed Despatch makes no reference to the Appendix, which exists, unattributed, as "Evacuation of Forces from Crete," PRO WO 201/2661.

56. War Diary, 2/8 Bn, 30 May, 1400 hrs, Item 8/3/18, AWM 52, reports an ambush that caused the Germans to lose "100 men." Griffiths-Marsh, *Sixpenny Soldier,* 200–01, recalls the devastating effect of the fire his unit directed at Germans trying to pass below them. Beevor, *Crete*, 220, and "Note," 227, recall the incursion of a German patrol into a ravine on May 30th that was "annihilated." He believes this action shows Sphakia vulnerable on May 31st. On the contrary, it helped persuade the Germans to remain inactive on May 31st.

57. Davin, *Crete*, 441, quotes German documents confirming this intention and date.

58. Weston, Despatch, para. 36, PRO.

59. Maj. Gen. I. S. O. Playfair, *The Mediterranean and the Middle East,* Vol. 2, History of the Second World War (London: Her Majesty's Stationery Office [HMSO], 1956), 146: "These [encircling movements] had not taken effect on the morning of 1 June, so that the final embarkation was not directly interfered with by the enemy."

60. Beevor, *Crete*, 220, and "Note," 227.

61. War Diary 5 NZ Inf. Bde, Sat. May 31, 0700 hrs, PRO. As a precaution against *unlikely* German infiltration, 5 Bde and others set up the wide perimeter screen. Layforce and others took over New Zealand positions in the evening. It is absurd to imply that German "detachments" were located within this screen.

62. *Naval Operations in the Battle of Crete,* 29.

63. Weston, Despatch, para. 45, PRO, records "preference for fighting troops"; para. 42 sets out the list.

64. Weston, Despatch, paras. 42–45, PRO, outlines basic arrangements. Detail is from unit War Diaries.

65. Laycock Papers, Folder 23, LHC: "Warning Order" 31/5/41, penciled on very small sheets: "LAYFORCE will take up the positions . . . held by 5 Bde . . . 17 Bn (Aus) will take up the positions at present held by 28 Maori Bn . . . WELSH RGT AND RAINGERS [*sic*] will move into Wadi alongside HQ and stay in reserve."

66. "Evacuation of Forces from Crete," PRO WO 201/2661.

67. *Naval Operations in the Battle of Crete*, 29, sets out all relevant Navy signals. Allowing the ships to fill up was a significant concession because a heavily laden ship is difficult to maneuver during air attack.

68. Staff Capt. W. W. Mason, letter to Davin, June 2, 1951, ATL.

69. See also W. G. McClymont, Crete Campaign, para. 1751, note 1, Campaign Narrative of 2 NZ Division, Vol. V, MS Papers 5079–257, ATL.

70. Weston, Despatch, para. 44, PRO: "At 1830 hrs I was handed a signal from M.E. stating that 3,600 would be lifted that Saturday night." *Naval Operations in the Battle of Crete,* 29, details the incremental increases in lift.

71. For accounts of unscheduled New Zealand troops leaving, see Capt. R. Dawson (Bde Maj.), 5 Inf. Bde on Crete, 31 May, Afternoon, MS Papers 5079–256, ATL: "Message that there would be more boat accommodation. We warned everyone we could see . . . we tried to collect stragglers." Night: "March to the beach—collected everyone we could find, scouting the vicinity for stragglers." See also J. F. Cody, *New Zealand Engineers, Middle East* (Wellington: War History Branch, Department of Internal Affairs, 1961), 158. Stopped by the guards because he had no orders to embark, Captain Morrison "got a chit from Brig. Hargest" for 90 men. These examples can be multiplied.

72. Brigadier Hargest's Narrative, qtd. in Davin, *Crete*, 446.

73. Tension was inevitable because losses were unevenly spread and some commanding officers felt aggrieved. Christopher Buckley, *Greece and Crete 1941,* Popular Official History Series (London: HMSO, 1952), 291, analyzes the losses (mostly POWs). As a percentage of total British and Dominion losses, Britain's were 57 percent, Australia's 24 percent, New Zealand's 18 percent. As a percentage of their own forces on Crete, British losses were 51 percent, Australian 51 percent, NZ 35 percent. Layforce lost 75 percent. Some British units, e.g., 1 Welch, were very harshly treated. Lt. Col. Geoffrey Keyes, VC, MC, recalls in his unpublished diary (June 23, 1941) that Laycock told "C" Bn of Layforce, which Keyes commanded, "all about" Crete, "where Layforce seems to have been made scapegoat to evacuate the Aussies." There were also special arrangements (recorded in no history), e.g., for 64 Med. Rgt to take over picketing from New Zealand at midnight and then to embark all of its members.

74. Brigadier G. Vasey, "Account of Operations of AIF in Crete," 19 Aust. Inf. Bde, 13 July 1941, 5, AWM 54 535/1/10. Vasey gave the 500 places to 2/7 Bn and his HQ. His 2/8 Bn had received orders to embark earlier, and they followed the New Zealand troops onto the ships. The sudden change of orders gave units from thirty to ten minutes to organize their withdrawal: see War Diary of 2/7 Aust. Bn 1941, 31 May 20 hrs, AWM 52 Item 8/3/17.

75. Garrett, "Report on R. M. Battalion," 2–3, RMM; and Madoc, Journal, Box 3, 99–103, LHC. On their way to Sphakia with the 300 men, Garrett and Madoc were told to embark themselves (as specialists) and "to take with us 100 from the battalion. The remainder were to await instructions." Lots were drawn for the 100 places. Garrett ordered the remainder to move to the beach in an hour.

76. Davin, *Crete*, 446.

77. Ibid., says that Weston "sent for" Laycock. Beevor, *Crete*, 219, says Laycock "collared" Weston. Waugh says, "Bob and I went to get further orders" (*DEW* 508).

78. Only at 2000 hrs did Admiral Cunningham receive a message from General Wavell for transmission to Weston authorizing capitulation. See also note 84.

79. After quoting Weston's "fighting troops had precedence over others," Waugh writes: "We interpreted this to mean troops who had retained their arms and organization, but I

believe he may have meant soldiers as opposed to civilian refugees" (*DEW* 508). Waugh's overactive conscience was quite mistaken, as Weston's War Diary, which includes "LAYFORCE 500" in a list of "fighting troops," demonstrates.

80. Graham, "Cretan Crazy Week," 9, IWM. Emphasis added.

81. Beevor, "First Casualty," 26: "Graham . . . never thought to disbelieve . . . Laycock's lies."

82. Graham, "Cretan Crazy Week," 9, IWM; Graham, letter to Michael Davie (editor of *DEW*), June 9, 1976, IWM.

83. Kevin Baker, *Paul Cullen: Citizen and Soldier* (Dural, NSW: Rosenberg, 2005), 88, 92–93, records three instances of Weston's countermanding the orders of senior subordinates. Major Cullen served on Weston's staff and found him "brave and efficient" but markedly idiosyncratic.

84. Weston, Despatch, para. 45, PRO: "On my return at 2130, I sent for the senior officer available." Cunningham's Papers, Add. 52573, Folio 131, BL: "At about 2000 hours on 31 May [I] received a . . . personal message from Gen. Wavell to Maj. Gen. Weston . . . authorizing the capitulation of any troops who had to be left behind. As transmission of the message would mean an irrevocable decision to cease the evacuation, it was given careful consideration before [I] finally [sent] it on."

85. Weston, Despatch, para. 45, PRO: Weston sends for Colvin; Graham, "Cretan Crazy Week," 9, IWM: Weston summons Graham, dictates the order, and addresses it to Colvin; Graham keeps one of two carbon copies.

86. Graham, Papers, IWM: "I order you to go forward at first light and capitulate to the enemy."

87. Weston, Despatch, para. 47, PRO: "I embarked in a Sunderland flying boat at 2350 hrs." Madoc, Journal, 99, LHC: When on his way to the flying boat, Lt. Col. A. F. Hely, the evacuation officer, gave Madoc a pass for 100 Marines.

88. Graham, "Cretan Crazy Week," 9, IWM.

89. Beevor, "First Casualty," 26.

90. Ibid. Beevor, *Crete*, 220. In "Officers, but Not Gentlemen" (2000) Beevor writes: "That evening, however, Laycock . . . buttonholed Gen. Weston just before he left and persuaded him that . . . he should be allowed to leave." Because Weston left at 11:50 p.m., this passage seems to indicate more realistic timings than do *Crete* and "First Casualty"— but only if Beevor knew when Weston's plane took off. See note 6.

91. Graham, "Cretan Crazy Week," 9, IWM.

92. Log of HMS *Phoebe*, PRO ADM 53/114864: "23.20. Let go port anchor in Spharkia [*sic*] Bay; 23.35. Embarked first load of troops."

93. Lawrence, *Irregular Adventure,* 14; Cheetham, letter to Davin, undated, 5, ATL.

94. Graham, "Cretan Crazy Week," 9, IWM.

95. Beevor, *Crete*, 223. Emphasis added.

96. Garrett, "Report on R.M. Battalion," 3, RMM: "I proceeded . . . to find the embarkation staff and found there was no staff officer."

97. Beevor, *Crete*, 220.

98. Lt. Col. W. R. S. Windham, Royal Signals, "Minute 6: CIPHERS," addressed to the Inter-Services Committee on Crete, 10 June 1941, PRO WO 201/2663.

99. "Report by an Inter-Services Committee on Operations on Crete (1 November 1940 to 31 May 1941)," Part IV, "Summary of Lessons," paras. 61, 62, 72, PRO WO 106/3126.

100. "Beach Organization for Evacuation," PRO WO 201/2663.

101. Ralph Tanner, in *Touch and Go: The Battle for Crete 1941,* ed. David Smurthwaite (London: National Army Museum, 1991), 53. In *Crete,* Beevor has Tanner set off "around 11.00 pm." In "Officers, but Not Gentlemen," Beevor has Tanner set off "after Weston had gone . . . by running as fast as he could, he only just made it back to the beach in time." Weston left at 11:50 p.m., but whether Beevor was aware of this time it is impossible to tell. See notes 6 and 90.

102. Beevor, "First Casualty," 26.

103. Beevor, "Note," 227.

104. Officer Commanding G Troop, "A" Bn [Capt. Jocelyn Nicholls], letter to Col. Laycock, 24/6/1941, Personal Papers of Layforce Commander, PRO WO 201/717.

105. "A" Bn War Diary 31 May, PRO WO 218/168, says "about midnight." "D" Bn War Diary 31 May, PRO WO 218/172, says "later on in the evening." Contradictory evidence exists for who sent the withdrawal order. The Layforce War Diary says that Laycock sent it, as does Dr. Tanner, who writes (May 6, 2004): "The order was verbal, from Laycock." By contrast, the War Diary of "D" Bn records it as being sent by "the Brigade Major" (Graham). Messenger (with Lieutenant Colonel Young), *The Middle East Commandos,* 92, says: "Freddy Graham sent a runner to [Lt. Col.] George Young . . . telling him to withdraw." For "if possible," see also Lt. R. F. Mount, letter to the father of Cpl. N. A. Burford, 23 February 1942, LHC: "As the commando's task of holding the Germans back . . . was now completed, Captain Nicholls was given the order to evacuate the troops if possible."

106. "The Account of Sgt Charles Stewart, Who Was Himself Taken Prisoner at Crete," 5, IWM 93/17/11. Stewart waited for his "1–2 Sections," ran to Sphakia, briefly helped an injured man, and just failed to board.

107. Beevor says in *Crete,* 221, and in "Officers, but Not Gentlemen" that "the battalion [*sic*] was too dispersed to react in time" to reach Sphakia. In fact, as the following note demonstrates, most Commandos did reach Sphakia but could not get through the crowds to the boats. For the 2:00 a.m. time, see Madoc, Journal, Box 3, 103, IWM: the Marines had already reached the houses close to the sea when the Commandos arrived.

108. War Diary "D" Bn, PRO 218/172, records frustration at arriving outside Sphakia in time to embark but being unable to penetrate the crowds blocking entry to the beach.

109. Trooper H. Sparrow, letter to Officer Commanding Mid. East Commando Depot, 9 July 1941, PRO WO 201/2663, explains that his unit could not reach Sphakia by 2:30 a.m. because the distance was too great.

110. War Diary "D" Bn, PRO 218/172, records that "27 men, most Spanish Republicans," returned from Crete. This could not have been legal, but it is likely that these were the men detected on a transport on the night May 29. See Cox, *A Tale of Two Battles,* 105.

111. War Diary of "A" Bn, PRO 218/168; Layforce War Diary, 31 May 2200 hrs, PRO 218/166: "flank det[achments]s were able to reach beach"; Waugh: "Tanner was on another destroyer with about 120 officers and men of A Battalion who had got to the beach by a side lane" (*DEW* 509). Laycock Archive, LHC: Waugh's two-page summary of Crete records the escape.

112. War Diary of "A" Bn, 31 May 1941, PRO 218/168. See also "Account of Sgt Charles Stewart," 5, IWM. So close a run was it that Stewart, who briefly helped an injured comrade, arrived "just in time to witness the ALC . . . bear out to sea." See also Papers of Capt. F. R. J. Nicholls, IWM 93/17/1, who wrote to his mother, "We were the last to be

evacuated and there was a great deal of confusion." Two officers of "A" Bn told Geoffrey Keyes about "[getting] out of Crete by sheer luck" (Keyes, MS Diary, 22 June 1941).

113. Lt. R. F. Mount, letter to the father of Cpl. N. A. Burford, February 23, 1942, Laycock Archive, LHC. Burford narrowly failed to board.

114. War Diary 2/8 Aus. Bn, Appendix 1, 4, AWM. The 2/8 Bn embarked under New Zealand command.

115. W. G. McClymont, Crete Campaign, para. 1751, note 1, Campaign Narrative of 2 NZ Division, Vol. V, MS Papers 5079–257, ATL.

116. War Diary of 5 NZ Inf Bde May 1941, Sat. May 31 1610 hrs, PRO; Maj. H. G. Dyer, letter to J. F. Cody, January 14, 1953, 28 NZ (Maori) Battalion in Greece and Crete, Correspondence Collected by Unit Historian, NANZ WAII DA 68/15/15. These documents best recount New Zealand preparations for evacuation and operation of the cordons. For the control exercised, see "Account of Sgt Charles Stewart," 4, IWM: when the Commandos were moving through Sphakia to take over from New Zealand in the west, the Maori picket closely scrutinized their orders before allowing them to pass. See also Cody, *New Zealand Engineers, Middle East,* 158: "Capt. Morrison [tried to] tail on [after another unit but] the guards discouraged unauthorized bodies of men with rifle fire and grenades. They would not allow the Company [of NZ Engineers] to pass."

117. After each campaign a narrator is appointed to compile a Narrative for Infantry, Artillery, etc. It draws on orders, signals, War Diaries, and the memories of senior participants. A draft is submitted to senior participants for comment. British, Australian, and New Zealand services each compiled a Narrative of the Crete campaign.

118. McClymont, Crete Campaign, para. 1778, ATL: "The Maoris . . . formed an inner cordon until 2400 hrs when the line was taken over by 64 Medium Bty [Battery, *sic*]."

119. Christopher Buckley, *Greece and Crete 1941,* Popular Official History Series (London: HMSO, 1952), 286, alone hints at the withdrawal of the cordons but does not mention the handover to 64 Med. Rgt.

120. War Diary of 28 NZ (Maori) Bn, Report on Activities of 150 Who Stayed Behind, NANZ DA 68/1/17: "Carried out the duties of inner cordon till about 2400 hrs when its duties were taken over by 64 Medium Bty [*sic*]"; War Diary of 64 Med. Rgt 31.5.41, PRO WO 169/1492: "Complete unit, 8 Officers and 235 O[ther]R[ank]s, picketed approach to beach and gradually withdrew . . . as unit embarked without loss." See also Dyer, letter to Cody, January 14, 1953, cited in note 116.

121. Dyer, letter to Cody (note 116) gives a full account of the handover, disturbance, and restoration of order. For other eyewitness accounts, see Tony Simpson, *Operation Mercury: The Battle for Crete, 1941* (London: Hodder & Stoughton, 1981), 271–72.

122. The War Diary of 22 NZ Bn does not make clear when the battalion withdrew. But the most realistic historian of the evacuation explains, "The guards at the approaches were either withdrawn too early or were overwhelmed . . . and confusion reigned." See Buckley, *Greece and Crete,* 286. Because 22 NZ Bn embarked, we may conclude that it was not "overwhelmed" and must have withdrawn "too early."

123. Qtd. in Gavin Long, *Greece, Crete and Syria* (Canberra: Australian War Memorial, 1953), 305.

124. Ralph Tanner, letter to the author, May 6, 2004. This raises two questions: (1) Did Laycock issue his order later than is commonly believed, especially since Tanner returned to the beach just in time for the last boat? (2) Or did Tanner take a route not covered by the cordons?

125. Long, *Greece, Crete and Syria*, 305: "Captain Forbes managed to get his men to the beach [after traveling across country] about 0100 hrs . . . as a disciplined unit. All were embarked on the last boat to leave the island."

126. W. E. Murphy, Narrative of the 2 NZ Div. Artillery, Vol. 4, 189, NANZ DA 401.22/1. See two contradictory statements in McClymont, Crete Campaign, ATL: (1) Para. 1782, Brigadier Hargest tells Major Bull that "it was out of the question to embark [NZ Artillery] on the night 31 May–1 June"; (2) Para. 1790, "Major Bliss [of NZ Artillery] with some men . . . was able to embark when it was found that space was available after 5 Bde had embarked. *Other odd personnel got away at the same time.*" Emphasis added.

127. Major Marshall, Diary, AWM 54, gives a justly famous account of the journey to Sphakia. Many other harrowing narratives are attached to the War Diary of 2/7 Bn or can be found in W. P. Bolger, et al., *The Fiery Phoenix: The Story of 2/7 Australian Infantry Battalion 1939–1946* (Parkdale, VIC: 2/7 Battalion Association, n. d.), 96–98.

128. General Weston's Sunderland fixes the time of arrival at Sphakia. It took off at 11:50 p.m. By then Major Madoc had been at Sphakia for some time, behind the Australians. Madoc, Journal, 101–02, LHC: "The queue moved on by slow stages with frequent halts. . . . We heard and just saw the Sunderland taking the General to Egypt."

129. Weston, Despatch, para. 44, PRO: "It was impossible . . . to take more than 300 of 2/7 Bn." Since only 16 members of 2/7 Bn escaped, Weston was confused. This suggests that the pickets' orders were also confused. Buckley, *Greece and Crete,* 286, writes bluntly of "faulty transmission of orders." Brigadier Vasey directly attributes the loss of 2/7 Bn to movement control's not having the necessary orders. See note 130.

130. War Diary of 2/7 Bn, 1941, AWM 52 8/3/17: vivid appendixes describe difficulties of movement and misunderstandings that prevented progress. Brigadier Vasey, "Account of the Operations of the AIF on Crete, 19 Aust. Inf. Bde," 7, AWM 54/1/10, is the most authoritative account of the loss of 2/7 Bn. David Horner, *General Vasey's War* (Melbourne: Melbourne University Press, 1992), 130, adds vital detail.

131. AWM 2/7 Bn War Diary, qtd. in Horner, *General Vasey's War*, 130; Brigadier Vasey, "Account," 7, AWM 54/1/10.

132. Lt. A. W. F. Sutton R[oyal] N[avy], letter to The Rear Admiral, Med[iterranean] Aircraft Carriers, June 1941, Davin Papers, ATL. Sutton was on the beach on May 30th and reported: "The Army had taken charge. . . . There was chaos and terribly slow working until various Naval officers intervened. . . . Thus nearly an hour of valuable time was wasted and only 700 men were taken off instead of the 1000 or more who could have been carried."

133. Beevor, *Crete*, 220.

134. Ibid., 223.

135. War Diary of "D" Bn, 31 May, PRO WO 218 172: "In all 2 officers and about 25 other ranks (15 Spaniards) got back to Egypt." Re HQ, see Waugh: "Bob and I and Freddy, with servants, therefore set off to find the beach officer" (*DEW* 509); re escapees after the surrender, see Waugh: "Two men from brigade HQ and five from D Battalion made their escape by MLC [motor landing craft]" (*DEW* 510).

136. Beevor, *Crete*, 220.

137. Ibid.

138. Beevor, "First Casualty," 26.

139. Layforce War Diary, 31 May 1400 hrs, PRO 218/166. Emphasis added.

140. Beevor, "First Casualty," 26; Beevor, *Crete*, 219.

141. Beevor, "Note," 227. Emphasis added.

142. Col. E. E. Rich, "The Campaign in Crete: Nov. 1940 to June 1941," chap. 4, para. 93, PRO CAB 44/121.

143. Beevor, *Crete*, 216.

144. Beevor, "Note," 227.

145. Ibid.

146. Ibid.

147. Beevor, "First Casualty," 26.

148. Beevor, *Crete*, 216.

149. Ibid., 219.

150. Ibid., 222.

151. Young in Messenger, *Middle East Commandos, 92–93.*

152. Beevor, *Crete*, 223.

153. Ibid.

154. Laycock, letter to Davin, September 17, 1951, ATL. Laycock told Davin that General Weston had ordered Lt. Col. F. B. Colvin to surrender "after I had frankly refused to do so!" This remark was unprompted. Laycock did not elaborate, because he was suggesting possible reasons why Colvin had not answered Davin's letters. See note 7.

155. Weston, Despatch, para. 45, PRO; Graham, "Cretan Crazy Week," 9, IWM.

156. Graham, letter to Davie, June 9, 1976, and "Cretan Crazy Week," 9, IWM. Graham clearly writes, and repeats, "Weston's staff officer." Beevor gratuitously asserts that Waugh made the comment: see "First Casualty," 26, and *Crete*, 219.

157. G. C. Kiriakopoulos, *Ten Days to Destiny: The Battle for Crete, 1941* (New York: F. Watts, 1985), 361–62. The scene is probably not directly from Laycock: LHC Laycock papers hold no related correspondence, and Kiriakopoulos gives no source.

158. Sykes, letter to E. H. Hanson, June 13, 1976, Sykes Papers, Box 25, Folder 11, GU.

159. Kiriakopoulos, *Ten Days*, 362; Kiriakopoulos wrongly says that Laycock "commanded Lt Col. Young" to surrender. In fact Laycock nominated Lieutenant Colonel Colvin for the task.

160. Davin, *Crete*, 446.

161. Cunningham's Papers, Add. 52573, Folio 131, BL: "At 200 hrs 31 May" Cunningham received a "personal message" for Weston "authorizing capitulation." Presumably paraphrasing Wavell, Cunningham used the words quoted. Emphasis added. S. W. C. Pack, *The Battle for Crete* (London: Ian Allan, 1973), 83: "There seems to have been no final authorization for surrender" other than this "personal message."

162. Weston, Despatch, para. 45, PRO; see also Graham, "Cretan Crazy Week," 9, IWM. In the event, because the evacuation went awry, two battalion commanders senior to Colvin—Lt. Col. G. Young (Layforce) and Lt. Col. T. G. Walker (2/7 Australian Battalion) —were left behind. Messenger, *Middle East Commandos,* 93, says that Colvin handed the order to Young, who capitulated. But notes taken by Gavin Long (Australian Official War Historian) from Lieutenant Colonel Walker, AWM 67 2114, prove Messenger incorrect: "I [Walker] went down [to the beach]. Young of the Cdo was there—both Colvin and Young." Young handed the order to Walker, his senior, who in fact capitulated.

163. Beevor, "Note," 227.

164. Layforce War Diary 31 May, 1400 hrs, PRO.

165. Waugh says that Weston issued the embarkation order when "the wireless was no longer working," and he knew it was "the last night for evacuation" (*DEW* 508–09). It is therefore hard to understand how a "1400 hrs" order could be called "Final."

166. Weston, Despatch, paras. 42, 44, 45, PRO. The list is not in priority order. The quotas total 4,000.

167. Rich, "The Campaign in Crete," chap. 4, paras. 93–95, PRO CAB 44/121.

168. "Report by an Inter-Services Committee on Operations on Crete (1 November 1940 to 31 May 1941)," PRO WO 106/3126. This report is a uniquely important source of information about the Crete campaign. Based on the evidence of all major participants who returned from Crete, it was written within weeks of the end of the battle and contains information available nowhere else. Released only in 1972, it was not available to the official historians and most other major authorities.

169. Beevor, "Note," 227.

170. Brigadier Erskine prepared "Extracts from Report by an Inter-Services Committee," PRO 201/2652. He removed criticisms of GHQ Mid-East but did not alter the passages relating to Layforce. Paul Freyberg, Memorandum, Davin Papers, ATL, made a detailed study of the committee and its report. He emphasizes Salisbury-Jones's independence. Maj. Gen. G. Salisbury-Jones complains in a letter to the Army Council of being kept in South Africa ("as far away from the war as it is possible to be") and details the way the report was suppressed. See IWM 67/201/1–3 (3). See also Papers of Sir Basil Liddell Hart, LHC. In a letter to Liddell Hart, August 24, 1966, Salisbury-Jones says the report was "destroyed."

171. "Report by an Inter-Services Committee on Operations on Crete," part III, para.73, PRO.

172. Tanner, *Touch and Go,* 53.

173. Weston, Despatch; Appendix, List of Awards and Mentions, PRO: "6970623 Private Ralph Esmond Selby Tanner, C. in C's [commander in chief's] Award." I have been unable to trace an award with this title, and it is possible that Weston, a Marine, had in mind a naval "Commendation." In the event, the award conferred was "Mentioned in Despatches for Distinguished Service." Although the citation is not available, Dr. Tanner understands that the decoration was for carrying the withdrawal order (letter to the author, May 6, 2004).

174. Beevor, "Note," 227.

175. "Report by an Inter-Services Committee on Operations in Crete," part II, para. 73, PRO WO 106/3126: "The bulk of Layforce were left behind through a misunderstanding. But the difficulties were great and there were no means of communication except by runner."

176. Beevor, "Note," 227.

177. Beevor, *Crete,* 219.

178. Beevor, "First Casualty," 26.

179. Beevor, *Crete,* 220.

180. Beevor, "First Casualty," 26.

181. Beevor, "Note," 227.

182. Waugh telegraphed Fleming, "Of course there is no possible connection between Bob and Claire." See Amory, ed., *Letters of Ann Fleming,* 155. But in *Diaries* he wrote, "If she breathes a suspicion of this cruel fact it will be the end of our friendship" (728). Some read "cruel fact" as damning, not recognizing that *fact* can mean "alleged" or "untrue" fact. A lawyer wrote to *Private Eye* on May 30, 1997: "I did accept . . . 30,000 pounds." The editor replied: "This fact is not correct." Older editions of *Oxford English Dictionary* give many relevant meanings of *fact.*

183. Edward Hulton, "Bloody Fiasco!" *Picture Post,* June 21, 1941: 9–13. Hulton, proprietor of the popular Leftish weekly, expressed vehement disgust at the defeat, the excuses made for it, and the state of the British Army.

184. Christopher Sykes, *Evelyn Waugh: A Biography* (London: Collins, 1975), 216.

185. Gerard de Winton, qtd. in Beevor, *Crete*, 230.

186. Qtd. in Stewart, *Struggle for Crete,* 372: "The failure in each case seems to me that [the commanders on Crete] . . . adopted a course that made victory impossible— fundamental mistakes irretrievable by the valour and devotion of the men under their command."

187. "Intelligence Reports on Crete after 1 June," Report No. 32, NANZ DA 21/13/2.

188. John Manifold, "The Tomb of Lt John Learmonth": "Say Crete, and there is little more to tell / Of muddle tall as treachery."

189. V. West, 1 Rangers, 127–33, IWM PP/MCR/239. Waugh wrote: "The English are a very base people. I did not know this, living as I did. Now I know them through and through and they disgust me." See Artemis Cooper, ed., *Mr Wu and Mrs Stitch: The Letters of Evelyn Waugh and Diana Cooper* (London: Hodder & Stoughton, 1991), 77.

190. Madoc, Journal, Box 3, 97, LHC.

191. J. C. Whelan RM, "War Memoirs of Gunner Whelan," chap. 6, 28–29, IWM 93/ 17/1.

192. C. J. Hamson, *Liber in Vinculis* (Cambridge: Trinity College, 1989), 44: "Cowardice, oh no! merely the final and most disastrous failure in the inner core." In a preface to the book, Hamson's daughter observes: "The Allied defence degenerated into the chaos that Jack felt was exactly described by Evelyn Waugh." Waugh's Major Hound is not so much a coward as a man lacking an "inner core." Without orders he cannot act. He issues orders not expecting them to be carried out.

193. R. H. Thompson, in Callum McDonald, *The Lost Battle: Crete 1941* (London: Macmillan, 1993), 293.

194. Charles Jager, *Escape from Crete* (Smithfield, NSW: Floradale, 2004), 30.

195. W. E. Murphy, "The NZ Army on Crete," 191, MS Papers 5079–227, ATL: "His [Major Bull's] men were thunderstruck. The thought of surrender smacked of treachery."

196. Waugh, letter to Davin, September 7, 1951, qtd. in Stewart, *Struggle for Crete,* 469.

197. Evelyn Waugh, *Sword of Honour: A Final Version of the Novels* Men at Arms *(1952),* Officers and Gentlemen *(1955) and* Unconditional Surrender *(1961)* (1965; rep., London: Eyre Methuen, 1980), 545. Hereafter cited as *SoH.*

198. Guy queries the justice of England's not declaring war on Russia after Russia invaded Poland: "'Justice?' said the old soldiers. 'Justice?'" (*SoH* 29–30). When Russia defeats Finland, Guy feels that "courage and a just cause are quite irrelevant to the issue" (*SoH* 156).

199. Waugh, September 25, 1939: "The papers are all smugly jubilant at Russian conquests in Poland as though this were not a more terrible fate for the allies we are pledged to defend than conquest by Germany" (*DEW* 443). See also May 15, 1943: "The Poles are generally blamed for minding about the murder of 8000-odd officers by the Russians" (*DEW* 537). This is an underestimate of the 15,000 Polish officers shot by the NKVD in camps around Katyn, a fact that the British at the time tried to conceal. For Poland under Nazi and Soviet rule, see Richard C. Lukas, *Forgotten Holocaust: The Poles under German Occupation 1939–1944* (Lexington: University Press of Kentucky, 1986)

and Norman Davies, *Rising '44: "The Battle for Warsaw"* (London: Macmillan, 2003). Waugh was aware of these atrocities through Catholic sources such as Moray McLaren, and through his brother-in-law, Auberon Herbert, who served with the Polish Army. See Evelyn Waugh, *The Letters of Evelyn Waugh*, ed. Mark Amory (London: Weidenfeld & Nicolson, 1980), 166, 200–01.

200. A random sample of the *Tablet* in April 1939 reveals the intensity of prewar Catholic opposition to a Soviet alliance. Inter alia, under the heading "Alliance with the Soviet" on April 22nd and 29th, Arnold Lunn, the Catholic apologist, reveals that he has been asked to organize a petition assuring the prime minister that "Catholics will take no part in a war against Germany if Russia is our ally" (April 29, 557)—and that he refused. An editorial argues that once a Russian army had entered a country, great difficulty would be experienced in getting it out. Presciently, it adds that Soviet imperialism would install weak left-wing regimes as a prelude to "more Soviets" ("Britain Approaches Moscow," April 22, 506). Many Catholics welcomed the Molotov-Ribbentrop pact because it saved them from the "moral dilemma" that a British alliance with the Soviet Union would have created. See E. M. Andrews, *Isolationism and Appeasement in Australia* (Canberra: Australian National University Press, 1970), 181.

201. Garrett, "Report on R. M. Bn formed for Rearguard Duties," 1, RMM; Madoc, Journal, Box 3, 96–97, LHC. Formed from RM batteries on May 29th, the battalion fought under Australian command on May 30–31.

202. Sykes, *Evelyn Waugh,* 215: "I intend to give no space [to Crete because Waugh] related the whole story himself . . . in *Officers and Gentlemen.*"

203. Chan Ch'ao, epigraph to Evelyn Waugh, *Put Out More Flags* (London: Chapman & Hall, 1942).

The BBC *Brideshead,* 1956, or Whatever Happened to Celia, Sex, and Syphilis?

Patrick Denman Flanery

I<small>N THE</small> BBC W<small>RITTEN</small> A<small>RCHIVE IS A SINGLE MICROFILM COPY OF</small> L<small>ANCE</small> S<small>IEVEKING'S</small> 103-minute, 45-second script adaptation of Evelyn Waugh's *Brideshead Revisited* (1945); another copy exists in the Sieveking archive at Indiana University's Lilly Library. No sound recording of Sieveking's *Brideshead* adaptation survives in the BBC Archives, but his script, with its detailed list of sound effects and their reference numbers ("Lorry reversing—13B49 . . . Oxford clocks—3A36 . . . Paris chatter—20A27") gives one a sense of the sound world that the producer Donald McWhinnie created, no doubt with Sieveking's influence, either directly or through the by-then-established Sieveking production style.

Lance Sieveking was among the most influential pioneers of BBC Radio Drama. In addition to being a radio dramatist, he was a novelist and writer of nonsense verse, as well as an original member of the BBC Research Section, organized in 1928 with the often internally unpopular remit "to browse over the whole field of programmes, to initiate ideas, to experiment generally."[1] Sieveking championed the short-lived but nonetheless stylistically influential Dramatic Control-Panel, and its "playing" by the radio producer as a kind of proto-synthesizer, blending sound effects, music, and actors' voices as they performed.[2]

At least as early as 1948, the BBC was considering a radio adaptation of *Brideshead.* In an internal memo, Stephen Potter in the Features Department asserted, "Douglas Cleverdon . . . is strongly interested in an adaptation of *Brideshead Revisited.* I agree with him that this would make much better radio [than *Work Suspended* (1942)], and feel that he should be the one to do it."[3] Waugh had famously fraught relations with the BBC, and in 1953 when an attempt was made to secure the adaptation rights for the stories "An Englishman's Home" and "Excursion in Reality," Charles Lefeaux, acting script editor of drama (sound), wrote an internal memo to Mary Hope Allen asserting, "The eccentric gentleman [Waugh] told Lance Sieveking that there were no actors or actresses good enough to interpret his works, and that consequently he would never allow any of them to be dramatised; and he has apparently not even replied to his agent's request for permission. I am afraid, therefore, that we must put the project on one side until after his demise."[4] Whether this was obstructionist bluster or a reaction to his earlier dealings with the BBC, Waugh eventually bowed to financial pressures and on March 29, 1955 wrote to his agent, A. D. Peters, saying that he would need to sell the radio rights of his novels to the BBC or the film rights to *Scoop* (1938) to see him through the summer.[5]

Assistant head of drama (sound) Donald McWhinnie stated in an internal memo of March 18, 1955 that he wished to adapt *Brideshead* for the Home Service's Monday night drama slot. In the memo, McWhinnie stated that Waugh's friend, the writer Christopher Sykes (former deputy controller of the Third Programme and at that time working in the Features Department) would be "willing to meet the extra expense which would clearly be involved in negotiating terms for the use of [*Brideshead*] with Mr. Waugh."[6] After negotiations with Peters, the BBC paid £250 for the broadcasting rights to *Brideshead*, for a radio dramatization "to last for ninety minutes on the understanding that the first performance . . . shall be given within twelve months of the date of agreement, 26th April 1955, and any repeat performances within twelve months of the date on which the adaptation is completed."[7]

Sykes was initially the intended scriptwriter—Waugh had stipulated in a 1954 letter to Peters's associate John Montgomery that Sykes was the sole allowable adapter (for radio) of any of his works—but Sieveking ultimately (and inexplicably) undertook the project.[8] (In the same note to Montgomery, Waugh stipulated that the combined radio dramatization rights for *Put Out More Flags* (1942) and *Brideshead* should be sold to the BBC for not less than £500.) McWhinnie hoped that the adaptation broadcast of *Brideshead* would "prove to be something of an occasion."[9]

In its issue of April 6, 1956, the BBC's *Radio Times* advertised the April 9 broadcast of *Brideshead* with an illustration by the artist Leonard Rosoman and accompanying text by Peter Forster, which describes Waugh's story as

a rope of several strands, one being the development of Charles Ryder (who acts as narrator), and the others concern in the main his relationships with

the various members of the Flyte family—Lord Marchmain who lives in
Italy, his wife who lives in England, and their children, Cordelia and Julia
and the pathetic, unforgettable Sebastian, whom Charles meets in early
days of never-to-be-repeated happiness and freedom at Oxford. The story
is set in the pre-war period, but the occasion for its telling is the unexpected
wartime billeting of Ryder, now temporarily "a middle-aged infantry officer," at the Flytes' country seat, Brideshead Castle.[10]

The prominence of Lord Marchmain in the list of Flyte family members,
his placement in Italy, and the reference to the "Flytes' country seat" au-
gurs the adaptation's construction of the story as a chiefly secular microcosm of upper-class life, with reference neither to Roman Catholicism nor
to Charles's adulterous relationship with Julia, and only a deftly inconclusive description of Charles and Sebastian's friendship and their Oxford
milieu.[11] As do so many other publicity and marketing materials for *Brideshead* and its adaptations, Rosoman's illustration emphasizes Sebastian,
Charles, Aloysius, alcohol, floppy hair, and stately surroundings. With no
information apart from Forster's blurb and Rosoman's sketch, one could be
forgiven for thinking that Julia was a not very important secondary character. The accompanying broadcast listing, in the fourth column of the same
page, credits the actors playing Charles, Sebastian, Julia, and Bridey over
the title, followed by Waugh's and Sieveking's names, a cast list in order
of speaking, and finally a credit for the producer, Donald McWhinnie. As
with the marketing of Granada Television's 1981 adaptation and its afterlife
on VHS and DVD, there is a disjunction between the visual and textual
marketing components. While the characters of Charles and Sebastian are
portrayed (often to the exclusion of all others), advertising and marketing
text typically lists the actors portraying Charles, Sebastian, and Julia, in
that (entirely proper) order.

On April 19, 1956, the BBC periodical the *Listener* printed J. C. Trewin's
laudatory review of Sieveking's adaptation, which provides some insight
into the character of the lost recording.[12] Trewin awards highest praise to
the actor Hugh Burden for his performance as Charles Ryder, hyperboli-
cally claiming, "He can magnify a comma. One feels that if Mr. Burden
raised an eyebrow before the microphone, we should be aware of it." Further, Trewin claims that the actor Robert Eddison "found for Sebastian the
pouting charm that belonged to that doomed youth in love with his own
childhood. . . . Mr. Burden and Mr. Eddison made a happy interlude of the
Brideshead wine-tasting—yes, . . . there we knew everything. '*Everything*
to do with wine is wonderful'—poor Sebastian!"[13]

More significantly, however, both Trewin's review and Sieveking's script seem to assume the listener's (and the *Listener* reader's) prior familiarity with Waugh's novel, suggesting that the accepted purpose of a radio drama adaptation of a novel was not so much to create a separate and distinct work of art, but rather to provide a species of *aide-mémoire* for the reader who had not dusted off her edition of *Brideshead* in the eleven years since its first publication, encouraging a return to an already familiar narrative. Alternatively, such adaptations might have been regarded by their producers as a unique literary experience for a certain segment of the listening audience, or as Waugh more tartly put it, "the lower classes dont read books but they do listen to the wireless."[14]

In his 1981 book *British Radio Drama*, John Drakakis argues that radio adaptation typically "took the form simply of 'cutting'" and that the "process of adapting plays, novels, and short stories has . . . grown to such an extent that radio must be considered a primary means by which many people gain access to the literature and drama of the past. Thus, historical self-awareness and the natural desire to assert an individual identity in the face of alternatives were never clearly disentangled from the larger, clearly irresistible task of generating in radio audiences an awareness of cultural heritage and the aesthetic judgements that supported it."[15] In his review of Sieveking's *Brideshead*, Trewin describes the production not as an adaptation, but as Sieveking's "most subtle *treatment* of the novel, a re-piecing of its jigsaw" (my emphasis), requiring that the dramatist decide what to "select" and what to "delete" from the source text(s). Trewin's language is revealing: "Most of the family came up as we had hoped. . . . It left us strangely wistful, not perhaps 'unusually cheerful,' after Hugh Burden— 'homeless, childless, middle-aged, loveless'—has expressed both the 'fierce little human tragedy' of Brideshead and the certainty of the flame that burned afresh among the old stones."[16] Trewin's use of "we" rather than "I" facilitates inclusion of the listener in the club of the initiated: those who know the novel and, on the basis of that knowledge, have specific expectations about the manner in which it might be adapted.

Certainly on paper, Sieveking's script does not make any radical changes to the plot or themes of the novel, though it accomplishes a great deal in ellipsis—even greater ellipses than Waugh dared use—and is marred by awkward expository dialogue that suffers from the familiar syndrome "Dear Listener, this is what happened in the lives of the characters between the last scene and this one." It does, however, eliminate either thematically or narratively significant characters such as Nanny Hawkins, Cousin

Jasper, Boy Mulcaster, Mr. Samgrass, Kurt, and, perhaps most astonishingly, Celia—deletions that Frederick L. Beaty classes merely as "abridgements."[17] Some of these characters survive by reference, as in the case of Mr. Samgrass, whom Sebastian describes as "A ghastly little snob" who "Sucks up" to Lady Marchmain.[18] These selections and deletions, by their very nature, emphasize, and in one instance problematize, certain of the novel's intertwined themes—class and Catholicism—to the detriment of others: romantic friendship and profane love.

Waugh's attempt to realize a more overtly literary style in *Brideshead* is mostly lost in Sieveking's populist and often excessively melodramatic treatment, which occasionally approaches caricature as it reworks Waugh's dialogue, adding stereotypical verbal traits as class identifiers. This kind of dramatic manipulation may not violate the ethos of the source material, but its lack of subtlety reduces the complexity of Waugh's characterizations and looks like an attempt at appealing to the "popular listener." According to Drakakis, "The [BBC] policy of distinguishing between serious and popular drama . . . meant that among committed experimentalists . . . the Home Service became a byword for mediocrity."[19]

For example, when Sebastian first takes Charles to Brideshead Castle, he says: "One always ought to have a fountain just outside one's window. It's *necessary*" (Sieveking, "Brideshead," 7). Showing Charles around the rest of the house, he opens up the ball-room and says, (*"Indifferently"*), "You see. It's all like this. Marble pillars, frescoed ceilings. The usual thing. Seen enough?" (Sieveking, "Brideshead," 8). Granted, Waugh describes "vast, twin fireplaces of sculptured marble, the coved ceiling frescoed with classic deities and heroes, the gilt mirrors and scagliola pilaster," but having Sebastian voice these qualities in such an offhand way constructs him more starkly as a member of the superficial gilded youth. Unconvincingly borrowing a verbal tic from Agatha Runcible in *Vile Bodies* (1930), on showing Charles the art nouveau Brideshead chapel, Sebastian says, "It *is* a bit shy-making, isn't it?" (Sieveking, "Brideshead," 9). On his first night at Brideshead after responding to Sebastian's telegram, Charles says good night to Julia, rather absurdly addressing her directly as "Lady Julia" (Sieveking, "Brideshead," 16).

The most extended and extreme example occurs in Charles and Sebastian's interactions with the butler, Wilcox. In Sieveking's script, Wilcox answers Sebastian's summons with "Yes, m'lord?" and while his dialogue closely follows Waugh's own, Sieveking makes small but significant adjustments that reduce him to a stock comic domestic. When describing the state of the cellar, Sieveking's Wilcox says: "Ah, m'lord. There's a lot of old wine wants drinking up. Some of 'em vintages fifty years old! . . . We ought to have laid down in [*sic*] the eighteens and twenties. I've had several letters about it from the wine merchants, but her ladyship says to ask Lord Brideshead, and *he* says to ask his lordship, so I writes and his lordship answers that I'm to ask the lawyers. That's how we get low. . . . I'm afraid that you may find some of the older vintages have gone back to earth, as they say." Wilcox leaves, indicated by the sound of a shutting door, and Charles chirps, "Gone back to earth? What a wonderful phrase" (Sieveking, "Brideshead," 18).[20]

Wilcox's "so I writes" and his repetitive, obsequious "m'lord's" (a total of six over two pages of script) were perhaps meant to inject some comedy into a dry exchange. In the original text(s), Wilcox does not use "m'lord" and the social markers of his idiolect are infinitely more discreet: "There's been nothing added since his Lordship went abroad. . . . A lot of the old wine wants drinking up. We ought to have laid down the eighteens and twenties. I've had several letters about it from the wine merchants, but her Ladyship says to ask Lord Brideshead, and he says to ask his Lordship, and his Lordship says to ask the lawyers. That's how we get low."[21] In contrast with Sieveking's script, Jeremy Front's 2003 adaptation for BBC Radio 4 uses Waugh's dialogue almost verbatim, without a single "m'lord."

In reference to his drunkenness at Ma Mayfield's—which survives in Sieveking's script only in allusion as "that *sordid* night-club"—Sebastian concedes that he "*was* a bit squiffy" (Sieveking, "Brideshead," 31). During Sebastian's extended period of insobriety at Brideshead, Julia draws Cordelia away from the audible action with her admonition to attend to the call of the "dressing gong" (Sieveking, "Brideshead," 34). On the morning of the hunt, instead of imploring Sebastian, "Do go and change," Cordelia says "Do buck up and change" (*BR* 141; Sieveking, "Brideshead," 37). These are all fairly minor points, but they do seem potentially to act as audible labels for the listener, as aids to identifying either the speakers or their particular classes. Taken as a whole, Sieveking's changes suffuse the adaptation with a pungent air of arch class caricature, which can only have served to entrench the critical (and popular) perception that Waugh and the world he portrayed were rooted in snobbery.

Sieveking's most significant acts of "selection" and "deletion" result in the near elimination of all suggestions of sex, in contrast to Beaty's assertion that "sexual innuendoes" in Sieveking's adaptations of Waugh's novels "remained unaltered when they were verbally sophisticated."[22] Sieveking cuts Charles's reunion with Celia in New York, which in the editions of the novel then publicly available did not include the allusion to sexual intercourse that occurs in the Private Edition of 1944 and the Revised Edition of 1960. He also cuts Charles and Julia's love scene on the liner, which could only be described as (verbally) sophisticated to the point of aridity. Sieveking even eliminates Anthony Blanche's discussion of his affair with Stefanie, Duchess of Vincennes, though inconsistently (and confusingly for the listener who might not have read the book) he includes Charles and Sebastian's discussion of the affair and Sebastian's assertion that it was not a "grand passion." Sieveking spares only the occasional tame (and not terribly sophisticated) sexual innuendo, such as Mr. Ryder's description of a mixed-sex sketching club with its intimations of "free love" ("Brideshead" 13). Sebastian's references to the "woman in Hull" who used an instrument, and the "naughty scout-master" reported in the *News of the World* are sanitized in Sieveking's script with Sebastian's merely exclaiming, "Ah! I do like these frightful Sunday papers" (*BR* 77–78; "Brideshead" 20). Sieveking eliminates Charles's indecently sunbathing on the roof when Cordelia arrives, transferring Charles's introduction to her indoors ("Brideshead" 22).

In the Venetian sequence Sieveking retains Cara's assessment of Charles and Sebastian's romantic friendship but seems, more significantly, to insert a thematically inconsistent note of anticonversion caution. Cara says of Lady Marchmain: "She is deeply religious . . . but she does not understand that one must not *press* religion on other people." After Cara worries aloud about the nature of Sebastian's drinking, Charles asks her: "You think it is his mother's fault?" Cara: "Ah! It may be . . . it may be . . ." (Sieveking, "Brideshead," 29–30). Cara's view as introduced by Sieveking certainly is not openly expressed in Waugh's text(s) and is perhaps best understood in light of the adaptation's own social and institutional context.[23]

When recounting his trip through the Levant with Samgrass in Waugh's text(s), Sebastian refers to his meeting with Anthony Blanche and his "Jew boy" (*BR* 140). In Sieveking's script, Sebastian says, more ambiguously, that he "met Anthony Blanche with a beastly Armenian," and avoids mentioning the American sailor in Constantinople ("Brideshead" 37). During Charles's trip to Tangier there is no mention of Kurt's being infected with syphilis, though Charles demands to know whether Sebastian means to spend his life "with that septic, lisping Teuton" (Sieveking, "Brideshead," 52). Upon Charles's return to Great Britain, Sieveking retains the exchange with Bridey about the possibility of there being "anything vicious" in Sebastian's connection with Kurt. Charles says, verbatim from the public 1940s editions of *Brideshead*, "No. I'm sure not. It's simply a case of two waifs coming together" ("Brideshead" 52).

The most significant cuts are in reference to Celia and Julia. Sieveking's script uses a huge ellipsis to skip from Bridey's commissioning Charles's paintings of Marchmain House to Julia's asking Charles to marry her and plan for the two divorces, effectively eliminating all reference to Charles's trip to South America and his reunion with Celia. Sieveking does not even mention Celia's name, let alone the return passage to Britain, Charles's budding affair with Julia, Celia's realization of his adultery, the exhibition of his paintings, and his final encounter with Anthony Blanche ("Brideshead" 53). This ellipsis eliminates any explanation for Charles's adultery. There is no gradual crescendo of affection between Charles and Julia, as in Waugh's text(s); no consummation; no maddening Celia to explain why Charles might turn to another woman instead of his wife. The answer must be, in part, that Sieveking assumed a prior familiarity with the novel among his listeners or, failing that, a willingness by uninitiated listeners to find inspiration in his adaptation, spurring them to read the book and discover all the nuance lacking in the radio treatment. Nameless, Celia survives only in a single line, when Charles says to Julia, "I wonder which is more horrible. My wife's art and fashion, or your husband's politics and money" (Sieveking, "Brideshead," 53).

Time constraints no doubt played some part in this massive editing, which effectively pushes the narrative emphasis toward the first half, to Sebastian and Charles's friendship. The mores of the mid-1950s were, no doubt, the chief reason behind the deletions. In *British Radio Drama: 1922–1956*, Val Gielgud, head of BBC drama, asserted: "My selection of plays was not subject to the Lord Chamberlain's veto. And, apart from having to observe the amber warning-lights at the cross-roads of Sex, Religion, and Politics, I could drive straight ahead with reasonable confidence of security. It is, of course, true that the aforesaid amber lights would flash red on occasion with disquieting rapidity."[24] As a novel being considered for radio adaptation, *Brideshead Revisited* must have set the warning lights into low-level panic, just as it had set off alarm bells in Hollywood in 1947, when MGM realized it would be impossible to film a book whose plot hinged on divorce and adultery, with liberal helpings of implied homosexual relationships.[25]

In contrast, Jeremy Front's 2003 adaptation does not flinch from the two sex scenes (or other passages of sexual innuendo) and sources the dialogue and narration from the text of the 1960 Revised Edition. In the New York hotel room Celia asks whether she should put her face to bed. Charles replies, "No, not at once" and in voiceover states, "Then she knew what was wanted." There is the sound of rustling sheets "AS THEY CLIMB INTO

BED," and Celia whispers "Oh, Charles, my darling . . . It's been such a long time," and Charles says in narration, "She had neat, hygienic ways for that too, but there were both relief and triumph in her smile of welcome."[26] Further, in the love scene with Julia, Front again uses the text of the 1960 Revised Edition as Charles narrates the encounter without sound effects.

There is a final change, albeit slight, on the last page of Sieveking's script. In a segue from Charles and Julia's final scene together to the "Epilogue" scene, Sieveking expands on Julia's dialogue as it occurs in Waugh's text(s). Literally echoing through time, Charles recalls Julia's saying (in Sieveking's version), "perhaps, however bad I am, God won't despair of me in the end . . . or of you either, Charles." To himself, and very much in the present tense of the Epilogue scene (rather than in the "*full echo*" of the remembered past), Charles wonders, "Or of me, either?" This question would seem to imply that Charles is still, several years on, pondering the validity of Julia's words. Sieveking eliminates Charles's tour of occupied Brideshead Castle and focuses instead on his exchange with Hooper. There is no indication that Charles prays in the chapel at Brideshead, but after Hooper leaves him alone, he says "(*To himself*)" "Vanity of vanities, all is vanity . . . and yet . . . and yet . . . something quite remote from anything the builders intended has come out of their work . . . the small red flame in the beaten copper lamp in the chapel burns again—The flame which the old knights saw from their tombs and saw put out. That flame burns again now for other soldiers, far from home, farther, in heart, than Acre or Jerusalem" (Sieveking, "Brideshead," 65). This ending is altogether more ambiguous than Waugh's own. The combination of Charles's continued rumination about whether or not God will despair of him in the end and his failure to pray (consider how easily a prayer might be conveyed over radio) casts his "Vanity of vanities" speech in a quite different light: nostalgic, universal, and only slightly personal. If Charles is meant to convert to Roman Catholicism in Sieveking's script, it is a conversion that transpires after the final fade out.[27]

How, then, should one regard Sieveking's 1956 version, and what can be said about its potential influence on the reception of Waugh's text? BBC Listener Research for 1955 calculated an average of 2.75 million listeners to Monday night plays on the Home Service.[28] The Home Service was, according to Burton Paulu, "the keystone—the broad middle strand—of British radio broadcasting, and offered the widest program range of the BBC's domestic services," carrying "principal newscasts and news analyses; programs for in-school use; the children's hour; much serious music and some light and popular music; variety and other entertainment features; dramas; religious programs; and many talks and discussions."[29]

The Third Programme, later Radio 3, was then the preserve of more overtly and unapologetically intellectual programming. The placement of *Brideshead* in such a middle range, bridging the cultural gulf between the populist Light Programme and the often highbrow quarters of the Third Programme, reflects the unstable position of Waugh's novel in the literary canon. This downward positioning in the popular consciousness, along with its further popularization in Granada Television's ITV-broadcast adaptation, has aided its construction, at least in Britain, as rather mediocre melodramatic entertainment: a window on the eccentricities of the English upper classes and specifically on that even smaller minority, the Catholic upper classes.

The history of *Brideshead* on BBC Radio did not end in 1956. In January 1970, the program *Woman's Hour* (then on Radio 2) broadcast a fifteen-part reading of the novel by the actor Hugh Burden, who had portrayed Charles Ryder in the Sieveking adaptation. Waugh's literary value had appreciated only slightly since 1956 (and since his death in 1966), as the BBC paid £1.6.10 per minute of broadcast ("the normal rate plus one-sixth"), for a total broadcast time of presumably some 225 minutes.[30]

The BBC Radio 4 production of Jeremy Front's four-part three-hour and fifty-minute serial adaptation of *Brideshead*, directed by Marion Nancarrow with original music by Neil Brand, was broadcast in March 2003, in observance of Waugh's centenary. Front's script, liberated both by its extended serial format and the liberalized mores of British broadcasting, provides a rounded adaptation of the novel that manages to include all the major characters, does not shrink from representing scenes and themes that set the amber warning lights flashing in the past, and bravely adapts elements of Waugh's text(s) that might inflame politically correct post-Christian, postcolonial sensibilities today. Where Sieveking's adaptation acts as reminder and outline of the novel, always reliant on knowledge of the prior text to understand the adapted text, Front's adaptation exists at once as a recognizable "version" of *Brideshead Revisited* and as an autonomous "text" whose frame of reference remains artfully its own.

NOTES

Thanks to the staff of the BBC Written Archive Centre (WAC) for their assistance and permission to quote from internal correspondence and Lance Sieveking's script, and Jeremy Front for permission to quote from his script.

1. Val Gielgud, *British Radio Drama: 1922–1956* (London: George G. Harrap, 1957), 27.

2. Lance Sieveking, *The Stuff of Radio* (London: Cassell, 1934), 58–59.

3. Stephen Potter, "Adaptation of 'Work Suspended' by Evelyn Waugh," July 14, 1948, Written Archive Centre, British Broadcasting Corporation. Hereafter cited as WAC, BBC. Cf. Winnifred M. Bogaards, "Evelyn Waugh and the BBC," *Evelyn Waugh: New Directions*, ed. Alain Blayac (London: Macmillan, 1992), 102.

4. Charles Lefeaux, internal memo to Mary Hope Allen, April 17, 1953, WAC, BBC.

5. Robert Murray Davis, *A Catalogue of the Evelyn Waugh Collection at the Humanities Research Center, the University of Texas at Austin* (Troy, NY: Whitston, 1981), E880. Less than a year earlier, when radio adaptations of *Put Out More Flags* (1942) and *Work Suspended* were in discussion, Waugh wished to stipulate that any radio script should use only his words and that any additional dialogue would be provided by him at a high fee. See Davis, *Catalogue*, E856.

6. Donald McWhinnie, internal memo to E. M. Layton, Copyright Department, March 18, 1955, WAC, BBC.

7. E. M. Layton, internal memo to Script Editor, Drama (Sound), April 27, 1955, WAC, BBC.

8. Frederick L. Beaty and Winnifred M. Bogaards agree that the cause behind the switch remains unexplained by Sykes or Sieveking. See Beaty, "Evelyn Waugh and Lance Sieveking: New Light on Waugh's Relations with the BBC," *Papers on Language & Literature* 25, no. 2 (1989): 193; Bogaards, "Waugh and the BBC," 106; and Davis, *Catalogue*, E862. See also E878, in which Waugh reasserts to Montgomery that radio adaptation rights for *Brideshead* and *Put Out More Flags* should not sell to the BBC for less than £500 and that Sykes should adapt and cast the productions.

9. Donald McWhinnie, internal memo, June 1, 1955, WAC, BBC.

10. Peter Forster, untitled notice, *Radio Times: Journal of the BBC*, April 6, 1956, 16.

11. The influence of the *Radio Times* in the mid-1950s should not be underestimated; in 1955 it reached a publication peak with weekly sales in excess of eight million copies. The effect of illustrations such as Rosoman's was analogous to that of today's movie "trailers" and advance advertising for forthcoming programs on television. See David Linton, "*Radio Times*," in *Consumer Magazines of the British Isles*, ed. Sam G. Riley, (London: Greenwood Press, 1993), 166–71.

12. In 1939, on the occasion of the *Listener*'s tenth anniversary, the then director-general of the BBC wrote that one aspect of the *Listener*'s mission was to "promote the influence of broadcasting, particularly in the field of arts and letters." See Alan Thomas, "A Long Line of 'Listeners,'" *Listener*, August 3, 1967, 141.

13. J. C. Trewin, "Sound Drama," the *Listener*, April 19, 1956, 477–78. Coincidentally, Eddison portrayed Troutbeck in the 1987 television adaptation of *Scoop*.

14. Evelyn Waugh, *The Letters of Evelyn Waugh*, ed. Mark Amory (New York: Ticknor & Fields, 1980), 230. Hereafter cited as *LEW*.

15. John Drakakis, Introduction, in *British Radio Drama* (Cambridge: Cambridge University Press, 1981), 3.

16. Trewin, "Sound Drama," 477–78.

17. Beaty, "Waugh and Sieveking," 198.

18. Lance Sieveking, "Brideshead Revisited," MS, WAC, BBC, 30. Hereafter cited as Sieveking, "Brideshead."

19. Drakakis, Introduction, 16.

20. Sieveking here apparently misreads the line from the novel, which suggests that vintages from those years should have been put down; Sieveking's version suggests that the cellars of Brideshead should have been stocked *during* the period.

21. Evelyn Waugh, *Brideshead Revisited: The Sacred and Profane Memories of Captain Charles Ryder* (London: Chapman & Hall, 1945), 74. Hereafter cited as *BR*.

22. Beaty, "Waugh and Sieveking," 198.

23. Frederick L. Beaty ably sets out the evidence in support of Waugh's never having read Sieveking's script or hearing the broadcast, though he was given ample opportunity. Beaty attributes this lack of meddling to Waugh's respect for and "confidence in" Sieveking, which he sees expressed in a selection of "unpublished postcards and letters from Waugh." It may be a mistake, however, to extrapolate confidence in Sieveking's artistry from what seems to be little more than a polite epistolary style of Waugh's. See Beaty, "Waugh and Sieveking," 191–94. Correspondence in the BBC WAC reveals that Barbara Bray, the BBC script editor for drama (sound), provided A. D. Peters's associate, John Montgomery, with a copy of Sieveking's script on March 14, 1956, eleven days before the adaptation was recorded, and nearly a month before its first broadcast.

24. Gielgud, *British Radio Drama*, 36.

25. Robert Murray Davis, *Mischief in the Sun: The Making and Unmaking of* The Loved One (Troy, NY: Whitston, 1999), 30–53.

26. Jeremy Front, "Brideshead Revisited Episode 3," MS, Casarotto Ramsay & Associates Limited, London, 69. A sound recording of Front's adaptation is available for purchase from the BBC. In the production, the sound effects of the scene are muted: rustling of sheets, a single modest sigh from Celia.

27. Sieveking does, inconsistently, retain Hooper's line from the prologue: "There's a sort of little R.C. church, attached. I looked in and there was a kind of service going on—just one padre and one old man. I felt very awkward. More in your line than mine" ("Brideshead" 4).

28. Gielgud, *British Radio Drama*, 30

29. Burton Paulu, *British Broadcasting in Transition* (London: Macmillan, 1961), 148.

30. BBC Copyright Department to Anthony Jones, February 5, 1969, and Virginia Brown-Wilkinson to B. H. Alexander, internal memo, WAC, BBC.

Eyes Reopened:
A Tourist in Africa

Dan S. Kostopulos

IN HIS INTRODUCTION TO *WHEN THE GOING WAS GOOD* (1946), EVELYN WAUGH wrote, "My own travelling days are over and I do not expect to see many travel books in the near future."[1] While it is certainly true that the rough travel of the 1930s typified by *Remote People* (1931) and *Ninety-Two Days* (1934) was at an end for him in the years following the Second World War, Waugh continued to journey abroad frequently, although usually by himself and as a tourist. His motives for doing so were often mixed: perhaps to escape an English winter or to restore his failing health, sometimes to relieve boredom or to gather material for a commission, and once, as *The Ordeal of Gilbert Pinfold* (1957) painfully records, to escape the demons of madness within himself. As with his first travel book, *Labels* (1930), thirty years before, it was the first of these reasons that supposedly drove him out of England and served as the genesis of his last book of travel writing.

Among his travel books, *A Tourist in Africa* (1960) provokes the widest variety of responses from Waugh scholars. Selina Hastings writes that it is "almost as boring to read as evidently it was to write,"[2] while Douglas Lane Patey calls it his "wisest travel book."[3] The result of a two-month trip to Kenya, Tanganyika, and Rhodesia in early 1959, Waugh's journal-style book is an engaging portrait of British colonial rule of Africa in transition. While this is not his first time back in Africa since covering the Italo-Ethiopian war in 1936, *A Tourist in Africa* records his first extended visit to that continent in over twenty years. Why Africa? The book explains: "It is not so easy as it was thirty years ago to find retreat. Tourism and politics have laid waste everywhere. Nor is 55 the best age for travel; too old for the jungle, too young for the beaches, one must seek refreshment in the spectacle of other people at work, leading lives quite different from one's own. . . . Africa again without preoccupations with eyes reopened to the exotic. That's the ticket."[4] While the nature of travel had significantly changed by the late 1950s, exactly what Waugh expected to find in Africa is not clear in his opening chapter. However, by allowing his eyes to be "reopened" to Africa, Waugh provoked the most profound confrontation with colonialism found in his work. As Martin Stannard points out, "In 1931 [Waugh] had offered confidently eccentric opinions on whatever crossed his path. In 1959 Africa was no longer a white man's joke. Colonialism and apartheid could not be dismissed as the bugbears of lunatic liberals."[5] Nevertheless, *A Tourist in Africa* is perhaps Waugh's most neglected book and is often dismissed as evidence of literary decline in his final years. It is not funny like *Labels* or *Remote People*, polemical like *Waugh in Abyssinia* (1936) or *Robbery under Law* (1939); nor is it haunting like *The Ordeal of Gilbert Pinfold*.

Indeed, its neglect can be traced all the way back to publication in 1960, when it was treated quite roughly. Alan Sillitoe ridiculed Waugh's "sense of tolerance of a cast-bound mind," and the renowned African historian Basil Davidson declared that Waugh's political opinions were "out of touch with reality."[6] Fifty years later, this neglect continues. Indeed, it might still be easy for historians and postcolonialists to point out what Waugh got wrong about Africa during decolonization. But what is almost never done, and certainly more interesting and beneficial, is to point out what he got right. Postcolonialism in Africa has been painful, as endless coups, civil wars, brutal dictatorships and kleptocracies, acts of genocide, and continued exploitation by the West have all revealed. While it may not contain his finest travel writing, *A Tourist in Africa* resolves Waugh's ambiguous and conflicted views on empire as he struggles to understand the overwhelming reality of its decline in Africa, as well as its movement toward new forms of "independence" such as apartheid and postcolonialism.

Waugh's convictions about imperialism are neither clear-cut nor easy to explain. *Remote People* certainly contains numerous passages that debunk any notion of British and European superiority in Africa, while also reveling in the atmosphere of places such as the plantations of colonial Kenya. And while *Waugh in Abyssinia* is certainly pro-Italian in its point of view, it also expresses misgivings about the colonial endeavors of other countries, particularly Britain. At what point in Waugh's imagination is the issue finally resolved? Certainly the Second World War (in which Waugh was a combatant) had shown that war and conquest, once thought by him to be "inevitable,"[7] had led the way to nothing less than global disaster: "Had we known that all that seeming-solid, patiently built, gorgeously ornamented structure of Western life was to melt overnight like an ice-castle, leaving only a puddle of mud; had we known man was even then leaving his post. Instead we set off on our various stern roads . . . with the belief that barbarism was a dodo to be stalked with a pinch of salt" (*WTGWG* 8). Instead, the West had witnessed and perpetrated barbarism in quantity; the notion of Western superiority's maintaining a civilizing influence over other peoples must have seemed pure hypocrisy. And the process of de-colonization that was to follow shortly thereafter was not simply a matter of handing back power to local peoples. As Waugh comments near the end of *A Tourist in Africa*, "the foundations of Empire are often occasions of woe; their dismemberment always" (157). Traveling through Africa in 1959, Waugh could have easily insulated himself from the problems he saw and been contented with nostalgia for the past. Instead, *A Tourist in Africa* confronts current issues and is a significant work in the canon of postcolonial discourse that provides a unique glimpse of colonial African culture in transition.

Before his arrival in colonial Africa, Waugh's journey aboard the *Rhodesia Castle* provided an opportunity to revisit some points in his early travels. The voyage south partially repeated the honeymoon cruise of his doomed first marriage in 1929, as well as that of his first journey to Africa in 1930. The sense of repetition was not lost on him. Paris, Italy, the Mediterranean, the Middle East were all noted with varying degrees of fondness and disappointment. At Port Said, where Waugh had his first contact with the Orient through Arab Town in 1929, he found only the familiar. "No tarboushes to be seen," he writes. "The touts have discarded their white gowns for shoddy western suits, exemplifying the almost universal rule that 'Nationalists' obliterate national idiosyncrasies. Even the 'gully-gully' man wore trousers" (*Tourist* 25). And Waugh is correct, for as Frantz Fanon and Edward Said both point out, one of the paradoxes of colonialism is that the new "national" culture often replicates the colonial master in a variety of aspects.[8] There is also Steamer Point near Aden, where the boyish public-school atmosphere of the British colony captivated Waugh in 1930. Instead of the rocky and barren coastline, he finds that the colony has "grown green," and that there are "portraits of Nasser in many of the Arab shops" (*Tourist* 28–29). Again, nationalism, which Waugh once thought endemic only to the West, shows itself within the margins of what was once the unfamiliar. But perhaps the most striking change is in the people traveling out to the colonies: "The great majority are the young, returning to work; not adventurers seeking a fortune, not, at this late age of Africa, empire builders; but the employees of governments and big commercial firms taking up secure posts as clerks and schoolmasters and conservators of soil; sons of the Welfare State; well qualified, well behaved, enjoying an easy bonhomie with the stewards. Many have young wives, children and infants in arms" (*Tourist* 23). There is no romance about them; nor is there reactionary contempt. Instead, the young colonials are simply members of a growing bureaucracy sent out to the remote places to do a job. To Waugh, their presence signifies that the Africa he is to reencounter is very different from the one he first knew three decades earlier.

While bureaucrats and bureaucracy are for Waugh "one of the evidences of original sin" (*Tourist* 9), their presence in colonial Africa illustrates that the old dichotomy established in *Waugh in Abyssinia* of the noble "explorer" ("doing what no men had done before them . . . in small companies, often alone, in unknown dangers") and lowly "financier" ("what they risked was a small thing but it was what they valued most highly") no longer functions as neatly in Waugh's colonial imagination.[9] Recognizing this shift, he attempts to demystify some of white colonial Africa's greatest heroes. The first of these is Sir Henry Stanley, arguably the archetype of all African "explorers." Waugh characterizes his final expedition through central Africa in 1889 as "tragic and villainous, tempered only by farce" (*Tourist* 62). More bizarre but perhaps more sympathetic is Emin; a protégé of General Gordon, he was for a time the governor of southern Sudan. Born a German Jew named Schnitzer, he went "native," commanding his own personal army in Africa until Arab slave traders eventually murdered him.

Yet no white colonial figure is debunked as soundly as Cecil Rhodes. "He was a visionary," Waugh writes, "and almost all he saw was hallucination" (*Tourist* 149). After visiting Rhodes's massive estate in Rhodesia and standing at the foot of his grave, Waugh reflects: "He was not . . . a man of action. He was neither a soldier nor an explorer. . . . Rhodes was a financier. He made a huge fortune very young at a time when other huge fortunes were being made. . . . Rhodes' predominant skill was in the market, in negotiating combinations, monopolies and loans, in beguiling shareholders. . . . And money for him was not an end; it was not the means to pleasure or even personal power; it was the substance of his dreams" (*Tourist* 149–50). As the "financier" of Waugh's familiar imperial dichotomy, Rhodes has nothing attractive about his character, and no good can come of his legacy. Whereas some might justify Rhodes's presence because he seemingly introduced order and culture to a chaotic wilderness, Waugh makes no attempt at rationalization. Rather, he sees Rhodes as a megalomaniac absurdly "dedicated to the supremacy of the Anglo-Saxon race" (*Tourist* 151). Waugh reduces his legacy to "imprudence and dishonesty": "He had seen Afrikaaners and British in South Africa hopelessly embittered. Today his great project of the all-British Cape to Cairo route has lost all meaning; the personal, honourable ascendancy of Great White Chiefs has degenerated into 'apartheid'" (*Tourist* 149). And apartheid, according to Waugh, is "alien and . . . outrageous" to the "explorer" sensibility because both the white settler and the native are connected to the land in the same manner as the English landed gentry and the peasants (*Tourist* 142). That is, the gentry act on land's potential while the peasants remain close to the land through their labor. It is easy to argue that Waugh's depiction is merely a naive attempt to debunk the reputation of an imperial icon. Yet by 1959, Rhodes hardly needed to be "exposed" for what he really was. While Rhodesia offered an ordered and prosperous society in both the city and the country, Waugh cannot ignore the obvious racism that is the basis for its continuation. In addition, his sympathy with black Africans is not based on the comic juxta-position of savagery with the West as it is in *Remote People*, *Black Mischief* (1932), or *A Handful of Dust* (1934). Rather, Waugh recognizes that their cultures' significance is largely unrecognized—"Rhodesians seem to me morbidly incurious about native customs and beliefs" (*Tourist* 141)—and those cultures cannot be sustained (at least in their present form) in the wake of colonial dissolution because they are being absorbed and eclipsed by the rise of different African nationalisms.

But of all the places that Waugh visits in *A Tourist in Africa*, none embodies the spirit of postcolonial uncertainty as much as Kenya. It had been an idyllic place in his imagination, an attempt to "recreate Barsetshire on the equator," all that is good about colonialism.[10] When the *Rhodesia Castle* pulls in at Mombasa, he is uncertain of what he will encounter: "Why should not this equatorial Arcadia, so lately and lightly colonized, go the way of Europe?" (*Tourist* 36). Kenya was on the verge of indepen-dence (in 1963) and still reeling from the bloody Mau Mau uprising against the British. In contrast with Waugh's former idealism about "the enchant-ing contradictions of Kenya life" in *Remote People* (151), this trip allows him to delve deeper into current political realities. In 1931, "officials" and "settlers" in Kenya struggled over a new policy: "Where the interests of the immigrant and native races conflicted, the interests of the native were 'paramount'" (*Tourist* 37). For the first time, Waugh argues, the Kenyan settlers became "politically-conscious." They "saw the Colonial office as their declared enemy who sought to rob them of the lands they had cleared and ploughed and watered. The officials, they said, had no stake on the country; they were in transit, thinking only of promotion and pension; they would retire to die in Europe. The settlers were transforming a wilderness where they intended to found families" (*Tourist* 38). As in *Remote People*, Waugh's sympathy is naturally with the settlers in their struggle against the bureaucracy of colonial officials. However, he approaches the argument as something altogether more complicated. While the settlers are certainly white, as in *Remote People* (and as is certainly true today in Kenyan politics), their lives center on Kenya, so they too regard their interests as largely "native." Indeed, when one stops being a "settler" and becomes a "native" is an issue of critical significance in the discussion of nationalism and post-colonialism. As can various "black" African nationalisms, the nativism of white Kenyans can be seen as an example of what Benedict Anderson calls an "imagined community" that tries to intensify its own sense of self by establishing a sense of difference between Kenyans and the English.[11] Unlike Rhodesians, the Kenyans (and Waugh) have previously regarded the English officials as ideological fools: "There was then a simple division between two groups of Englishmen, one trying to run the country as a Montessori School, the other as a league of feudal estates, each sincerely believing that it understood better the natives and knew what was best for them" (*Tourist* 38). However, in 1959 conditions were altogether different as the country moved closer to independence. Waugh does not say a great deal about current politics, except to remark that all the past resentment between officials and settlers "seems now to have subsided" (*Tourist* 38). The reason is clear in the next line. Waugh hints at the collective anxiety: "Officials, settlers and Indians have a common uncertainty of their future," and "since the Mau-Mau 'emergency' no one pretends to understand the natives" (*Tourist* 38). As in Rhodesia, the struggle between black and white, "native" and "settler," threatens to overwhelm the peaceful transition toward independence.

According to Waugh, "no one talked of African 'Nationalism'" in Kenya in 1931 (*Tourist* 38). Disputes were largely among officials, settlers, and Indians. By 1959, the dispute had changed to a contest between African nationalism on one side and all immigrants on the other. The black Kenyans asserted their rights as an indigenous people, while the "other" Kenyans justified their power because they acted on Kenya's economic potential. Such nationalist enterprises are always problematic because, as Seamus Deane points out, "The terms of the dispute can be crude. The 'native' . . . can say they came first; the . . . planters can say they were the first to create a civil society. . . . Priority is a claim to power."[12] National issues, especially regarding the possession of land, are an inherent part of the process of decolonization. As Deniz Kandiyoti writes, nationalism "presents itself both as a modern project that melts and transforms traditional attachments in favour of new identities and as a reaffirmation of authentic cultural values culled from the depths of a presumed communal past. It therefore opens up a highly fluid and ambivalent field of meanings which can be reactivated, reinterpreted, and often reinvented at critical junctures of the histories of nation-states."[13] Those "meanings" are often the subject of struggle as a new Kenya begins to emerge beyond the parameters of colonialism. The degree to which Waugh is conscious of this ambivalence is uncertain. Clearly, while he is uncomfortable discussing such topics as "a stranger" (*Tourist* 104), he understands that such issues are a critical part of understanding contemporary Africa. Even in Tanganyika, a "nationalist" movement awaited the transfer of power from the colonial government, though as Waugh points out, "nationality" is irrelevant to people so heterogeneous and arbitrarily assigned to the territory (*Tourist* 58–59). Waugh is certainly conscious of the irony inherent in such a situation, viewing it with a degree of impatience and skepticism. He later remarks: "For someone as unpolitical as myself it is difficult to guess what is meant by 'a nation' of peoples as dissimilar as the Chagga, the Masai, the Gogo, the Arabs of Pagani, the fishermen of Kilwa, the Greek and Indian magnates of Dar-es-Salaam, whose frontiers were arbitrarily drawn in Europe by politicians who had never set foot in Africa" (*Tourist* 98). Waugh's comments anticipate Fanon's argument that the "native's" reconstruction of a national "culture, extracted from the past to be displayed in all its splendour, is not necessarily that of his own country."[14] However, at their base, nationalist programs are movements of liberation, not historical reconstruction. Just as Europeans envisioned Africa as a savage blank space in its era of colonization, decolonization makes it essential for natives to rethink Africa without its imperial heritage "and proclaim the existence of another culture."[15]

Despite the transitional nature of imperial Africa in 1959, one thing for Waugh remains wholly good and uncorrupted in the midst of decolonization. Not surprisingly, this is Christianity. While visiting Father Groeber's Serima mission in Rhodesia, Waugh has only praise and admiration for the distinctive African-Christian religious and artistic culture that thrives there. The church, according to Waugh, is "one of the most beautiful and original . . . of the modern world" (*Tourist* 131), largely because its carvings are "symbolic and didactic, like that of the European Middle Ages; entirely novel and entirely African." "There is no suggestion of self-expression or of aesthetic emotion," he writes, "nor of acquiring a marketable skill or titillating national pride at doing as well as the white man" (*Tourist* 128–29). It is a haven away from the nationalism and endless political discussion that have followed him everywhere else. Although conceived by Father Groeber, everything at Serima is devoted to the glorification of God in a manner that follows no prescribed Western model for aesthetics or worship. Looking around the ingeniously constructed church and the outlying mission, Waugh pauses to consider the fate of such a place in the midst of decolonization: "What will happen when Fr Groeber is no longer there to direct them? . . . Their technical skill will remain ripe for well-intentioned exploitation by collectors and museums. How long can their vision remain uncontaminated by Europe and America? Those eager apprentices I saw today will find that there are larger rewards awaiting them for inferior work" (*Tourist* 131). At Serima he finds something essentially superior to what he has left behind in the West and that he has not encountered in his earlier African travels. While it is done under the supervision of Father Groeber, who is inscribed up to a point with the "explorer" mystique (*Tourist* 126), even his presence is diminished by the distinctly "African" aesthetic triumph that Waugh encounters: "It would be an absurd presumption to suggest a tradition has been founded at Serima. But to say that is not to belittle the present achievement. . . . Fr Groeber's achievement has been to make Africans do what none but Africans could have done and what no Africans in this huge region ever did before; to leave a church where they and their descendants can worship, which their descendants will cherish with the pride and awe with which we in Europe survey the edifices of our Middle Ages" (*Tourist* 131–32). At Serima, Waugh sees a new "African" community that moves beyond the boundaries of nationalism and cultural reclamation. Unlike colonialism, which empties "the native's brain of all form and content . . . and distorts, disfigures, and destroys" the past,[16] Serima is, according to Waugh, about the creation of a new and authentic culture that is neither colonial nor native but, like the Virgin of Guadalupe in *Robbery under Law* (220–34), wholly different and unique. Perhaps most significant of all is that Serima allows Waugh to conceive of an Africa free of white authority and beyond the various nationalist enterprises that anticipate independence. Arguably, it is a flawed vision. One could claim that, in fact, little has changed. Led by a white European, the Africans worshipped the god of the West in a controlled environment that was simply a haven and a distraction from the internecine struggle outside its boundaries. Nevertheless, its existence allows Waugh to envision Africa beyond imperialism. It is an ideal, another imagined community, but it is Waugh's recognition that Rhodesia's descent into "racial insanity" (*Tourist* 158) is as untenable as the idealism that led to its creation.

At the end of his journey, Waugh echoes another sentence found in his first record of African travel, *Remote People*: "I went abroad with no

particular views about empire and no intention of forming any. The problems were so insistent that there was no choice but to become concerned
with them" (120). In *A Tourist in Africa*, he writes, he traveled to Africa
"eschewing 'problems' and . . . seeking only the diverting and the picturesque." "Alas," he continues, "that is not possible. 'Problems' obtrude"
(*Tourist* 156). Imperialism cannot continue to exist as a fact in the minds
of white Europeans; nor can simply "giving" the colonies self-rule dimin-
ish the painful problems of decolonization: "From Algeria to Cape Town
the whole African continent is afflicted by political activities which it is
fatuous to ignore and as fatuous to dub complacently an 'awakening.' Men
who have given their lives to the continent can do no more to predict the
future than can the superficial tourist" (*Tourist* 157). It is an ending rooted
in trepidation, but was Waugh really "defeated" by the "complexity of
African politics," as Stannard maintains?[17] One need only consider, for example, his concise, detailed, and accurate account of the ill-fated Groundnuts Scheme in Tanganyika, an altruistic agricultural enterprise conceived
by the Labour government, which was supposed to provide margarine for
postwar Britain as well as a degree of financial prosperity for Kenya. The
entire project was, according to Waugh, "conceived in an ideological haze,
prematurely advertised as a specifically socialist achievement and unscru-
pulously defended in London when everyone in Africa knew it was inde-
fensible" (*Tourist* 78), principally because the site chosen for the scheme
had no water. And while Waugh lists myriad local problems that go terribly
wrong at the site at Kongwa and doom the project to failure, ultimately,
he concludes, the blame rests with the home government and "the hubris
that leads elected persons to believe a majority at the polls endues them
with inordinate abilities" (*Tourist* 79). As with the politicians who drew
lines and defined borders even though they knew nothing about Africa,
the Groundnuts Scheme proves that the old system of "knowing" what is
best for the natives is no longer supportable. Moreover, Waugh simultaneously recognizes that any notion of independence and self-rule engenders
a cynical expectation of failure in British officials: "What does seem plain
to me is that if the Groundnuts Scheme had been conceived and executed
by natives, everyone would point to it as incontrovertible evidence that they
were unfit to manage their affairs" (*Tourist* 104–05). Rather than slipping
into resignation and boredom, as some have accused his final travel book
of doing, *A Tourist in Africa* shows Waugh investigating, discussing, and
listening, all the while demonstrating that there are infinite shades of complexity to the enterprise of decolonization.

Written from the center by a former advocate and critic of empire, *A Tourist in Africa* shows Waugh to be at odds with the values of the colonizer in the midst of colonial decline. Postcolonialism is not simply a textual occurrence for those who have been marginalized by imperial structures. Indeed, such a narrow definition would be just as hegemonic as the old notions of "English" literature. Rather, postcolonialism "foregrounds a politics of opposition and struggle, and problematizes the key relationship between centre and periphery."[18] Waugh may be skeptical of the transformation, but he recognizes that the old system is no longer supportable. "It is hard to realize now," Waugh reflects, "that at the time of the Diamond Jubilee many men of goodwill thought the Pax Victoriana a reality" (*Tourist* 144). Moreover, he foresees and accepts independence (something he could not do in his other travel books), albeit with some misgivings. And why should he not be skeptical? In *A Tourist in Africa*, Waugh knows that what Anne McClintock calls "deep settler colonization"[19] will tragically prevail over the best democratic efforts of decolonization, especially in Rhodesia. Waugh writes: "I heard people of 'pioneer stock' say: '*You* can't understand. *We* remember the time when these people threatened to kill us,' while at the same time cordially entertaining Germans. The more recent, more civilized immigrants have none of these unreasoning emotions . . . but if their sons go to local schools they are in danger of picking up more than an unattractive accent" (*Tourist* 158). Was he very far off the mark? After a brutal civil war in the 1970s, the Lancaster House Agreement (ironically orchestrated in Britain) gave over one third of the arable land in Rhodesia/Zimbabwe to the minute white population when full independence was granted in 1980.[20] Can one say that such a country has truly undergone decolonization when such blatant injustice and vast inequalities uphold the legacy of imperialism? Similarly, the kleptocratic rule of president and former guerrilla leader Robert Mugabe expropriated thousands of white-owned farms two decades later; the resulting hyperinflation, shortages, massive internal displacement, and disintegration of Zimbabwe's once-stable economy show that the problems of decolonization still obtrude upon the present and will continue to do so in the future. Therefore, instead of being regarded as a marginal book that is somehow evidence of "declining" powers in Waugh's oeuvre, *A Tourist in Africa* should instead be thought of as a significant work of postcolonial discourse because it demonstrates a shift in consciousness, a new awareness that the relationship between the colonized subject and the colonizer is in the midst of a profound transformation.

Notes

1. Evelyn Waugh, *When the Going Was Good* (1946; rep., London: Penguin, 1951), 9. Hereafter cited as *WTGWG*.

2. Selina Hastings, *Evelyn Waugh: A Biography* (Boston: Houghton Mifflin, 1994), 590.

3. Douglas Lane Patey, *The Life of Evelyn Waugh: A Critical Biography* (Oxford: Blackwell, 1998), 347.

4. Evelyn Waugh, *A Tourist in Africa* (1960; rep., Boston: Little, Brown, 1986), 7. Hereafter cited as *Tourist*.

5. Martin Stannard, *Evelyn Waugh: The Later Years 1939–1966* (New York: Norton, 1992), 415.

6. Qtd. in Patey, *Evelyn Waugh*, 347.

7. Evelyn Waugh, *Robbery under Law: The Mexican Object Lesson* (1939; rep., London: Catholic Book Club, 1940), 17. Hereafter cited in the text.

8. Frantz Fanon, *The Wretched of the Earth* (1961; rep., Harmondsworth, UK: Penguin, 1967), 166, and Edward Said, *Culture and Imperialism* (New York: Knopf, 1993), 223–24.

9. Evelyn Waugh, *Waugh in Abyssinia* (1936; rep., London: Penguin, 1986), 12.

10. Evelyn Waugh, *Remote People* (1931; rep., London: Penguin, 1985). 141. Hereafter cited in the text.

11. Benedict Anderson, *Imagined Communities: Reflections on the Origin and Spread of Nationalism* (London: New Left, 1983), 15.

12. Seamus Deane, introduction to *Nationalism, Colonialism, and Literature* (Minneapolis: University of Minnesota Press, 1990), 17.

13. Deniz Kandiyoti, "Identity and Its Discontents: Women and the Nation," *Millennium: Journal of International Studies* 20, no. 3 (1991): 431.

14. Fanon, *Wretched of the Earth*, 169.

15. Ibid.

16. Ibid.

17. Stannard, *Later Years*, 414.

18. Vijay Mishra and Bob Hodge, "What Is Post(-)Colonialism?" *Textual Practice* 5, no. 3 (1991): 399.

19. Anne McClintock, "The Angel of Progress: Pitfalls of the Term 'Post-Colonial,'" *Social Text*, Spring 1992, 5.

20. Ibid.

Contributors

BARON ALDER is a solicitor in New South Wales and an occasional contributor to the *Australian Literary Review*, the *Australian Financial Review*, the *Sydney Morning Herald*, the *Age*, and *Quadrant*. He has published essays in the *Journal of the Royal Australian Historical Society* and *Literature & Aesthetics*, and he is convener of the Australia and New Zealand branch of the Evelyn Waugh Society.

PETER G. CHRISTENSEN was an Assistant Professor of English at Cardinal Stritch University, where he had taught since 1995. He had well over two hundred scholarly publications and presentations on diverse authors including Thornton Wilder, Jean Cocteau, Vernon Lee, and Marguerite Yourcenar. He passed away in 2007.

ROBERT MURRAY DAVIS, Professor Emeritus at the University of Oklahoma, compiled the catalogue of the Waugh papers at the Humanities Research Center, University of Texas; helped to compile two editions of Waugh bibliography; and published *Evelyn Waugh, Writer* and other books on Waugh. He has also published books on the American West and on Central European writing, two volumes of poetry, and four volumes of personal writing. He has completed another volume of memoir/family history and is working on a book of impressionistic travel sketches and a book on the literature and culture of the American West. He now lives at the edge of metropolitan Phoenix, Arizona.

MARCEL DECOSTE is an Associate Professor of English at Regina University. He has published essays in *Twentieth Century Literature*, *Modern Fiction Studies*, the *Journal of Modern Literature*, *Contemporary Literature*, *Style*, and *Renascence*, and he has completed a book on wartime British fiction.

PATRICK DENMAN FLANERY is an Honorary Fellow of the School of English Literature, Language and Linguistics, University of Sheffield. He is writing a monograph on adaptation and literary reputation for Manchester University Press, and he has research interests in adaptation studies, modern and contemporary Anglophone literature, and South African and American film.

DONAT GALLAGHER edited a comprehensive selection of Waugh's journalism in 1983 under the title *The Essays, Articles and Reviews of Evelyn Waugh,* having already made a significant contribution to establishing the extent and motivation of Waugh's occasional writings. He has published widely in areas where Waugh became involved in public controversy: Abyssinia, the operation and proper role of the press, Roman Catholicism, and the Second World War, with emphasis on Yugoslavia and Crete. Having taught within the English Department of James Cook University in North Queensland since 1964, he now holds an adjunct position there. He is the Honorary Secretary of the Foundation for Australian Literary Studies and a judge for the Colin Roderick Award for the best book published in Australia in the preceding year.

IRINA KABANOVA is a Professor and Head of the Department of World Literature at Saratov State University. She has published books and essays on world literature, English literature, and critical theory.

DAN S. KOSTOPULOS has published and presented a number of essays on the travel writing of Evelyn Waugh. He is an Instructor in Humanities at the Arkansas School for Mathematics, Sciences, and the Arts in Hot Springs.

LEWIS MACLEOD is an Assistant Professor at Trent University. He writes about British, West Indian, and African literature, and he is working on a series of essays dealing with violation and transgression in contemporary fiction. He has published essays in *Modern Fiction Studies*, *Critique*, *Mosaic*, and *ARIEL*.

JOHN W. MAHON, Professor of English at Iona College in New Rochelle, New York, coedits the *Shakespeare Newsletter*, an international scholarly journal published three times per year in forty-page issues. In addition to editing several collections of original essays on Shakespeare, Mahon publishes on modern and contemporary writers, including contributions to the *Evelyn Waugh Newsletter* and essays on James Joyce (in *Christianity and Literature*), as well as on Mary Gordon, Paul Theroux, Brian Moore, and Piers Paul Read. His teaching includes upper-level and graduate courses in Shakespeare, nondramatic Renaissance literature, the Bible as literature, and Irish literature.

RICHARD W. ORAM is Associate Director and Hobby Foundation Librarian at the Harry Ransom Center, the University of Texas at Austin. He has co-edited one volume from the Knopf Inc. Archive in the *Directory of Literary Biography* series, and he has published essays on English literature, special collections, and library history.

ANN PASTERNAK SLATER is the Eardley-Wilmot Fellow in English at St. Anne's College, Oxford. She is the author of *Shakespeare the Director* (Barnes & Noble, 1982) and the translator of Alexander Pasternak's *A Vanished Present* (Oxford University Press and Cornell University Press, 1984) and Lev Tolstoy's *The Death of Ivan Ilyich* and *Master and Man* (Modern Library, 2003). She is the editor of George Herbert's *Complete English Works* (Everyman's Library, 1995) and Evelyn Waugh's *Complete Short Stories* (Everyman's Library, 1998) and *Black Mischief, Scoop, The Loved One,* and *The Ordeal of Gilbert Pinfold* (Everyman's Library, 2003).

JOHN HOWARD WILSON is an Associate Professor of English at Lock Haven University of Pennsylvania. He has published *Evelyn Waugh: A Literary Biography, 1903–1924* (FDUP, 1996) and *Evelyn Waugh: A Literary Biography, 1924–1966* (FDUP, 2001). He edits *Evelyn Waugh Newsletter and Studies*, available at http://www.lhup.edu/jwilson3/newsletter.htm.

Index